# Unlocking The Mysteries of Revelation

## Using the Keys of the Feasts of the Lord

G. Carlton & M. Mineer

Copyright © 1999 by G. Carlton & M. Mineer
All rights reserved

ISBN: 0-9668678-0-7

*First printing, March 1999*
*Second printing, January 2002*
*Third printing, June 2003*

Published by G. Carlton & M. Mineer
10751 W. Ashland Way, Avondale, AZ 85323

Unless otherwise noted, all Scripture quotations marked NIV are from the HOLY BIBLE, NEW INTERNATIONAL VERSION. Copyright © 1973, 1978, 1984 by International Bible Society. Used by permission of Zondervan Publishing House. All rights reserved.

Scripture quotations marked KJV are from the King James Version of the Bible.

Scripture quotations marked Amplified are from The Amplified Bible © 1965 by Zondervan Publishing House. All rights reserved.

Illustrations by G. Carlton and M. Mineer unless otherwise noted.

Cover design by: Asano, Murillo, Germir, and Lopez, El Cajon, California

Printed in Canada

# DEDICATION

The concept of this book was not born out of the lofty ideal of sharing our revelation with the world. It was born out of our need to justify our obsession, in an understandable way, to family that made comments like:

"How can you spend so much time on that terrible stuff in Revelations? I have little children, I don't want to think of things like that ahead."

"I can't even keep track of who Jacob's wife was, Mom, I'll never understand what you're doing."

"If you'd devote this much time to your business we could retire early."

AND SO . . .

To my children, who have always given me faith and love even when they couldn't understand me.

To my husband, who has set me on a quest to know God the Covenant Keeper.

And for Jaimie: We may know in part, but you know fully (I Corinthians 13:12).

All my love, Marilyn

AND FINALLY . . .

To my husband, thanks for your patience and endurance through all the years of study, chasing back and forth, and being glued to the computer.

And to my sons, for all your love and encouragement throughout the years when I'm sure you thought mom was obsessed with this book and it would never become a reality.

All my love, Ginger

# ACKNOWLEDGEMENTS

Thank you and a line in print cannot compensate for the debt we owe to:

Judy Witt, who offered expert English skills in tiny threadlike hand, when illness prevented even the holding of a fork.

Sue Proulx who tried, often unsuccessfully, to hone our sentence structure and paragraph construction.

Roxanne Bryan, our coach and cheerleader in so many transitions in the labor of life.

Christine Bailey, our Mentor, who taught us to hear the voice of God.

Peggy Coates, one of our most loyal fans whose "no nonsense" focus plowed through tedious chores of detail, never missing a dot or tittle.  Thanks "mom".

Anna Hunt, ever young—our spiritual mom and faithful intercessor.


*See us about a discount!*

Love,  Ginger and Marilyn

# Contents

| Chapter | Page |
|---|---|

## Charts & Illustrations

# PREFACE

We began studying the book of Revelation nearly 20 years ago, separately and whenever possible for long days together. Beginning with microscopic examination of word meaning and symbolism we labored tirelessly. By this means we continued for many years, discovering wonderful insights into the Word of God but never really unlocking the mystery of this book.

Then, we discovered the Feasts of the Lord celebrated in the Tabernacle and the subsequent Temples. Having been so long steeped in the language of Revelation, the language of the Feasts seemed immediately familiar to us and suddenly opened a floodgate of understanding.

As Gentile Christians we frankly were ignorant of the Jewish culture. As we began to research the subject of the Feasts we found ourselves in the midst of Jewish laws, traditions and folklore. At times they seemed a people laboriously legalistic and superstitious, but ultimately we were thrilled and inspired by a people who know and love their God.

It is not the writers' purpose to give credence to Jewish apocryphal works or Jewish legend. These things are noted to give enlightenment regarding word usage and thinking during the times of the biblical texts noted. Much insight can be gained by examining the scriptures in the context of their Jewish setting.

As we began to explore Jewish sources we were amazed that our findings led us to new insights into the things Jesus did and said; for he was a Jew speaking to Jewish people. In researching the celebration of the Feasts, we were often confused by sources that gave conflicting accounts of the form and content of the traditions. In truth the rituals underwent changes from generation to generation. While the nation enjoyed a fixed territory in their God-given land and with a standing Temple, they celebrated in one manner. Dispersed throughout nations in captivity and exile they developed other traditions. It is not our purpose to follow these changes sequentially; it is apparent that by God's guidance many profound truths were instituted and preserved through these changes. We have endeavored to bring to you the most prominent aspects of the Feasts that prevailed throughout our sources.

We found, through surveying, that most Christians have little knowledge of the Feasts and think of them as being a part of the Mosaic Law that has passed away in the New Covenant. However, the Feasts established by God are described and decreed in Leviticus 23 as a "lasting ordinance for the generations to come, wherever you live."

Viewed in the light of Jesus, the Feasts of the Lord are not so many strange rituals that the Jewish people observed back in the Old Testament. They are the connecting points to other revelations in His Word, as well as the evidence that the Word is Divine in its authorship. Each part fits perfectly into the other and they all point to Him in whom the love of God was manifested.

> *This is how God showed his love among us: He sent his one and only Son into the world that we might live through him. This is love: not that we loved God, but that he loved us and sent his Son as an atoning sacrifice for our sins.*
> *1 John 4:9,10*

God was so faithful to meet us each time we came together to study and we know that He will meet you when you begin to study the Scriptures and read through this book. We believe you will discover keys for unlocking passages that may have been a mystery to you in the past.

It is our goal to provide you with an understanding of the Feasts. With this information placed solidly in your grasp, we will take you into the book of Revelation where you will begin to see the fulfillment of Jesus' work through the Feasts.

As we put together the myriad of information gathered over years of research, we realized how much we have yet to learn. Through each step of the way in the development of this book, the Lord proved himself Faithful and True and we were each strengthened in our Christian faith. We hope you will likewise be strengthened in your faith.

The Authors

# INTRODUCTION

At the time that Adam and Eve sinned, in the Garden of Eden, God revealed to them his provision for a Redeemer that would be empowered by the Holy Spirit to defeat Satan and restore to man his lost glory. This Redeemer came to be known to the Hebrews as Messiah, the Anointed One. As God's revelation began to unfold about this coming Messiah, there seemed to be some contradictions regarding the nature of this expected one.

By the time of the first century, the Jewish people had developed the concept of two Messiahs to reconcile this confusion. There was Messiah, the Conquering King, who came to be known among the Jewish people as Messiah ben David; and a Suffering Messiah, who came to be known as Messiah ben Joseph.

This confusing expectation regarding the Messiah was the basis for John the Baptist's question from prison asking Jesus whether he was the Messiah or should they expect another (Matthew 11:2). Because of the lack of Jewish understanding of this Messianic expectation, Christians have concluded that John the Baptist was in doubt as to whether Jesus was the Messiah. It is imperative that we examine these redemptive revelations within the context of their Jewish origin. In truth, John had already declared Jesus to be Messiah ben Joseph, the Suffering Messiah (John 1:29-34; 3:22-36). John was questioning Jesus as to whether he would also fulfill the prophecies regarding Messiah ben-David or if God would send another.

> The Kingly Messiah - *Isaiah 9:7*
> *Of the increase of his government and peace there will be no end. He will reign on David's throne and over his kingdom, establishing and upholding it with justice and righteousness from that time on and forever. The zeal of the Lord Almighty will accomplish this.*
>
> The Suffering Messiah - *Isaiah 53:8-10*
> *By oppression and judgment he was taken away. And who can speak of his descendants? For he was cut off from the land of the living; for the transgression of my people he was stricken. He was assigned a grave with the wicked, and with the rich in his death, though he had done no violence, nor was any deceit in his mouth. Yet it was the Lord's will to crush him and cause him to suffer, and though the Lord makes his life a guilt offering, he will see his offspring and prolong his days, and the will of the Lord will prosper in his hand.*

Jesus' answer was recognized in Jewish thinking as referring partially to the Suffering Messiah and partially to the Messiah, the Conquering King. Jesus was expressing that he would fulfill all of the Messianic prophecies. God was not sending two Messiahs, but one Messiah in two separate appearances.

A means to understanding the two messianic themes is in the study of the Feasts. It is significant to this truth that God divided the Feasts celebrated in the Tabernacle into two groups, Spring and Fall. These two groups related prophetically to the first and second coming of the Messiah.

## OUR PROMISE TO YOU

We've stumbled upon some surprising answers to questions we had never thought to ask. Questions such as:

Why didn't Jesus know the day of his return?
What did Jesus really mean when he said 'It is finished'?
Why the lake of fire?
What's being served at the Wedding Supper?

*"Like all of Biblical Judaism, the festivals (feasts) in some way teach us about the Messiah. Leviticus twenty-three is one of the key chapters for unlocking the entire Bible. If one can obtain a good working knowledge of the festivals, then he will have in his possession G-d's blueprint for mankind."*[1]

One of our discoveries was that the Feasts of Israel are keys to end times prophecy. When you were in school, the teachers wouldn't give you the answers to your math problems, but they gave you the tools to figure it out yourself. We won't be giving you all the answers either, but we'll point you in the right direction for your own study and give you some tools to work with.

We have attempted to lay out a foundation of information regarding the Spring and Fall Feasts of the Lord. In order to understand some of the concepts about the timing of the Feasts, we have included information about the Hebrew calendar. We have also included chapters on the Tabernacle, Marriage & Adultery, and Kingship to better help you understand the point of view from which John wrote the book of Revelation. We have used the New International Version Bible for all scripture references, unless otherwise noted.

When God established the nation of Israel, He showed Moses the heavenly Temple and instructed him to build a Tabernacle on the earth after the pattern he had seen. Scripture gives us many descriptions of its construction, furnishings, rituals and its prophetic significance. The Tabernacle structure and its furnishings symbolize the redemptive work of the Messiah, as do the Feasts that are celebrated there, the sacrifices offered and the work of the Priesthood.

The keys you will discover in the following pages will help to open the way for your own exploration of the mysteries of the Second Coming of Christ.

## OUR FORMAT

We have chosen a large size format to encourage you to use this as a guide for your own notes and study. It was our intent to make it easy for you to find related information for reference. At the top left of the page you will see chapter titles and on the top right subjects being discussed.

In the margin of our layout you will find key and lock symbols identified with a chapter and number. These keys highlight important words, phrases, or concepts that will be used to unlock the mysteries of the first and second coming of Christ.

A key is presented only once and it is not necessary to do anything with it at that time. It merely indicates that the concept being referred to in the text next to it will be appearing again later in the book. At that time, the same concept or idea will be noted as a lock. Just as an actual key may be created as a master key to open many locks, so a single key from our text will have several locks. The keys and their locks are linked together much like a chain reference.

For example, in Chapter 2 the first key appears on page 14 and is called "Heavenly Pattern". It is, therefore, numbered 2-1.

Key 2-1
Heavenly Pattern

The paragraph that this key appears next to is discussing the Lord's instructions to Moses to build a tabernacle according to the *heavenly pattern* he had seen. At the appearance of the key simply note it and move on. When you reach page 23, however, you will find a lock symbol with the number 2-1 and the name "Heavenly Pattern". It appears next to text that is also referring to *copies of heavenly things*. These two portions of text relate to each other.

Lock for 2-1
Heavenly Pattern
Page #14

In addition to a number and name, the lock includes a page reference. Returning to page 14, a key which opens this lock is found. The concept that is referred to in the text beside the key can then be reviewed providing clarification if it was not clear when reading page 23.

Using this system, you will find locks for Key 2-1 appearing on pages 157and 161. The lock on page 157 refers back to the previous lock on page 23. The lock on page 161 refers back to page 157. Therefore, when you reach page 161, by going backward in chain fashion, you will be able to tie together points of interest regarding the concept of the "Heavenly Pattern" until you return to its original reference in our text indicated by the Key 2-1.

A complete index of the Keys and Locks can be found at the back of this book.

For the sake of space we have added a heading at the beginning of some sections called, **Before you begin, read:** It would not be practical to write out every scripture reference for you, so it will be <u>**important**</u> that you take the time to read the references indicated before you continue with the text.

> In addition, we have included boxes in the margins which contain items of interest to the subject being discussed.

GOD'S PROMISE TO YOU

*"Blessed—happy, fortunate [to be envied] — are the people who know the joyful sound [who understand and appreciate the spiritual blessings symbolized by the feasts]; they walk, O Lord, in the light and favor of Your countenance!"*

*Psalms 89:15 Amplified*

# QUICK REFERENCE
# TO CALENDAR

## MONTHS

| Sacred Number | Common or Civil Number | Sacred Name | English Name |
|---|---|---|---|
| 1 | 7 | Nisan (Abib)-*New Year* | Mar/Apr |
| 2 | 8 | Iyar (Zif) | Apr/May |
| 3 | 9 | Sivan | May/Jun |
| 4 | 10 | Tammuz | Jun/Jul |
| 5 | 11 | Ab (Av) | Jul/Aug |
| 6 | 12 | Elul | Aug/Sep |
| 7 | 1 | Tishri (Ethanim)-*New Year* | Sep/Oct |
| 8 | 2 | Bul (Cheshvan) | Oct/Nov |
| 9 | 3 | Kislev (Chisleu) | Nov/Dec |
| 10 | 4 | Tebeth (Tevet) | Dec/Jan |
| 11 | 5 | Shebat (Shevat) | Jan/Feb |
| 12 | 6 | Adar | Feb/Mar |
| 13 | | Adar Sheni (in case of leap year) | |

# Chapter 1

## THE BIBLICAL CALENDARS

### OVERVIEW

The Old Testament records two calendars that regulated the lives of the Jewish people. The first, we call the Civil Calendar, begins in the Fall of the year with the month of Tishri. The second we refer to as the Sacred Calendar begins in the Spring with the month of Nisan. These two calendars existed simultaneously in Jewish life, the first regulating their secular life and the second their religious practices. At the outset this may seem a strange and confusing concept, living by two calendars at the same time, but many aspects of our own lives have differing calendars.

If you own a business you may manage it year round by a fiscal calendar. Your business or fiscal calendar may begin on April 15th. This is the 15th day of the fourth month of our common calendar which begins on the first day of the first month or January 1st.

Your children may attend school on a nine month schedule, the school year, commencing in the Fall of the common calendar and ending in late Spring. This is a strange calendar indeed, spanning only nine months rather than the accepted twelve.

Your church may divide its weekly scripture readings to complete the whole Bible during the course of a year. However, the cycle may begin in December with the gospels' recording of the birth of Jesus and continue through the months that follow being completed and begun again on the following December.

All the while these varied calendars regulate your life you date your correspondence, financial matters and personal lives by the twelve month, 365 day calendar beginning in January and ending in December.

It will be necessary for you to have some understanding of the biblical Sacred and Civil Calendars as we approach our study of the Feasts. In this chapter we will give a brief description of each.

**Before you begin, refer to: Quick Reference diagram on the facing page of this chapter and Feasts of the Lord Calendar at the end.**

### THE CIVIL OR COMMON CALENDAR

Key 1-1
Time

*"In the beginning. . ."* The beginning of time as we know it is described for us in the narrative of creation found in Genesis. In this account a day is measured from sunset to sunset:

> *God called the light "day", and the darkness he called "night." And there was evening, and there was morning— the first day. Genesis 1:5*

Key 1-2
1st of Tishri

Key 1-3
Sevens

Key 1-4
10th of Tishri

According to some accounts, the first day of creation was known in Hebrew as the first day of the month of Tishri. This day came to be designated as New Year's Day of the Civil Calendar which regulated the secular life of Israel. By this reckoning the first Sabbath would have taken place on Tishri 7. This account was the first example in scripture of a unit of time being measured in sevens. Jewish tradition says Adam and Eve sinned on the 10th day of Tishri. On that day God came into the garden of Eden and provided a sacrifice to clothe them (Genesis 3:21) and gave the first promise of a redeemer (Genesis 3:15).

The names of the months underwent changes as the nation of Israel was dispersed through the generations. For this reason the months were referred to most commonly by numbers, providing some consistency for business and government purposes.

The first month of the Civil Calendar corresponds with our modern calendar as the last part of September and the first portion of October. Occurring in the Fall of the year, it was the time of the year's final harvest consisting of the fruits of the orchard and vineyard. This period marked the beginning of the Fall rainy season and was perhaps the reason this first month was also called *Ethanim* (Hebrew) meaning 'flowing rivers'.

## THE SACRED CALENDAR

At Mt. Sinai, God gave a pattern for a Tabernacle to be built and instructions for events to be celebrated there. Among His provisions was a yearly schedule of events to commemorate His historical interventions on Israel's behalf. This was to remind Israel that all she had was from the hand of the Lord. For this purpose God established a religious calendar.

> *The Lord said to Moses and Aaron in Egypt, "This month is to be for you the first month, the first month of your year." Exodus 12:1-2*

As we study the Feasts, we will be referring to the Sacred calendar for it is from this calendar the Feasts of the Lord are marked.

The first month of the Sacred Calendar, Nisan, corresponds to the seventh month of the Civil Calendar. The Sacred Calendar is measured by the circuit of the moon and the solar rotation. Each month begins with the new moon. It takes slightly over 29 days for the moon to make its trip around the earth, each phase lasting approximately seven days. For this reason the calendar was measured in alternating 29 and 30 day months. This Sacred Calendar arrangement provided for the Feasts to be anchored to certain phases of the moon and certain seasons.

Key 1-5
New Moon-One Long Day

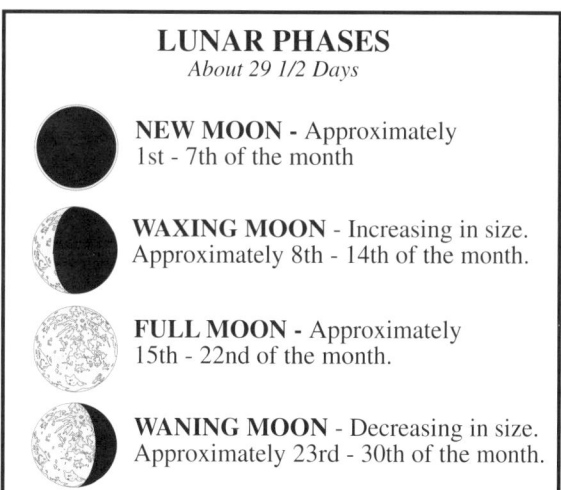

**LUNAR PHASES**
*About 29 1/2 Days*

**NEW MOON -** Approximately 1st - 7th of the month

**WAXING MOON** - Increasing in size. Approximately 8th - 14th of the month.

**FULL MOON -** Approximately 15th - 22nd of the month.

**WANING MOON** - Decreasing in size. Approximately 23rd - 30th of the month.

A twelve month period of such 'shortened months' would only account for 353-355 days compared to the solar year of 365. Therefore, adjustments were made by creating a leap year seven times in every 19-year cycle. On leap year a 13th month was added.

A Jewish source explains the significance of the lunar calendar as it relates to Israel:

*'Before God took Israel out of Egypt He hinted to them that their kingdom would not set for thirty generations... The month consists of thirty days, and their kingdom would endure for thirty generations. On the first of the month the moon begins to shed light, and its light grows till the fifteenth to the thirtieth of the month, its light diminishes till it is no longer seen on the thirtieth. Likewise Israel: Fifteen generations passed from Avraham [Abraham] till Shlomo [Solomon] . . .When Shlomo came, the disc of the moon was full. From then, the kings continuously diminished for another fifteen generations... When Tzidkiyahu [Zedekiah] came... the light of the moon was completely lacking'."* (Shmot Raba 15). [1] [Brackets authors' addition.]

Unique to Israel is her capacity for spiritual renewal. It is for this reason that the lunar month, which is in constant renewal, is the basis of Israel's religious calendar.

Another Jewish source offers an explanation for the lunar symbolism:

*The nations of the world count by the sun, which has no regular pattern of renewal. The people of Israel, however count by the moon—which is diminished, and enlarged, again and again—but which is always renewed. The lunar month is a sign to Israel. Though their light may be dim in comparison to the light of the sun; though their light may at times seem completely lacking—nevertheless, they have the perpetual capacity for renewal. ... It seemed as if Israel's light had been completely extinguished. But, behold! A new molad [appointed time]—like the molad of a new moon. Israel's light began to shine again. It shone again in exile; it shone again in its land; above all it was constantly renewed.'* [2] [Brackets authors' addition.]

## THE NEW MOON—ONE LONG DAY

Lock 1-5
New Moon-One
Long Day
Page #5

Each month of the Sacred Calendar was to begin with the new moon. In determining the precise time of the new moon, witnesses were employed from different regions of Israel to visually confirm the appearance of the moon. Inclement weather could be a problem in precisely determining this appearance, therefore, the need for reputable witnesses. At the beginning of each month messengers brought the news of the witnesses' sighting to Jerusalem. A proclamation was then made by the Sanhedrin establishing the appearance of the new moon. It was on this proclamation that the celebration of the Feasts depended. This determined the first day of the month. However, because many Jews lived a great distance from Jerusalem, causing the announcement to take some time to reach them, important observances were extended over a two-day period known as 'one long day'.

## THE WEEK—SEVEN

The measurement of time in scripture is interlaced again and again with the number seven. In Jewish understanding the number seven is a perfect number signifying a complete unit of time. The Hebrew word for 'week' simply means seven. The first account of creation in the scriptures is measured in a complete unit of time, called a 'week of days'.

Lock 1-3
Sevens
Page #4

In the marking of the Day of Pentecost a week of weeks or seven weeks are counted, 49 days plus one making 50 days.

> *Count off seven weeks from the time you begin to put the sickle to the standing grain. Deuteronomy 16:9*

The Feasts themselves are celebrated within a period of seven months called a 'week of months'. Seven years mark a 'week of years', the seventh year being a Sabbath year, a sabbath of rest for the land.

A Jubilee year was counted by seven sets of seven years called a 'week of weeks of years', plus one year. The 50th year was known as Jubilee and all debts were canceled, land was returned to family inheritors and slaves set free. The year of Jubilee was consecrated on the Day of Atonement, the 10th of Tishri.

Key 1-6
Jubilee

Lock 1-4
10th of Tishri
Page #4

These patterns of weeks or sevens are said in the book of Hebrews to have prophetic significance pointing to a day of rest for all people who are obedient to God.

> *Therefore God again set a certain day, calling it Today, when a long time later he spoke through David, as was said before: "Today, if you hear his voice do not harden your hearts." For if Joshua had given them rest, God would not have spoken later about another day. There remains, then, a Sabbath-rest for the people of God; Hebrews 4:7-9*

*Week of Redemption...*

Many Bible scholars speak of a Week of Redemption, citing the following scriptures to interpret this period as 7,000 years.

*For a thousand years in your sight are like a day that has just gone by, or like a watch in the night. Psalms 90:4*

*But do not forget this one thing, dear friends: With the Lord a day is like a thousand years, and a thousand years are like a day. II Peter 3:8*

Lock 1-3
Sevens
Page #7

Lock 1-1
Time
Page #4

Key 1-7
Redemptive Week

By their interpretation, scripture indicates that God views a thousand years as a day. Four days of the Lord or 4,000 years are marked from Adam to Christ's first coming; and two days or 2,000 years transpires until the return of Christ. The Redemptive Week culminates in a Sabbath rest for the people of God, on the seventh day, and this last thousand years (one day) is known as the Millennial Age.

This Redemptive Week is demonstrated in the following diagram:

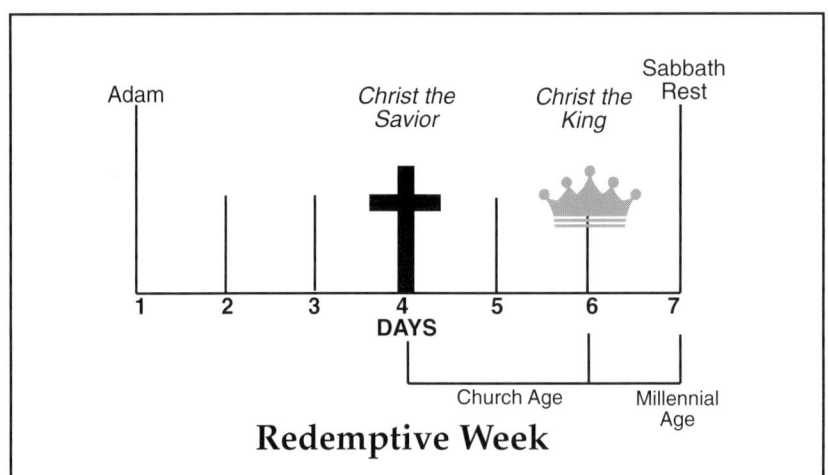

**Redemptive Week**

*Daniel's Weeks . . .*

The angel Gabriel instructed Daniel in a redemptive timetable for Israel as recorded in Daniel 9:

*"Seventy 'sevens' are decreed for your people and your holy city to finish transgression, to put an end to sin, to atone for wickedness, to bring in everlasting righteousness, to seal up vision and prophecy and to anoint the most holy." Daniel 9:24*

Seventy sevens will be the manner of Israel's redemption and the Holy City Jerusalem. Sixty-nine sevens are the numbers of time until the Anointed One is cut off. One seven remains for the completion of transgression and to bring everlasting righteousness.

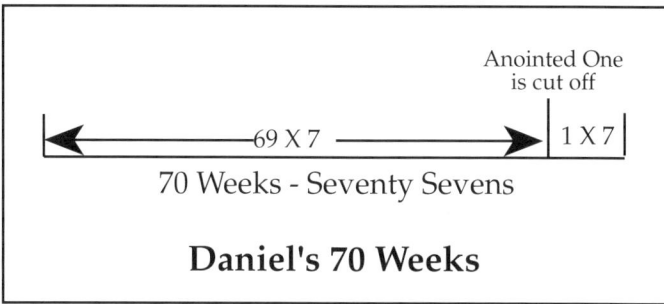

## THE DAY

The biblical day as stated in Genesis 1 was marked from sunset to sunset. The day itself, in the Temple, was divided into two 12-hour segments. *Evening* was marked from roughly 6 p.m. to 6 a.m. The *day* ran from approximately 6 a.m. to 6 p.m. Each 12-hour segment was also divided into smaller portions. From 6 a.m. to noon was the 'morning of the day'. From noon to 6 p.m. was considered the 'evening of the day'.

'Between the evening', as in Exodus 12:6, refers to the mid-portion of the evening of the day which would be 3 p.m. Therefore, counting from 6 a.m. this would be the ninth hour of the day. The third and ninth hours were the regular times of worship in the Temple, the times for the morning and evening sacrifice.

Key 1-8
The Hour

## AUTHORS' COMMENT

Because of the changing calendar through the ages, calculating and recalculating the day and hour of biblical events can be time consuming and unproductive. Jewish tradition has also changed through time attributing historical events to a variety of significant dates. Like the changing feast rituals, we have chosen the more common customs found in our research. This is not to be construed to mean the exactness of time is not important to God. It simply means man is not able to calculate it with God's accuracy. God's timing is perfect; it is man's calculations that lack perfection.

It is interesting to note, in regard to the Antichrist, that Daniel 7:25 indicates the following:

*He will speak against the Most High and oppress his saints and try to change the set times and the laws. . .*

For this reason we will point to the timing of events histori-cally, ritually and prophetically, as they reveal God's purpose. But we will not engage in lengthy calculations. Those inter-ested will find much and varied material in other sources to stimulate their thinking.

We do suggest, however, while studying scripture, you take note when references are made to the date i.e., *'it was on the 10th day of the first month'*. Oftentimes these references will have connections to feast days and bring new insights to the lessons being taught.

# Feasts of the Lord — Calendar

*Feasts of the Lord - Calendar*

| Sacred Number | Civil Number | Sacred Name | Modern Name | Day | Feast Name | Jewish Name | Other Feast Names |
|---|---|---|---|---|---|---|---|
| | | | **Latter or Spring Rains begin in the First Month** | | | | |
| 1 | 7 | Nisan(Abib) | Mar/Apr | 10 / 14 / 15 / 16 / 21 | *Select Pascal Lamb* / Passover / Unleavened Bread / Feast of Sheaf of Firstfruits / Last Day of Passover | Pesach | Sheaf of First Fruits |
| 2 | 8 | Zif (Ijar) | Apr/May | | | | |
| 3 | 9 | Sivan | May/Jun | 29 days / 50 days after waving of sheaf | Pentecost | Omer / Shavuot | Feast of Weeks |
| 4 | 10 | Tammuz | Jun/Jul | 29 days | | | |
| 5 | 11 | Ab (Av) | Jul/Aug | 30 days | | | |
| 6 | 12 | Elul | Aug/Sep | 29 days | *Month for Repenting in preparation of Day of Atonement* | Teshuvah *Elul 1-Tishri 10* | |
| | | | **Former or Early Rains begin in the Seventh Month - Plowing & Sowing start** | | | | |
| 7 | 1 | Tishri — Tishri 1-10 Days of Awe — A time of preparing in repentance | Sep/Oct | 1-2* / 10 / 15 / 22-23* | Day of Trumpets / Day of Atonement / Feast of Tabernacles / Great Day of Feast / 8th Day of Feast / 9th Day of Feast | Rosh Hashanah / Yom Kippur / Sukkot / Hashanah Rabah / Shemini Atzeret / Simchat Torah | New Year / Feast of Tabernacles / Feast of Ingathering / Rejoicing in Torah |
| 8 | 2 | Bul (Marcheshvan) | Oct/Nov | 29 days | | | |
| 9 | 3 | Chisleu | Nov/Dec | 30 days | | | |
| 10 | 4 | Tabeth | Dec/Jan | 29 days | | | |
| 11 | 5 | Shebat (Sebat) | Jan/Feb | 30 days | | | |
| 12 | 6 | Adar | Feb/Mar | 29 days | | | |

*Known as one long day

-11-

**N**

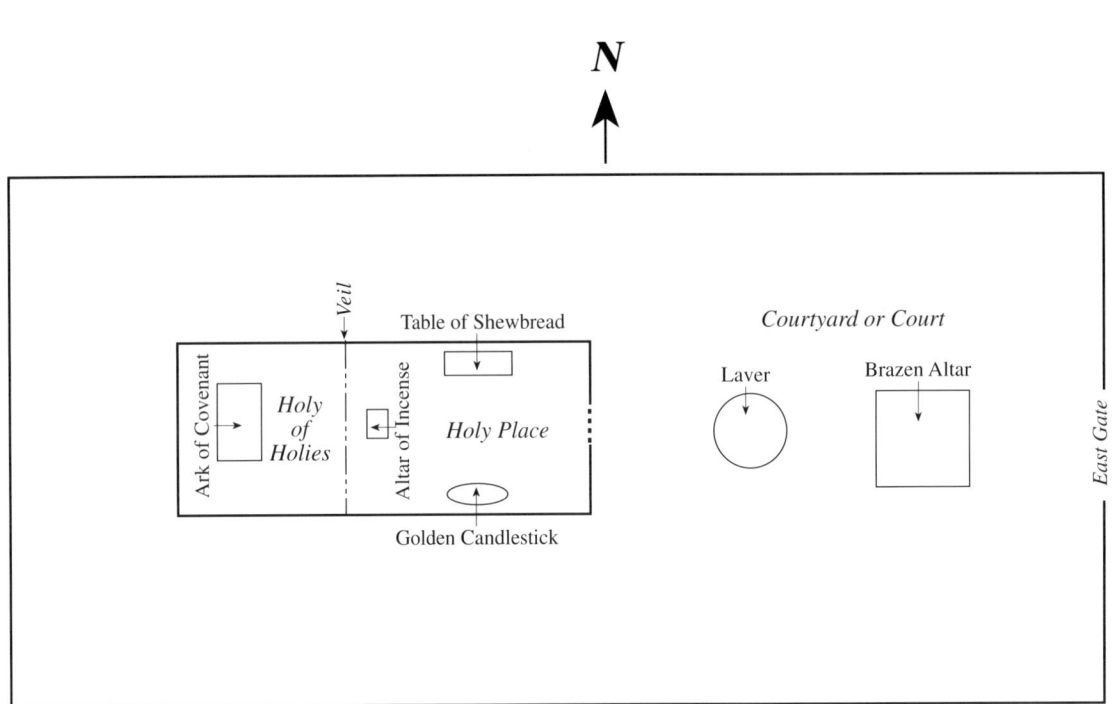

## Moses' Tabernacle

# Chapter 2

## THE TABERNACLE OF MOSES

### Overview

We were fortunate when we began our study of the Feasts to have a background in the mysteries and symbolism of the Tabernacle of Moses and the subsequent Temples built in the same pattern. We highly recommend the study of the construction and furnishings of the Tabernacle and their prophetic significance regarding the redemptive work of Jesus the Messiah. The Jewish people also attach much symbolic meaning to these structures from which we can be enriched.

Just as the Tabernacle was instructive of the Plan of Redemption, so were the Feasts celebrated in it. In this chapter we will provide a brief description of the divisions or rooms and furnishings of the Tabernacle. We also outline the activities of the priesthood and the sacrifices offered. The locations of the activities and the types of offerings will be referred to as we study the Feasts.

Please refer to the diagram of Moses' Tabernacle on the facing page to assist you as you explore this chapter.

# THE STRUCTURE

**References: Exodus chapters 25-27, 30, 35-38, 40.**

Key 2-1
Heavenly Pattern

The Lord called Moses to come up to Him on Mount Sinai where he would be given the tablets of the Law and instructions for building the Tabernacle and the furnishings. Moses was instructed by God to make the Tabernacle and all of its furnishings according to the pattern he was shown.

> *They serve at a sanctuary that is a copy and shadow of what is in heaven. This is why Moses was warned when he was about to build the tabernacle: "See to it that you make everything according to the pattern shown you on the mountain." Hebrews 8:5*

## COURTYARD

Key 2-2
Courtyard

The Tabernacle of Moses was surrounded by a rectangular area enclosed by curtains on frames. This area was called the Court or Courtyard. God instructed that the gate to the courtyard was always to be located on the east when the Tabernacle was erected during the Israelites' wilderness travels.

### *Altar of Sacrifice and Laver . . .*
As the worshippers entered the curtained gate, before them was a large altar covered over with brass. This was known as the Brazen Altar or Altar of Sacrifice. It was on this altar that most sacrifices were burned and the blood poured out. Further into the courtyard was a brass basin of water called the Laver, this was where the priests washed.

## TABERNACLE

Within the courtyard to the west was a rectangular structure made of wood, cloth and animal skins. Its curtained entrance was also located on the east side. This was the Tabernacle proper which was also called the Tent of the Testimony or Tent of Meeting and was divided into two rooms: The Holy Place and the Holy of Holies.

### Holy Place . . .

The Holy Place was the first room entered from the Court-yard. In this room were three pieces of gold furniture. The Candlestick or Lampstand had seven branches and was located on the south side of the room. On the north stood the Table of Bread of the Presence (Shewbread) containing twelve loaves of bread, wine and incense. The Golden Altar of Incense stood straight ahead or to the west directly in front of a curtain called the Veil of the Holy of Holies.

Key 2-3
Holy Place

### Holy of Holies . . .

Behind the Veil which separates the Holy Place from the Holy of Holies was the Ark of the Covenant. It was also of gold and upon it was a lid, sometimes called a Mercy Seat, having two cherubim attached (NIV renders it an atonement cover).

> *There, above the cover between the two cherubim that are over the ark of the Testimony, I will meet with you and give you all my commands for the Israelites. Exodus 25:22*

While we will not be discussing the proportions of this Tabernacle in detail, it will be of interest to us later if we note here that the measurements of the 'room' called the Holy of Holies was foursquare, its four sides and height being equal.

Key 2-4
Holy of Holies

After the same manner of the pattern of the Tabernacle, David through inspiration of the Lord, planned and gathered materials which Solomon used to create the great Temple in Jerusalem. After its destruction, Herod built the Second Temple which stood at the time of Jesus. Though the Temples were more elaborate than the Tabernacle Moses built, their type and function remained the same.

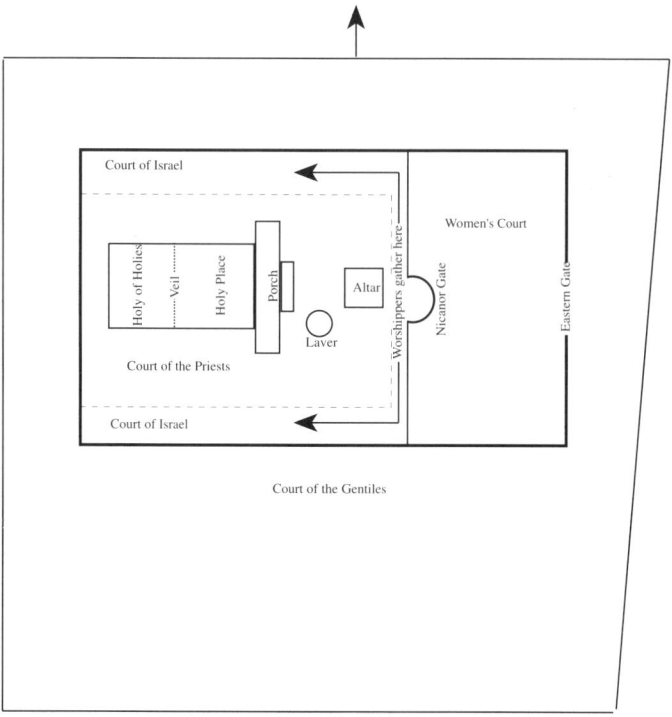

**Herod's Temple—The Second Temple**

# THE PRIESTHOOD

**References: Exodus 28 & 29, Leviticus 1-9, 10:6-18; 21, 22:1-16; Numbers 3:1-15 and Hebrews 8-10.**

## DUTIES

Key 2-5
Priestly Duties

By the time of the permanent Temple, the priesthood consisted of 24 courses or divisions. Half of these were permanent residents of Jerusalem and the rest were scattered throughout the land. These divisions of serving priests changed every Sabbath. The priests who served were given specific duties creating ranks among them. The highest of these ranks being that of the High Priest. Each of the divisions were responsible for certain duties of ministration in the Temple: porters of the gates, singers and musicians, timekeepers that determined the time for the Feasts and other ceremonies, those in charge of the fire, water, wood and ashes and many others. One of these ranks consisted of a council of elders that together with the High Priest constituted a court of judgment. It was one of the duties of this council to determine and announce the time of the new moon.

Key 2-6
Priest/King &
His Council

Lock 1-5
New Moon-
One Long Day
Page #6

During the rituals and Feasts, the priests moved among the furnishings and rooms of the Temple, performing their allotted duties. All of the priesthood served in the area of the outer courtyards, where the people entered to worship and make sacrifice.

Lock 2-3
Holy Place
Page #15

However, the Holy Place or Tent of the Testimony was only entered by the members of the priesthood of higher rank. Here they tended the lamps on the Lampstand, the bread on the Table, and the fire and incense of the Golden Altar.

Lock 2-4
Holy of Holies
Page #15

The Holy of Holies was only entered once a year by the High Priest bearing blood and a censor of incense from the Golden Altar. It was in this room where the cloud of God's presence dwelled.

As we will see, a general knowledge of these locations, the people who may enter them, and the activities that are performed there, provide us with clues or keys to recognize the

Feast rituals in the scriptures. The book of Hebrews abounds with information written to the Jews in terms they could identify with from their knowledge of the ceremonies of the Temple.

## GARMENTS OF THE PRIESTS

The ordinary priests wore four garments of white byssus, a white shining cotton fabric sometimes translated linen. First was a pair of linen breeches over which a coat reaching from the shoulder to the floor was worn. A girdle was worn about the chest or paps which held the garment together. A bonnet sometimes referred to as a turban or mitre was worn on the head.

Key 2-7
White Garments

In addition to the four garments worn by the priests, the High Priest wore four additional distinctive articles. These were called the golden vestments. The golden robes were only worn on the sabbaths, feasts and new moons. These golden garments are known as the 'golden vestments of the bridegroom'. They consisted of:

Key 2-8
Golden Garments

- Robe of the ephod - a dark blue garment that went to the knees somewhat like a tunic, the hem of which was decorated with alternating golden bells and pomegranate blossoms of blue, purple and scarlet. This garment was seamless and reinforced at the neck to prevent tearing.
- Ephod - a breastplate of 12 stones in 3 rows of 4, each stone bearing the name of one of the tribes of Israel.
- Mitre - a bonnet or turban like headdress.
- Ziz - a golden plate engraved with the words "Holiness to the Lord." This was fastened to the mitre above the forehead.

## ORDINATION OF THE PRIESTHOOD

### *Selection of the High Priest . . .*

The choice of Aaron as the first High Priest of the Tabernacle was revealed by the miraculous budding of the rod. Jewish tradition identifies the rod of Aaron with the rod of Moses and the staff or scepter of the kings of Israel. From this point on those who served in the priesthood were to be descendants of Aaron of the tribe of Levi. By this means God divinely demonstrated his choice:

Key 2-9
Selection by Divine Revelation

> *So Moses spoke to the Israelites, and their leaders gave him twelve staffs, one for the leader of each of their ancestral tribes, and Aaron's staff was among them. Moses placed*

*the staffs before the Lord in the Tent of the Testimony. The next day Moses entered the Tent of the Testimony and saw that Aaron's staff, which represented the house of Levi, had not only sprouted but had budded, blossomed and produced almonds. Numbers 17:6-8*

Key 2-10
Without Blemish

### Physical Attributes . . .
God instructed that those serving in the priesthood must be without blemish:

> *"'Listen, O high priest Joshua and your associates seated before you, who are men symbolic of things to come: . . .'"Zechariah 3:8a*

*The Lord said to Moses, "Say to Aaron: 'For the generations to come none of your descendants who has a defect may come near to offer the food of his God. No man who has any defect may come near: no man who is blind or lame, disfigured or deformed; no man with crippled foot or hand, or who is hunchbacked or dwarfed, or who has any eye defect, or who has festering or running sores or damaged testicles. No descendant of Aaron the priest who has any defect is to come near to present the offerings made to the Lord by fire. He has a defect; he must not come near to offer the food of his God. He may eat the most holy food of his God, as well as the holy food; yet because of his defect, he must not go near the curtain or approach the altar, and so desecrate my sanctuary. I am the Lord, who makes them holy.'" Leviticus 21:16-23*

Key 2-11
Anointed of God

### Baptism/Anointing . . .
Before the assembly, Aaron and his sons were washed with water, received the symbols of their authority and were anointed with oil.

*Moses said to the assembly, "This is what the Lord has commanded to be done." Then Moses brought Aaron and his sons forward and washed them with water. He put the tunic on Aaron, tied the sash around him, clothed him with the robe, and put the ephod on him. He also tied the ephod to him by its skillfully woven waistband; so it was fastened on him. He placed the breastpiece on him and put the Urim and Thummim in the breastpiece. Then he placed the turban on Aaron's head and set the gold plate, the sacred diadem, on the front of it, as the Lord commanded Moses. . . He poured some of the anointing oil on Aaron's head and anointed him to consecrate him. Then he brought Aaron's sons forward, put tunics on them, tied sashes around them and put headbands on them, as the Lord commanded Moses. Leviticus 8:5-9, 12-13*

At this time the Tabernacle and everything in it was also anointed and consecrated.

Key 2-12
Sanctuary
Cleansing

> *Then Moses took the anointing oil and anointed the tabernacle and everything in it, and so consecrated them. He sprinkled some of the oil on the altar seven times, anointing the altar and all its utensils and the basin with its stand, to consecrate them. Leviticus 8:10-11*

### *Sacrifices of Anointing/Communal Meal. . .*

A lengthy account is given in Leviticus 8:14-35 of the sacrifices made on the day of Aaron's ordination. A bull was offered for a sin offering to purify the altar and the blood applied to the horns of the altar and then poured out at the base. Two rams were sacrificed, one a burnt offering and the other a ram of ordination.

Key 2-13
Horns of the Altar

Lock 2-2
Courtyard
Page #14

During the ordination of Aaron and his sons, God instructed Moses that a communion meal be prepared from portions of the ordination sacrifices. These included three types of bread offerings and portions of the ram of ordination.

Key 2-14
Sacrifices of
Anointing

Offering commentary on the three types of bread offered at the ordination of the priesthood, Scherman in his anthology The Chumash stated:

Key 2-15
Meal Offering

> *"The breads were prepared with varying amounts of oil, from the unleavened breads that were kneaded with twice as much oil as the unleavened loaves, to the wafers that were kneaded without any oil. This symbolized that the Kohanim [priesthood] were to feel proud and content to be servants of God, whatever the degree of their personal wealth and possessions. (R. Hirch)* [1] *[Brackets authors' addition]*

From the ordination ram God instructed that the thigh portion together with one each of the three bread offerings was to be given as a burnt offering. Josephus in his Antiquities of the Jews called this thigh portion the 'royal portion':

> *"Consecrate those parts of the ordination ram that belong to Aaron and his sons: the breast that was waved and the thigh that was presented. Exodus 29:27*

God instructed that the ordination ceremonies of Aaron as High Priest and his sons as priests take place before the whole Israelite community at the entrance to the Tent of Meeting. God commanded the priests to remain for seven days at the en-

Key 2-16
Days of Ordination

trance of the Tent of Meeting for their ordination to be completed. During this time, daily sacrifices were offered according to God's instruction:

> *Moses then said to Aaron and his sons, "Cook the meat at the entrance to the Tent of Meeting and eat it there with the bread from the basket of ordination offerings, as I commanded, saying, 'Aaron and his sons are to eat it.' Then burn up the rest of the meat and the bread. Do not leave the entrance to the Tent of Meeting for seven days, until the days of your ordination are completed, for your ordination will last seven days. What has been done today was commanded by the Lord to make atonement for you. You must stay at the entrance to the Tent of Meeting day and night for seven days and do what the Lord requires, so you will not die; for that is what I have been commanded." So Aaron and his sons did everything the Lord commanded through Moses. Leviticus 8:31-36*

> *Do for Aaron and his sons everything I have commanded you, taking seven days to ordain them. Sacrifice a bull each day as a sin offering to make atonement. Purify the altar by making atonement for it, and anoint it to consecrate it. For seven days make atonement for the altar and consecrate it. Then the altar will be most holy, and whatever touches it will be holy. Exodus 29:35-37*

Key 2-17
Fire Kindled

### Sacred Fire . . .
At the end of the seven day ordination of Aaron and his sons, a fire is kindled.

> *On the eighth day Moses summoned Aaron and his sons and the elders of Israel. . . Fire came out from the presence of the Lord and consumed the burnt offering and the fat portions on the altar. And when all the people saw it, they shouted for joy and fell facedown. Leviticus 9:1, 24*

Lock 2-2
Courtyard
Page #19

Lock 2-5
Priestly Duties
Page #16

It was one of the duties of the priesthood to maintain this fire kindled by the Lord. For no other fire may be used upon the altar. See Leviticus 10 for the account of Hadeb and Abihu offering strange fire and of the consequences of being disobedient regarding this mandate.

# JESUS THE HIGH PRIEST

The concept of Jesus as High Priest is developed for us in Paul's letter to the Hebrews.  Just as the Tabernacle had its deeper meaning in the Messiah, so does the High Priesthood.  We cannot develop the full concept of Jesus as High Priest, but you will be enriched to pursue this study at another time.

*Selection as High Priest . . .*
Just as in the case of Aaron, God divinely appointed Jesus as High Priest for, *"No one takes his honor upon himself; he must be called by God, just as Aaron was." Hebrews 5:4*

Lock 2-9
Selection by
Divine Revelation
Page #17

However, God set down a regulation that the High Priest must come from the tribe of Levi.  Jesus was appointed as High Priest after the order of Melchizedek as Paul explains:

> *And what we have said is even more clear if another priest like Melchizedek appears, one who has become a priest not on the basis of a regulation as to his ancestry but on the basis of the power of an indestructible life.  For it is declared: "You are a priest forever, in the order of Melchizedek."  The former regulation is set aside because it was weak and useless (for the law made nothing perfect), and a better hope is introduced, by which we draw near to God.  And it was not without an oath!  Others became priests without any oath, but he became a priest with an oath when God said to him: "The Lord has sworn and will not change his mind: 'You are a priest forever.'  Because of this oath, Jesus has become the guarantee of a better covenant.  Hebrews 7:15-22*

*Physical Attributes . . .*
Jesus' physical nature is described by Paul as follows:

> *Since the children have flesh and blood, he too shared in their humanity so that by his death he might destroy him who holds the power of death—that is, the devil—and free those who all their lives were held in slavery by their fear of death.  For surely it is not angels he helps, but Abraham's descendants.  For this reason he had to be made like his brothers in every way, in order that he might become a*

*merciful and faithful high priest in service to God, and that he might make atonement for the sins of the people. Because he himself suffered when he was tempted, he is able to help those who are being tempted. Hebrews 2:14-18*

And His perfection is described in the following verses.

Lock 2-10
Without Blemish
Page #18

*In bringing many sons to glory, it was fitting that God, for whom and through whom everything exists, should make the author of their salvation perfect through suffering. Hebrews 2:10*

*Although he was a son, he learned obedience from what he suffered and, once made perfect, he became the source of eternal salvation for all who obey him and was designated by God to be high priest in the order of Melchizedek. Hebrews 5:8-10*

### Baptism/Anointing . . .

Lock 2-11
Anointed of God
Page #18

The baptism and anointing of Jesus by John, himself of a priestly line, conformed to the law that a priest must be anointed by another priest.

*At that time Jesus came from Nazareth in Galilee and was baptized by John in the Jordan. As Jesus was coming up out of the water, he saw heaven being torn open and the Spirit descending on him like a dove. And a voice came from heaven: "You are my Son, whom I love; with you I am well pleased." Mark 1:9-11*

Paul speaks of Jesus' anointing by quoting Psalms 45:

*You have loved righteousness and hated wickedness; therefore God, your God, has set you above your companions by anointing you with the oil of joy. Hebrews 1:9*

### Sacrifices . . .

Lock 2-14
Sacrifices of
Anointing
Page #19

The other High Priests had to offer up sacrifices for their own sins as well as the sins of the people. Jesus, as our High Priest, does not need to offer sacrifices for his own sin because he was without sin.

*Unlike the other high priests, he does not need to offer sacrifices day after day, first for his own sins, and then for the sins of the people. He sacrificed for their sins once for all when he offered himself. Hebrews 7:27*

His sacrifice did, however, atone for the sins of his priesthood as they consumed their ordination ram.

> *. . . and with your blood you purchased men for God from every tribe and language and people and nation. You have made them to be a kingdom and priests to serve our God. . . Revelation 5:9b-10a*

> *While they were eating, Jesus took bread, gave thanks and broke it, and gave it to his disciples, saying, "Take and eat; this is my body." Then he took the cup, gave thanks and offered it to them, saying, "Drink from it, all of you. This is my blood of the covenant, which is poured out for many for the forgiveness of sins. . ."Matthew 26:26-28*

Moreover, as High Priest, Jesus' sacrificial offering for all people took on even greater significance:

> *And by that will, we have been made holy through the sacrifice of the body of Jesus Christ once for all. Day after day every priest stands and performs his religious duties; again and again he offers the same sacrifices, which can never take away sins. But when this priest had offered for all time one sacrifice for sins, he sat down at the right hand of God. Since that time he waits for his enemies to be made his footstool, because by one sacrifice he has made perfect forever those who are being made holy. Hebrews 10:11-14*

### *Consecration of the Heavenly Temple . . .*

Jesus our High Priest, after his death entered the heavenly Temple to obtain eternal redemption and to purify that Temple. Paul describes Jesus' service as High Priest in his letter to the Hebrews:

Lock 2-12
Sanctuary Cleansing
Page #19

> *When Christ came as high priest of the good things that are already here, he went through the greater and more perfect tabernacle that is not man-made, that is to say, not a part of this creation. He did not enter by means of the blood of goats and calves; but he entered the Most Holy Place once for all by his own blood, having obtained eternal redemption. Hebrews 9:11-12*

Lock 2-4
Holy of Holies
Page #16

> *It was necessary, then, for the copies of the heavenly things to be purified with these sacrifices, but the heavenly things themselves with better sacrifices than these. For Christ did not enter a man-made sanctuary that was only a copy of the true one; he entered heaven itself, now to appear for us in God's presence. Hebrews 9:23-24*

Lock 2-1
Heavenly Pattern
Page #14

## AUTHORS' COMMENTS

Two things came to our notice as we studied the garments of the priesthood. First, it was not a coincidence that John mentioned that Jesus had a seamless garment that was not torn by the soldiers at His crucifixion.

*When the soldiers crucified Jesus, they took his clothes, dividing them into four shares, one for each of them, with the undergarment remaining. This garment was seamless, woven in one piece from top to bottom. "Let's not tear it," they said to one another. "Let's decide by lot who will get it." John 19:23-24*

Lock 2-8
Golden Garments
Page #17

This seamless garment was representative of the one worn by the High Priest. Such a garment was reinforced around the neck to prevent it from tearing when it was put on. The law provided that if this garment was torn either accidentally or intentionally, the High Priest was disqualified from performing his duties, until certain rituals were performed. Thus, Jesus was still able to function in the capacity of a High Priest, even at His crucifixion. This is significant when we note that previous to the crucifixion, when Jesus stood before the High Priest Caiaphas for questioning, that at Jesus' response the High Priest tore his clothes. Even though Caiaphas was not of Aaronic line he was, however, acting High Priest at the time of Jesus' arrest. By the act of tearing his clothes he disqualified himself by law from acting as High Priest of the Passover to follow.

Second, Matthew's account of the appearance of Jesus, prior to His crucifixion, before the Sanhedrin provides an additional fact worth noting. Jesus did not respond to his accusers until the High Priest said:

*I charge you under oath by the living God: Tell us if you are the Christ, the Son of God" . . . Jesus responded: "Yes, it is as you say. . ." Matthew 26:63,64*

Key 2-18
Charge to Testify

Jewish law provided that under this phrase of questioning by the High Priest, a man MUST answer. If Jesus refused to answer, he would have broken the law.

*If a person sins because he does not speak up when he hears a public charge to testify regarding something he has seen or learned about, he will be held responsible. Leviticus 5:1*

It was an awakening experience for us to realize that these details given in the Gospels had such significance. They showed that Jesus fulfilled even the religious law of the Jews.

# THE SACRIFICES AND OFFERINGS

**Reference: Leviticus 1-8.**

Studying the sacrifices and offerings of the Bible may not be very appealing, but it nagged in the back of our minds that God didn't just toss those verses in to take up space. Our first spark of interest was ignited when our investigation brought to light new insights into Christ's work on the cross. We discovered that referring to Jesus as our sacrifice had richer meaning for us after our study.

Because of the destruction of the Temple and the dispersion of the Jews, the sacrificial ceremonies have ceased. Today, many Jews and Christians have declared that the sacrifices have become irrelevant.

God renewed His covenant with Abraham through his descendents at the time of the exodus from Egypt. The Passover Lamb and its blood was the means of sealing that renewed covenant. This first sacrifice became the basis upon which all other sacrifices rested when the ceremonies were instituted in the Tabernacle. All subsequent sacrifices were instituted to commemorate and enjoy the relationship of Israel with her God or to re-establish broken communion.

In this section, we will provide a brief reference on the different sacrifices. While we encourage you to read through this material now, do not labor to absorb everything at one time. As the subject of the Feasts unfolds, you will want to refer to this list to broaden your understanding of the meaning of the ceremonies. As we studied the Feasts we found that God specified certain sacrifices in conjunction with these celebrations. The instructions for sacrifices helped us to unravel some of the prophetic mystery of the Feasts.

### SACRIFICIAL SYMBOLISM

*To Restore Communion-those sacrifices made to re-establish broken communion. Both of these sacrifices were only valid if real repentance accompanied them. These are mandatory offerings.*

| NAME | SYMBOLIC MEANING | SACRIFICE | KEY |
|---|---|---|---|
| **Sin offerings** *(Hebrew - Chatat)* | Made atonement for the offender. They symbolize general redemption and are brought during Feast occasions on behalf of the whole congregation (nation). They have a retroactive effect on the worshippers. Where portions of the sin offering are eaten, it represents that the repentance and the offering has been accepted by the Lord and communion re-established. This is a mandatory offering. | Always a male animal in the case of public sacrifices and female in the case of private offerings. A bullock is the highest form of sin offering. It is used for the sins of the High Priest on the Day of Atonement and in the consecration of the priests. A kid of a goat is used for the sins of the king. (All 24 divisions of priests are needed for the offering of a bullock.) Female goats are offered as sin offerings for individuals.<br><br>Note: A ram is never used as a sin offering. The term lamb refers to a yearling. | Key 2-19 Sin Offering<br><br>Lock 1-4 10th of Tishri Page #7<br><br>Lock 2-14 Sacrifices of Anointing Page #22 |
| **Trespass Offerings or Guilt Offerings** *(Hebrew-Asham)* | Made atonement for a single offense. They symbolize ransom for a special wrong, for which a decided satisfaction is demanded. Hebrew word implies it covers the act of sin, the responsibility of the sinner and the natural result. They are never brought on behalf of the whole congregation, but only by the individual. This is a mandatory offering. | Always a male, generally a ram. No substitution could be made in the case of poverty. | Key 2-20 Trespass Offering |

### *Handling the Blood. . .*

Key 2-21
Blood Sprinkling

The method of handling the blood of the sacrifice was specified with each offering: for trespass, burnt, and peace offerings the blood was sprinkled against the altar on all sides. The blood of the sin offering was not thrown, but sprinkled by the priest dipping his hand into the vessel. The blood of the Passover lamb was neither thrown nor sprinkled from the priests' hand, but poured out directly from the vessel at the base of the altar. Note: This handling of the blood was unique to the Passover sacrifice.

Lock 2-3
Holy Place
Page #16

Lock 2-13
Horns of the Altar
Page #19

Lock 2-14
Sacrifices of
Anointing
Page #22

Blood which was to be sprinkled in the Holy Place between the Lampstand and the Altar of Incense, indicated the sin committed endangered the covenant relationship itself. The touching of the horns of the Altar of Incense with the blood symbolized the re-establishment of the covenant relationship.

## SACRIFICIAL SYMBOLISM

*In Communion-those offerings made when there is no breach in covenant relationship. These are voluntary offerings.*

| NAME | SYMBOLIC MEANING | SACRIFICE | KEY |
|---|---|---|---|
| **Burnt Offerings** *(Hebrew-Olah or Chalil)* | Symbolizes entire surrender and homage given to God the King. They are sometimes called the sacrifices of devotion and service given and done freely, willingly, and joyfully. They are the only sacrifice a non-Jew can bring (if they bring a peace offering it is treated as a burnt offering). | Always a male animal. Bull, ram or male bird; no defect. Except for the skin, they are wholly burned (consumed) with neither priest nor worshipper partaking of the meat. | Key 2-22 Burnt Offering |
| **Fellowship/Peace Offerings** *(Hebrew-Sevach)* | Symbolizes a time of happy fellowship with God. They are known as offerings of completion for they follow all other sacrifices and indicate complete peace with God. They are offerings of a grateful soul justified and accepted before God. The communion of the meal is the main point of importance and is a symbol of intimacy. | Any animal without defect from herd or flock. The sacrifice was eaten by the priests and the worshipper; with the exception that the Pentecost peace offering is eaten only by the officiating priest within the Holy Place. It was a unique provision that in the case of the peace offering, given as a voluntary offering of a loving heart, even an animal with defect may be offered. | Key 2-23 Peace Offering<br><br>Lock 2-3 Holy Place Page #26 |
| **Meal/Grain Offerings** *(Hebrew-Minchah)* | These are acts of worship and recognize the goodness of God and His provisions. Offered with burnt and peace offerings but never with sin and trespass offerings. They are therefore, considered voluntary offerings. | Firstfruits of the harvest, unleavened bread along with drink offerings. On Pentecost two loaves of leavened bread were offered. They were to be offered by fire. | Lock 2-15 Meal Offering Page #19 |

## *Most Holy Sacrifices . . .*

It is important to note that some sacrifices were considered more holy than others. Certain meal offerings and all burnt, sin, and trespass offerings, as well as public peace offerings were 'most holy'. These most holy offerings were offered on the north side of the altar.

Key 2-24
Most Holy Sacrifice

Other offerings were made to the east or south side of the altar. These were either eaten by the officiating priests or not eaten at all. In the case of other sacrifices, the worshipper often shared in eating a portion of the sacrifice.

## RESPONSIBILITIES OF PRIEST AND WORSHIPPER

As to the responsibilities of priest and worshipper in the sacrificial act, the following generalization will serve our needs:

The worshipper, having been duly purified, entered the Temple through the northern entrance to offer a 'most holy' sacrifice. If the offering was other than a 'most holy' sacrifice, the worshipper entered the Temple through the southern entrance. When offering personal sacrifices, the worshipper was responsible for the laying on of hands, slaying, skinning, cutting up, and washing the inner parts of the sacrifice. The laying on of the hands of the worshipper seems to have been an acknowledgment of ownership of the sacrifice and the transfer of the debt of sin and its confession in prayer. In the case of the peace offerings the prayer of praise was substituted for the prayer of confession of sin.

> In Romans 12:1 Paul exhorts us to present our bodies a living sacrifice, holy, acceptable to God. This refers to the act of the worshipper in the Temple placing his sacrifice so it faced the Most Holy Place to present it to the Lord before sacrifice.
>
> II Timothy 2:15 (KJV) speaks of rightly dividing the word of truth adopting the sacrificial term referring to the sacrifices that were divided into pieces for offering.

It was the priests' responsibilities to catch up the blood of the sacrifices and sprinkle it. They maintained the altar fire and brought the sacrificial pieces to the altar. The slaying of all public sacrifices was also their duty.

## THE PASSOVER SACRIFICE

Key 2-25
Passover Lamb

The Passover Lamb sacrifice was instituted by God at the time of Israel's exodus from Egypt. This was previous to the establishment of the Levitical sacrifices and was unique in the respect that it was a male ram and did not conform wholly to what later became known as the sin offering. A sin offering was never to be a ram nor was unleavened bread to be offered with it. By the same token the sacrifice did not conform strictly to that which became known as the peace offering, as it was a combination of both.

> *It was a sacrifice, and yet quite out of the order of all Levitical sacrifices. For it had been instituted and observed before Levitical sacrifices existed; before the Law was given; nay, before the Covenant was ratified by blood (Exod. 24). In a sense, it may be said to have been the cause of all the later sacrifices of the Law, and of the Covenant itself. Lastly, it belonged neither to one nor to another class of sacrifices; it was neither exactly a sin-offering nor a peace-offering, but combined them both.*[2]

The sin offering, as seen in the Sacrificial Symbolism chart, was for the purpose of restoring broken communion. During Feasts it was offered in behalf of the whole congregation and had a retroactive effect covering all sin. In addition, as the sin offering was eaten, it symbolized that communion with God was re-established.

Lock 2-19
Sin Offering
Page #26

The peace or fellowship offering was only offered after any sin offerings were made. It was known as an offering of completion, representing complete peace with God. The eating of the sacrifice as a communion meal was the main emphasis.

Lock 2-23
Peace Offering
Page #27

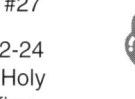

Lock 2-24
Most Holy
Sacrifice
Page #27

> *The meat of his fellowship offering of thanksgiving must be eaten on the day it is offered; he must leave none of it till morning. Leviticus 7:15*

## AUTHORS' COMMENT

For the student's reference Appendix A at the end of this chapter lists the sacrifices made at the different Feasts.

# JESUS THE OFFERING

*The law is only a shadow of the good things that are coming—not the realities themselves. For this reason it can never, by the same sacrifices repeated endlessly year after year, make perfect those who draw near to worship.*
*Hebrews 10:1*

Just as Jesus fulfilled the office of the High Priest, His offering of Himself also fulfilled all aspects of the sacrifices. The sacrifices of the Temple were prophetic of the true and complete work of Jesus the offering.

Lock 2-25
Passover Lamb
Page #28

*In short, just as the priesthood of Christ was a real Old Testament priesthood, yet not after the order of Aaron, but after the earlier, prophetic, and royal order of Melchisedek, so that sacrifice also of Christ was a real Old Testament sacrifice, yet not after the order of Levitical sacrifices, but after that of the earlier prophetic Passover sacrifice, by which Israel had become a royal nation.[3]*

Lock 2-19
Sin Offerings
Page #29

**Jesus the Sin Offering. . .**
*For this reason he had to be made like his brothers in every way, in order that he might become a merciful and faithful high priest in service to God, and that he might make atonement for the sins of the people. Hebrews 2:17*

Lock 2-24
Most Holy
Sacrifice
Page #29

*But when this priest had offered for all time one sacrifice for sins, he sat down at the right hand of God. Since that time he waits for his enemies to be made his footstool, because by one sacrifice he has made perfect forever those who are being made holy. Hebrews 10:12-14*

Lock 2-20
Trespass Offering
Page #26

**Jesus the Trespass or Guilt Offering. . .**
*And you, being dead in your sins and the uncircumcision of your flesh, hath he quickened together with him, having forgiven you all trespasses; Blotting out the handwriting of ordinances that was against us, which was contrary to us, and took it out of the way, nailing it to his cross;*
*Colossians 2:13-14 (KJV)*

Lock 2-24
Most Holy
Sacrifice
Page #29

*Be kind and compassionate to one another, forgiving each other, just as in Christ God forgave you. Ephesians 4:32*

*How much more, then, will the blood of Christ, who through the eternal Spirit offered himself unblemished to God, cleanse our consciences from acts that lead to death, so that we may serve the living God! Hebrews 9:14*

*Yet it was the Lord's will to crush him and cause him to suffer, and though the Lord makes his life a guilt offering . . . Isaiah 53:10*

### Jesus the Burnt Offering. . .

*Therefore, when Christ came into the world, he said: "Sacrifice and offering you did not desire, but a body you prepared for me; with burnt offerings and sin offerings you were not pleased. Then I said, 'Here I am—it is written about me in the scroll—I have come to do your will, O God.' Hebrews 10:5-7*

Lock 2-22
Burnt Offering
Page #27

Lock 2-24
Most Holy
Sacrifice
Page #30

### Jesus the Peace Offering . . .

*For he himself is our peace, who has made the two one and has destroyed the barrier, the dividing wall of hostility, by abolishing in his flesh the law with its commandments and regulations. His purpose was to create in himself one new man out of the two, thus making peace, and in this one body to reconcile both of them to God through the cross, by which he put to death their hostility. Ephesians 2:14-16*

Lock 2-23
Peace Offering
Page #29

Lock 2-24
Most Holy
Sacrifice
Page #30

*For God was pleased to have all his fullness dwell in him, and through him to reconcile to himself all things, whether things on earth or things in heaven, by making peace through his blood, shed on the cross. Once you were alienated from God and were enemies in your minds because of your evil behavior. But now he has reconciled you by Christ's physical body through death to present you holy in his sight, without blemish and free from accusation— Colossians 1:19-22*

### Jesus the Meal Offering. . .

*I am the living bread that came down from heaven. If anyone eats of this bread, he will live forever. This bread is my flesh, which I will give for the life of the world. John 6:51*

Lock 2-15
Meal Offering
Page #27

# APPENDIX A- SACRIFICES & OFFERINGS OF THE DAY

**DAILY OFFERINGS -** *These offerings were offered twice daily in the Temple, at morning and twilight, before any other special offerings were made.*

| OFFERING | TYPE |
|---|---|
| 1 lamb - 1 year old | Burnt offering |
| 1/10 ephah flour | |
| 1/4 hin of oil | |
| 1/4 hin-fermented wine | |

**SABBATH OFFERINGS -** *In addition to the daily offerings, on the Sabbath the following offering was made, which constituted a double portion of the daily offering.*

| OFFERING | TYPE |
|---|---|
| 2 lambs-1 year old | Burnt offering |
| 2/10 ephah of flour | |
| 1/2 hin of oil | |
| 1/2 hin-fermented wine | |

**NEW MOON OFFERINGS -** *On the first day of the month the following offerings were made in addition to the daily offering and any other offerings specified for special days.*

| OFFERING | TYPE |
|---|---|
| 2 bulls | Burnt offering |
| 3/10 ephah flour with oil for each bull | |
| 1/2 hin wine for each bull | |
| 1 ram | Burnt offering |
| 2/10 ephah flour with oil | |
| 1/3 hin wine | |
| 7 male lambs | Burnt offering |
| 1/10 ephah flour with oil for each lamb | |
| 1/4 hin wine for each lamb | |
| 1 male goat | Sin offering |

**PASSOVER SACRIFICES -** *The following sacrifices were made daily during the seven days of the Passover/Unleavened Bread Feast and were in addition to the daily morning sacrifices.*

| OFFERING | TYPE |
|---|---|
| 2 bulls | Burnt offering |
| 3/10 ephah flour with oil for each bull | |
| 1/2 hin wine for each bull | |
| 1 Ram | |
| 2/10 ephah flour with oil | |
| 1/2 hin wine | |
| 7 male lambs | |
| 1/20 ephah flour with oil for each lamb | |
| 1/4 hin of wine for each lamb | |
| | |
| 1 male goat | Sin offering |

**PENTECOST (Feast of Weeks) SACRIFICES** - *The following offerings are in addition to the daily offerings.*

| OFFERING | TYPE |
|---|---|
| 2 bulls | Burnt offering |
| 3/10 ephah flour with oil for each bull | |
| 1/2 hin wine for each bull | |
| 1 Ram | |
| 2/10 ephah flour with oil | |
| 1/3 hin wine | |
| 7 male lambs | |
| 1/10 ephah flour with oil for each lamb | |
| 1/4 hin wine for each lamb | |
| | |
| 1 male goat | Sin offering |

**FEAST OF TRUMPETS SACRIFICES** - *These are in addition to the monthly and daily burnt offerings.*

| OFFERING | TYPE |
|---|---|
| 1 bull | Burnt offering |
| 3/10 ephah flour with oil | |
| 1/2 hin wine | |
| 1 ram | |
| 2/10 ephah flour with oil | |
| 1/3 hin wine | |
| 7 male lambs | |
| 1/20 ephah flour with oil | |
| 1/4 hin wine with each lamb | |
| | |
| 1 male goat | Sin offering |

**DAY OF ATONEMENT SACRIFICES** - *These were the general sacrifices in addition to the sacrifices for the High Priest on this day and the special offering of two males goats and the burnt offerings and also were in addition to the daily offerings.*

| OFFERING | TYPE |
|---|---|
| 1 bull | Burnt offering |
| 3/10 ephah flour with oil | |
| 1/2 hin wine | |
| 1 ram | |
| 2/10 ephah flour with oil | |
| 1/3 hin wine | |
| 7 male lambs | |
| 1/10 ephah flour with oil | |
| 1/4 hin wine for each lamb | |
| | |
| 1 male goat | Sin offering |

**FEAST OF TABERNACLES - 15th of Seventh month** - *All of the following are in addition to daily offerings, freewill offerings, etc.*

| DAY | OFFERING | TYPE |
|---|---|---|
| 1 | **13 bulls** | Burnt offering |
| | 3/10 ephah flour with oil for each bull | |
| | 1/2 hin wine for each bull | |
| | **2 Rams** | |
| | 2/10 ephah flour with oil for each ram | |
| | 1/3 hin wine for each ram | |
| | **14 male lambs** | |
| | 1/10 ephah flour with oil for each lamb | |
| | 1/4 hin wine for each lamb | |
| | **1 male goat** | Sin offering |

*Flour, oil and wine offerings are typical as in Day 1 for each following day.*

| DAY | OFFERING | |
|---|---|---|
| 2 | **12 bulls** | |
| | 2 rams | |
| | 14 male lambs | |
| | 1 goat | |
| 3 | **11 bulls** | |
| | 2 rams | |
| | 14 male lambs | |
| | 1 male goat | |
| 4 | **10 bulls** | |
| | 2 rams | |
| | 14 male lambs | |
| | 1 male goat | |
| 5 | **9 bulls** | |
| | 2 rams | |
| | 14 male lambs | |
| | 1 male goat | |
| 6 | **8 bulls** | |
| | 2 rams | |

|     |                  |             |
|-----|------------------|-------------|
|     | 14 male lambs    |             |
|     | 1 male goat      |             |
| 7   | **7 bulls**      |             |
|     | 2 rams           |             |
|     | 14 male lambs    |             |
|     | 1 male goat      |             |
| 8   | **1 bull**       |             |
|     | 1 ram            |             |
|     | 7 male lambs     |             |
|     | 1 male goat      | Sin offering |

**SACRIFICES FOR THE CONSECRATION OF THE PRIESTS and THE CORONATION OF THE KING** - *In addition to the daily offerings.*

| OFFERING | TYPE |
|----------|------|
| 1 bull | Sin offering |
| 1 ram | Burnt offering |
| Unleavened bread and cakes mixed with oil and wafers spread with oil | Heave offering |
| 1 ram | For Ordination |

# QUICK REFERENCE
# TO SPRING FEASTS

| Month | Day | Name of Feast | Other Names |
|---|---|---|---|
| 1-Nisan | 1 | New Year's Day | |
| (Mar/Apr) | 14 | Passover | Pesach |
| | 15-21 | Unleavened Bread | Hag HaMatzah |
| | Day after Sabbath | Sheaf of Firstfruits | Omer |
| | | | Bikkurim |
| 3-Sivan | 50 days after Day of | Pentecost | Shavuot |
| (May/Jun) | Sheaf of Firstfruits | | Feast of Weeks |

# *Chapter 3*

## THE SPRING FEASTS

### OVERVIEW

During our study of the Feasts of the Lord, we discovered that the Fall feasts were prophetic of Jesus' second coming. Following the initial excitement of this discovery, our focus was understandably directed to the Feast of Trumpets, Day of Atonement and Feast of Tabernacles. As for the Spring Feasts the concepts of Jesus dying for our sins as the Passover Lamb and the Holy Spirit's appearance at Pentecost were familiar. We were not inspired to further investigation, but wanted to press on to Jesus the King of Kings and His coming.

> *Therefore do not let anyone judge you by what you eat or drink, or with regard to a religious festival, a New Moon celebration or a Sabbath day. These are a shadow of the things that were to come; the reality, however, is found in Christ. Colossians 2:16-17*

Then one day, in the midst of trying to understand the meaning of some of the sacrifices, we discovered an account of the High Priest offering the Passover Lamb. As he completed the sacrifice he declared, "It is finished!" We were startled to realize these same words were spoken by Jesus from the cross. How many sermons had we heard on Easter about what Jesus meant when he said those words? Could it be a coincidence? With new interest, we began to explore the Jewish perspective on the Spring Feasts.

*jesus was both!*

*more deeply.*

We found that the Passover Lamb did not strictly adhere to the concept of a sin offering as we had previously believed. That was enough to set us on a quest to know more of the work of Jesus in the context of the Spring Feasts.

> *"Do not think that I have come to abolish the Law or the Prophets; I have not come to abolish them but to fulfill them." Matthew 5:17*

We hope this chapter will deepen your understanding and faith that God watches over His Word to perform it and that Jesus came not to abolish the Law or the Prophets but to fulfill them. For in a spiritual understanding of the feasts we have also found keys to our personal relationship with Him.

This chapter will provide good practice for you to use the keys of the Spring Feasts as they relate to the fulfillment in Jesus' coming as Messiah ben Joseph, the Suffering Messiah and the outpouring of the Holy Spirit. From this experience you will be able to move into the Fall Feasts in search of keys to the coming of Messiah ben David, Christ the King.

There are three Hebrew words in the Bible that denote the Feasts:

1. Mo'ed—means an appointed time or season, a cycle, an assembly. "...*These are my appointed feasts, the appointed feasts [mo'ed] of the Lord, . . ."* Leviticus 23:2

2. Chag—means festival and is derived from a word meaning to move in a circle, dance, hold a feast or celebration. *"On the fifteenth day of the month the Lord's Feast [chag] of Unleavened Bread begins. . ."* Leviticus 23:6

3. Miqra—means a rehearsal for a coming event. In the King James Version of the Bible, 'assemblies' is translated 'convocation' both from the Hebrew word miqra. *". . .which you are to proclaim as sacred assemblies [miqra]."* Leviticus 23:2

**Key 3-1**
**Rehearsal**

The Feasts of the Lord were for the purpose of remembrance of past events and a rehearsal of events yet to be fulfilled. The following scriptures show that the feasts are rehearsals of coming events. The feasts, therefore, are prophetic in nature. (Bracketed words in the following scriptures are added by the authors for clarification.)

**Passover:** *On the first day hold a sacred assembly [miqra] and do no regular work. For seven days present an offering made to the Lord by fire. And on the seventh day hold a sacred assembly [miqra] and do no regular work.* Leviticus 23: 7,8

**Pentecost:** *On that same day you are to proclaim a sacred assembly [miqra] and do no regular work. This is to be a lasting ordinance for the generations to come, wherever you live.* Leviticus 23:21

**Feast of Trumpets:** *"Say to the Israelites: 'On the first day of the seventh month you are to have a day of rest, a sacred assem-*

bly [miqra] commemorated with trumpet blasts. Do no regular work, but present an offering made to the Lord by fire.'"*
*Leviticus 23:24*

**Day of Atonement:** *"The tenth day of this seventh month is the Day of Atonement. Hold a sacred assembly [miqra] and deny yourselves and present an offering made to the Lord by fire."*
*Leviticus 23:27*

**Feast of Tabernacles:** *The first day is a sacred assembly [miqra]; do no regular work. Leviticus 23:35*

God's set times for the feasts were not just for the purpose of gathering the people at appointed times but to fulfill prophecy as well.

It must be noted that not only were the Feasts to be celebrated in God's appointed time but in his appointed place. As the people came into the promised land, they were instructed to gather and observe these Feasts in Jerusalem. We will see that as these Feasts are fulfilled prophetically, Jerusalem will be the focus, the appointed place. It was here that: *'important events surrounding the redemptive plan of God would be accomplished'. . ."*[1]

This is not to be interpreted that the feasts were only for the Jews, but they were for others living among them as well. They are the Feasts of the Lord and not, as often stated, the Feasts of Israel. God instructed that the feasts include:

*". . .you, your sons and daughters, your menservants and maidservants, the Levites in your towns, and the aliens, the fatherless and the widows living among you."*
*Deuteronomy 16:11b*

In the Spring of the year, the Feast of Unleavened Bread is celebrated beginning on the 14th day of the first month (Nisan) of the Sacred Calendar. The Feast of Unleavened Bread actually consists of three parts: The Passover, The Feast of Unleavened Bread, and The Feast Day of the Sheaf of Firstfruits. These combined feasts were instituted by the Lord as a remembrance of the deliverance from bondage in Egypt and as a thanksgiving for the Spring harvest. These Feasts also pointed prophetically to the first coming of Jesus and His work as the Suffering Messiah. Connected to these feasts is the Feast of Pentecost celebrated fifty days after the offering of the Sheaf of Firstfruits. The Feast of Pentecost pointed prophetically to the pouring out of the Holy Spirit as described in Acts 2.

**Before you begin, read: Exodus 11 and 12.**

## GOD'S INSTRUCTIONS

God had sent a deliverer, in the form of the man Moses, to lead his people out of the land of bondage into the promised land. God gave Moses the authority to call down plagues as a warning and judgment upon Egypt to let his people go. After the first nine plagues had been poured out on Egypt, Pharaoh still refused to let the people of God leave.

Lock 2-25
Passover Lamb
Page #30

Now the tenth plague, the killing of all firstborn, was about to take place. God delivered special instructions to the people of Israel which would protect them from this final judgment on Egypt. Each head of a household was to take a lamb for his family on the tenth day of the newly established first month of the sacred calendar (Exodus 12:2) and he was to set it aside. The lamb was to be a male, one year old, the firstborn of its mother, perfect and without defect. It was to be examined until the 14th day so that no blemish would be found in it. The lamb was killed at twilight on the 14th day, but no bone was to be broken. A bunch of hyssop was used to sprinkle the blood on the top and sides of the doorposts of their homes.

Lock 2-21
Blood Sprinkling
Page #26

*It is interesting to note that hyssop is the plant that was used for Passover and purification ceremonies for the unclean who had leprosy or had touched the dead.*

The lamb was to be roasted by fire and eaten together with unleavened bread and bitter herbs. It was to be consumed before morning or the leftovers burned. No uncircumcised male was to partake in this Lamb.

Key 3-2
Passover Meal

At midnight, the Lord struck down all the firstborn of Egypt, but the blood on the doorposts of the houses of the Israelites was a sign that their houses were to be 'passed over' and spared. This became the source of the name, Passover.

Key 3-3
Sign on Hand &
Forehead

In remembrance of this historic event, Israel was commanded to celebrate the feast yearly. The children were to be instructed at this time in the meaning of the feast and of the miracle by which God brought them out of bondage. The Israelites were also instructed to eat unleavened bread for seven days, beginning with Passover.

Later, when Israel had entered the promised land and begun reaping harvests in season, God instructed them to bring the first grain of their harvest as an offering to Him. This came to be known as the Sheaf of Firstfruits and was offered in connection with the Passover Lamb and Unleavened Bread. These combined days came to be referred to as the Feast of Unleavened Bread.

# PASSOVER

**Before you begin, read: Exodus 12:1-30, Leviticus 23:4-8, Numbers 28:16-25, and Deuteronomy 16:1-8.**

## THE PREPARATION DAYS

During the time of the Temples, the whole nation of Israel assembled in Jerusalem for the Passover. At that time the instructions God had given took the following form.

### *The 10th Day...*

Four days before the Passover, on the 10th of the first month, a ceremonial procession of priests, musicians and a multitude of the people entered Jerusalem and the Temple from the east bringing the Passover Lamb. This was the lamb that would be the public sacrifice in addition to those sacrifices brought by each household. The crowds waved palm branches before the lamb and sang, *"O Lord, save us. . . Blessed is he who comes in the name of the Lord." Psalm 118:25,26*

Lock 3-1
Rehearsal
Page #38

Key 3-4
Processions

Remember a Lamb for a House!

Between the 10th and 14th day the lambs were examined by the priests to ensure that no blemish or defect was found. Also during this time, the people assembled in the courtyard to listen to the discussions of the scriptures by the learned men.

Lock 2-10
Without Blemish
Page #22

### *The Eve of Passover. . .*

The law of Israel provided that all tithes be set aside and offered in Jerusalem at the Temple. Because it was not practical for those living far away to bring the tithes regularly, the Law prescribed that these accumulated tithes be brought on special days. One of these days occurred on the Eve of Passover. After all the tithes and offerings had been presented on the Eve of Passover, the person offering them declared before God:

> *"I have cleared out that which is holy [tithes and offerings] from the house, and I have also given it to the Levite, to the stranger, to the orphan and the widow according to all Your commandments which You have commanded me. I have not transgressed any of Your commandments nor have I forgotten any of them. I have not eaten of it while mourn-*

Key 3-5
Offering of Tithes

*ing and I have not used up any of it in a state of impurity. I have listened to the voice of God, my Lord, I have done everything which you have commanded me. Look down from Your holy dwelling place and bless Your People, Israel, and the Land which You have given us as You have sworn to our fathers, a land flowing with milk and honey."* [2]  [Brackets authors' addition]

## IN THE TEMPLE ON THE 14TH DAY

Lock 2-24
Most Holy
Sacrifice
Page #31

Lock 2-2
Courtyard
Page #20

Lock 1-8
The Hour
Page #9

Lock 2-21
Blood Sprinkling
Page #40

Lock 3-2
Passover Meal
Page #40

Lock 3-1
Rehearsal
Page #41

### *In the Outer Court. . .*

On the 14th day at the third hour the Passover Lamb which had been displayed for four days was brought into the Temple and was bound to the altar. At the ninth hour, the High Priest took his knife and killed the lamb, proclaiming the words, "It is finished." In addition, the head of each household  brought a lamb for slaughter. The blood of these sacrifices was caught in a vessel and poured onto the ground at the base of the altar by the priests. Then the head of the household took the slain lamb to his home to partake of the Passover meal as instituted by the Lord.

We found the following eyewitness report by an unnamed Roman Commissioner in several Jewish source books on Passover.   We have included the whole account, because for the first time, it provided us with a graphic picture of the Passover Feast celebration during the Second Temple before its destruction.

*'When the beginning of the month, which they call Nisan, arrives, couriers and messengers are sent out by order of the king and the judges, to all the area surrounding Jerusalem that whoever possesses sheep and cattle should hurry to bring them to the capital so that there be a sufficient supply for the pilgrims, both for their sacrifices and for their food. If anyone did not obey this order, his money would be confiscated for the use of the Sanctuary. All owners of cattle would hurry to obey and, on the way to Jerusalem they would bring their herds through a river to cleanse them of any dirt. When they reach the mountains round Jerusalem, they are so numerous that the grass cannot be seen. It appears to have become completely white because of the many sheep there. The sacrifice is offered on the fourteenth, so when the tenth of the month comes, everyone goes to buy his sacrifice which they call the 'Pesach.' It is a rule among them that no one asks another to let him go first, even if it were King David or King Shlomo. When I suggested to one of the cohanim [priests] that this was not polite, he told me that*

*before the Omnipresent there is no greatness and in His service all are equal.*

'*When the fourteenth of the month arrives they go up a high tower of the Beit Hamikdash [Temple] which they call Lul— it has a platform made like our 'canapario'—and blow on three silver trumpets. Then they make a proclamation, 'O, people of God, hearken! The time has come to slaughter the Pesach offering for the One Who causes His Presence to dwell in this great holy House.' When the people hear this announcement, they put on their festive attire for, from midday onwards, it is a festival for the Jews, since that is the time for the sacrifice.*

'*At the entrance to the great courtyard twelve Levites stand outside with silver sticks in their hands. Inside stand another twelve with golden sticks. Those outside are to keep the pilgrims in order that they do not harm one another in their great haste, and so that they do not enter in confusion and cause quarrels. It once happened on Pesach that an old man and his offering were crushed by the pressure of the crowd. The Levites who stand inside have to keep order among those who are leaving the courtyard. These also used to close the gates of the courtyard when enough people had entered.*

'*At the place where the offerings are slaughtered there are several rows of cohanim, some with silver spoons\* and some with golden spoons in their hands. The cohanim in one row all have silver spoons and those in another row all have golden ones, so that it looks most beautiful. The cohen at the head of each row receives a spoon of blood from the slaughtered animal and passes it to his neighbor and he to his neighbor until it reaches the altar. The one standing nearest the altar would send back the spoon empty and this would be passed from hand to hand until it reached the other end of the row. This was done in such a way that each cohen received a full vessel with one hand and an empty one with the other. There was no delay in this procedure. The men were so nimble that it seemed as if the vessels were flying like arrows from the bow of a trained marksman. They used to practice this for thirty days before the required time so that there should be no mistakes and they would know their task perfectly.*

'*At the same place there are two high platforms on which stand two cohanim with trumpets of silver. These are*

Lock 2-5
Priestly Duties
Page #20

*King Agrippa once wished to know the number of people in Jerusalem. He asked one of the cohanim to set aside for him one kidney from each Pesach offering and the number came to one million and two hundred thousand, double the number of males who came out of Egypt. But this was not the full number, for there was not a single Pesach lamb that was shared by less than ten people.[3]*

*\*These vessels for passing the blood are described in other sources as being wide at the top and pointed at the bottom so they cannot be put down. The blood had to be kept in motion to prevent congealing which would render it unfit to sprinkle on the altar.*

**The trumpets were sounded three times each time the Hallel was sung.*

Key 3-6
Hallel

sounded whenever a new group of pilgrims begins to bring sacrifices so that the Levites who are standing on their platforms should know that they must now sing the Halel with joy and thanksgiving, accompanied by all the musical instruments which they possess**. The owner of the offering also says Halel and if all the offerings have not yet been slaughtered, then Halel is repeated. After the slaughtering the pilgrims go to the courtyards. Here all the walls have iron teeth and prongs so that the offerings can be hung up and skinned. There are also bundles of sticks so that if there is no hook vacant, a person will suspend a stick from his shoulder to that of his friend and skin the lamb on it. The parts that are to be offered on the altar are given, and then the owner goes away joyfully, like a victorious warrior returning from battle. For it is considered a great disgrace among the Jews if one does not bring the Pesach offering at the correct time.

'While the cohanim are engaged on this task they wear short red tunics reaching to the thighs. These are red so that any blood which is spilt does not show. They stand barefoot and their sleeves reach only to the elbow so that they should not be hampered while they work. On their heads they wear a small hat with three cubits of cloth wound round it into a turban. People have told me that the Cohen Gadol [High Priest] has a white turban made of forty folds of cloth.

'The ovens on which they roasted their sacrifices were at the entrance to their houses, and they told me that this was to demonstrate their faith and also to rejoice even more. They sing joyfully while they eat and their voices can be heard from afar. No one locks his door that night in Jerusalem out of respect for the many strangers passing through the streets.'⁴ [Bracket authors' addition]

Jewish sources teach that the pivotal message of the Passover service is that every person in every generation must regard himself as having been personally freed from bondage, as was Israel from Egypt. The message of Passover is a spirit of longing for redemption and freedom, and the unyielding belief in God's provision of salvation.

# JESUS OBSERVES PASSOVER

Sensitive to feast language, we soon discovered that the Gospels contained many accounts of Jesus' participation in the feasts in Jerusalem. We realized that the lessons Jesus taught, relating to the feasts being celebrated, were to open the peoples understanding of their prophetic meaning. He clearly related the prophetic meaning of the Passover to His own death as the sacrificial Passover Lamb.

In regard to Passover, Luke 2:41-42 records Jesus as a young man celebrating Passover with his family, *"Every year his parents went to Jerusalem for the Feast of the Passover. When he was twelve years old, they went up to the Feast, according to the custom.."* Upon this occasion we see Jesus sitting under the instruction of the Rabbis.

John more than any other Gospel writer chronicled the acts of Jesus in the time frame of the feasts. In John 2:13 he writes, *"When it was almost time for the Jewish Passover, Jesus went up to Jerusalem."* At this time Jesus' declaration to the Pharisees, clearly spoke of His death and resurrection: *"Destroy this temple, and I will raise it again in three days". John 2:19*

John 3 relates that during this same season Jesus encountered Nicodemus. He taught that a man must be born again and that the Son of Man must be lifted up, alluding to His crucifixion and its provisions of salvation.

# JESUS THE PASSOVER LAMB

Lock 2-25
Passover Lamb
Page #40

Fifteen hundred years after the time of Moses, God's prophetic Spring Feasts were fulfilled by Jesus as Messiah ben Joseph, the Suffering Messiah. John the Baptist declared, *"Look, the Lamb of God, who takes away the sin of the world! John 1:29.* As the ultimate Passover Lamb, Jesus fulfilled all of God's requirements for the sacrificial lamb: a male, first born of his mother, perfect and without defect.

Lock 3-1
Rehearsal
Page #42

Lock 3-4
Processions
Page #41

On the 10th day of the first month, Jesus entered Jerusalem to face his coming death as the Passover lamb that was set aside. The crowd went before him waving palm branches and shouting, *"Blessed is he who comes in the name of the Lord!" John 12:13b.*

During the four days that followed, Jesus joined the learned men teaching in the Temple. There He was examined by the spiritual leaders much as the Passover lamb was examined by the priests before the Passover. He taught the parable of the tenants (Mark 12). In that story the owner of the vineyard sent his son to his tenants, but the tenants rose up and killed the owner's son. Jesus was teaching the prophetic meaning of this feast pointed to his death.

On the Eve of Passover [see Passover/Resurrection Chart at the end of this chapter], while eating with his disciples Jesus prayed a prayer that resembled the declaration said at the presenting of tithes:

Lock 3-5
Offering of Tithes
Page #42

*I have brought you glory on earth by completing the work you gave me to do. . . I have revealed you to those whom you gave me out of the world. They were yours; you gave them to me and they have obeyed your word. Now they know that everything you have given me comes from you. For I gave them the words you gave me and they accepted them. They knew with certainty that I came from you, and they believed that you sent me. . . My prayer is not that you take them out of the world but that you protect them from the evil one. John 17:4, 6-8, 15*

After being arrested, Jesus was subjected to further examination; a lamb without defect or blemish had been found.

Lock 2-10
Without Blemish
Page #41

> *Pilate saith unto them, Take ye him, and crucify him: for I find no fault in him. John 19:6b KJV*

On the morning of the 14th day of the first month at the third hour, Jesus was bound to the cross at a place called Golgotha located north of the Temple, fulfilling the provision of the Most Holy Sacrifice. For six hours He awaited death. At the ninth hour He proclaimed, "It is finished" and gave up his Spirit and died.

Lock 1-8
The Hour
Page #42

Lock 2-24
Most Holy Sacrifice
Page #42

> *Later, knowing that all was now completed, and so that the Scripture would be fulfilled, Jesus said, "I am thirsty." A jar of wine vinegar was there, so they soaked a sponge in it, put the sponge on a stalk of the hyssop plant and lifted it to Jesus' lips. When he had received the drink, Jesus said, "It is finished." With that he bowed his head and gave up his spirit. John 19:28-30*

The other instructions regarding the Passover lamb were also profoundly fulfilled in Jesus. Not a bone of the lamb was to be broken (Exodus 12:46). Though it was the custom to break the legs of crucifixion victims, Jesus' legs were not broken. However, He was pierced and blood and water poured out on the ground, just as the blood of the Passover lamb was poured out from the vessel at the base of the altar.

Lock 3-1
Rehearsal
Page #46

Lock 2-21
Blood Sprinkling
Page #42

> *The soldiers therefore came and broke the legs of the first man who had been crucified with Jesus, and then those of the other. But when they came to Jesus and found that he was already dead, they did not break his legs. Instead, one of the soldiers pierced Jesus' side with a spear, bringing a sudden flow of blood and water. The man who saw it has given testimony, and his testimony is true. He knows that he tells the truth, and he testifies so that you also may believe. These things happened so that the scripture would be fulfilled: "Not one of his bones will be broken," and, as another scripture says, "They will look on the one they have pierced." John 19:32-37*

> *For Christ, our Passover lamb, has been sacrificed. 1 Corinthians 5:7b*

According to one source, the animals that were to be sacrificed in the temple must be raised by the temple shepherds in the valley near Bethlehem. It was a rule that a sheep could not be raised in Galilee and carried to Jerusalem for sacrificing, nor could one raise a sheep in Jericho and carry it down to Jerusalem. Sacrifices must be born within a perimeter around Jerusalem. The southern edge of the boundary for the sacrifice was known as Migdal Eder (Bethlehem). To be qualified for the sacrifice, Jesus would have to be born within that perimeter or boundary.

# FEAST OF UNLEAVENED BREAD

**Before you begin, read: Exodus 23:14-19, 34:18-26, Leviticus 23:4-14, Numbers 28:16-25, Deuteronomy 16:1-8.** Ex 13v7, Ex 12.15 ,

The Feast of Unleavened Bread began the evening of the 14th day of the first month and continued until the 21st day. The first and last days of this feast were Sabbaths. Thus, a High Sabbath was created between the weekly Sabbath in that month. It is this circumstance that will clarify some of the confusion regarding the crucifixion week of Jesus, as discussed in the diagram The Passover/Resurrection at the end of this chapter.

According to tradition, on the evening of the 13th day the head of the household must make sure that there is no leaven anywhere in the home. After the sun sets, he takes a lighted candle and goes about looking into every nook and cranny searching for any scraps of leaven. At the hour of midnight, the leaven or any leavened bread that was found is disposed of by burning, immersing into water, or scattering into the wind.

Before the head of the household began his search for the leaven, he prayed the following prayer:

> *'Blessed are you, O Lord our God, King of the world, who has made us holy with His commandments and commanded us to remove the chametz [leaven].'*[5]

And when he had completed the search he prayed:

> *'Any leavened bread or leaven which is in my possession and which I have not seen, nor disposed of, nor did I know of it, may it be considered as null and as ownerless like the dust of the earth.'* [6]

The following interesting explanation is recorded regarding the removing of leaven:

> *What does the Torah mean by the expression 'to cause the leaven to cease?' It means that a person must nullify it in his mind, he must think of it as dust and discount it from*

*his possession, — or to put it differently, any chametz which he possesses is, in his eyes, as useless as dust....For from that time onwards, it is forbidden to derive any benefit from it and it is as if it no longer belongs to him."* [7]

The source also went on to say that the attitude and understanding of a person in fulfilling this command could not be assured. The Lord's instruction was also that the leaven should not be seen, therefore, a tradition was established. All leaven was removed from every household rather than simply nullified. For the entire seven day period of this feast no leaven was to be eaten or found in the homes of the Israelites. If leavening was found in their home they were to be cut off or separated from the congregation. They were, however, allowed to eat of unleavened bread which they baked on a daily basis. This bread has become known as Matzah and has been called the bread of affliction because of the affliction they sustained in Egypt. It is also reminiscent of the manna that God provided while the Israelites were in the wilderness.

*Symbolism of the leaven . . .*

Lock 3-1
Rehearsal
Page #47

Most references to leaven in the Old and New Testament compare it to evil influences and corruption. Unleavened bread was used in all the Feasts of the Lord except the Feast of Pentecost. It was also a symbol of consecration and separation of members of the priesthood and was one of the elements used in the making of covenants. Jesus and Paul have clearly interpreted for us the symbolism of the putting away of leaven.

Jesus warned his disciples against the leaven of Herod in Mark 8:15, the Pharisees in Luke 12:1, and the Sadducees in Matthew 16:6. It was after Jesus taught these lessons that the disciples understood what he had meant when he spoke of the leaven.

> *Then they understood that he was not telling them to guard against the yeast used in bread, but against the teaching of the Pharisees and Sadducees. Matthew 16:12*

When Paul spoke to the church at Corinth, he spoke to them not so much of the yeast used in the making of bread, but rather of the concept of how sin infiltrates the whole. Here again we see the influence and corruption that sin has in our lives:

> *Your boasting is not good. Don't you know that a little yeast works through the whole batch of dough? Get rid of the old yeast that you may be a new batch without yeast—*

*as you really are. For Christ, our Passover lamb, has been
sacrificed. Therefore let us keep the Festival, not with the
old yeast, the yeast of malice and wickedness, but with bread
without yeast, the bread of sincerity and truth.
1 Corinthians 5:6-8*

And Paul spoke in the above scripture that even though Christ,
our Passover lamb had been crucified, we should continue to
keep the Passover Feast in regards to leaven. Paul speaks profoundly on the nullification of sin (leaven) in our lives:

*In the same way, count yourselves dead to sin but alive to
God in Christ Jesus. Therefore do not let sin reign in your
mortal body . . . Romans 6:11-12a*

## EATING THE FEAST MEAL

The feast which the Lord commanded Israel to eat was to include three things: the flesh of the lamb, the unleavened bread,
and bitter herbs.

Lock 3-2
Passover Meal
Page #42

During the feast the father of the household was to teach his
children of the miracle God performed in bringing Israel out
of bondage in Egypt. The telling of the historical events that
surrounded the feast was for the instruction of the future generations that it might not be forgotten. By teaching this historical lesson the father of the household had fulfilled the scripture:

*In days to come, when your son asks you, 'What does this
mean?' say to him, 'With a mighty hand the Lord brought
us out of Egypt, out of the land of slavery. When Pharoah
stubbornly refused to let us go, the Lord killed every firstborn in Egypt, both man and animal. This is why I sacrifice to the Lord the first male offspring of every womb and
redeem each of my firstborn sons. And it will be like a sign
on your hand and a symbol on your forehead that the Lord
brought us out of Egypt with his mighty hand.
Exodus 13:14-16*

Lock 3-3
Sign on Hand &
Forehead
Page #40

At times when the Israelites were in dispersion and after the
Temple was destroyed, the Passover lamb could not be offered
according to the regulations that God had given. In order to
fulfill the commemoration of the feast substitute rituals were
adopted.

Lock 3-1
Rehearsal
Page #50

The custom today is the Jewish Seder meal which consists of, among other things, three pieces of matzah that are placed in a unity bag. One explanation that is given for the three pieces of matzah is that they represent Abraham, Isaac and Jacob. The second piece of matzah (known as Isaac) is broken into two pieces and one half is wrapped in a linen napkin and hidden until the end of the meal. The broken piece of matzah is saved throughout the year and members of the household partake of it in times of illness and financial need.

# JESUS  THE  UNLEAVENED BREAD

Just as the Passover Lamb had the duality of functioning as a sin and peace offering, so the Unleavened Bread was both the bread of affliction and the bread of life.  The bread of affliction represented bondage and separation.  The bread of life or manna symbolized the joy of the communion of peace.

Lock 3-2
Passover Meal
Page #51

John 6:4 indicates that the Passover Feast was near.  It was at this particular time that Jesus fed the multitude of five thousand and taught them about who he was.  He told them he was the Bread of Life, referring to the manna that had come down from heaven while the Israelites were in the wilderness.

> *Jesus said to them, "I tell you the truth, it is not Moses who has given you the bread from heaven, but it is my Father who gives you the true bread from heaven.  For the bread of God is he who comes down from heaven and gives life to the world.....I am the bread of life.....I am the bread that came down from heaven....Your forefathers ate the manna in the desert, yet they died.  But here is the bread that comes down from heaven which a man may eat and not die.  I am the living bread that came down from heaven.  If anyone eats of this bread, he will live forever.  This bread is my flesh, which I will give for the life of the world."  John 6:32-51*

Lock 2-15
Meal Offering
Page #31

As you will recall, the Jewish Seder meal uses three pieces of Matzah which represent for them, Abraham, Isaac and Jacob.  In a Christian setting a more understandable explanation of the three matzah of the unity bag would be a representation of the unity of the Father, Son and Holy Spirit.  What reason would there be to break Isaac?  But certainly the breaking (crucifixion) of the Son has profound significance.  The wrapping in linen and hiding of the broken piece is a profound picture of Jesus being wrapped in linen and laid in the tomb.

> *Joseph took the body, wrapped it in a clean linen cloth, and placed it in his own new tomb that he had cut out of the rock. He rolled a big stone in front of the entrance to the tomb and went away. Matthew 27:59-60*

Just as the broken piece of matzah is partaken of in times of illness and need, Jesus through his death, provides for us in our times of illness and need:

> *Surely he took up our infirmities and carried our sorrows, yet we considered him stricken by God, smitten by him, and afflicted. But he was pierced for our transgressions, he was crushed for our iniquities; the punishment that brought us peace was upon him, and by his wounds we are healed.*
> *Isaiah 53:4-5*

# FEAST DAY OF THE SHEAF OF FIRSTFRUITS

**Before you begin, read:  Exodus 23:16-19, Leviticus 23:9-14.**

The Feast Day of the Sheaf of Firstfruits was instituted by God to be celebrated not in the wilderness, but when the people of Israel entered the promise land and reaped its harvest.  Since this was the spring season it was also the beginning of the year's harvest. Grain was harvested at that time of the year and a sheaf (a bundle of grain) of the first harvest was to be brought to the priest to 'wave' before the Lord as a representative of the whole harvest.   The sheaf of grain was the first cutting of the harvest and the rest of the harvest could not be used until that sheaf was made as an offering.

Lock 2-15
Meal Offering
Page #53

Lock 3-1
Rehearsal
Page #52

The first sheaf of the harvest was to be waved in the house of the Lord on *"the day after the Sabbath." Leviticus 23:11*.  This phrase became a source of disagreement between different Jewish sects.  Some claimed it referred to the weekly Sabbath, while others insisted it referred to the High Sabbath of the first day of the Feast of Unleavened Bread.  (Refer to the Passover/Resurrection Chart at the end of this chapter.)

The *offering* of the sheaf of firstfruits needs to be distinguished from the *harvest* of the firstfruits, which came to be known as Pentecost.  The sheaf offering was the first representation of the harvest yet to come.  It was the first of the firstfruits and additional offerings would be made at Pentecost, completing the spring harvest offerings.  The concept of firstfruits was the same as that of the firstborn in Passover: the first, the foremost, and the best were always set aside as a holy offering to the Lord.

In the scriptures, the sheaf generally symbolized a person.  In Genesis 37:5-11 we find the account of the dream Joseph had when eleven sheaves were bowing down to his sheaf.  Scripture interprets that dream for us in Genesis 42:6.  The sheaves were Joseph's brothers bowing down to him.

## In the Temple - Court

One account from <u>The</u> <u>Book</u> <u>of</u> <u>Legends</u> <u>Sefer</u> <u>Ha-Aggadah</u> described the following ceremony of the gathering of the Sheaf of Firstfruits [called the Omer in Hebrew]:

*What was the procedure for preparing the omer? Messengers of the High Court used to go out on the day before Passover and tie the unreaped stand of barley grain in bunches to make it easier to reap. [On the night following the first day of Passover] all the inhabitants of the nearby towns assembled at a particular field so that the sheaf of the omer might be reaped in the midst of great commotion. As soon as it became dark, the one assigned to reap the barley called out, "Has the sun set?" And they shouted, "Yes!" "Has the sun set?" And they shouted, "Yes!" [Shall I reap] with this sickle?" And they shouted, "Yes!" "[Shall I reap] with this sickle?" And they shouted "Yes!" "Into this basket?" And they shouted, "Yes!" "Into this basket?" And they shouted, "Yes!" If it was the Sabbath, he called out further, "On this Sabbath?" And they shouted, "Yes!" "On this Sabbath?" And they shouted, "Yes!" "Shall I reap on the Sabbath?" And they shouted, "Reap!" Three times he inquired concerning each act, and three times they answered, "Yes!" "Yes!" "Yes!" . . .*

*After they reaped the omer, they put it into baskets and brought it to the Temple Court. They singed it over fire by putting it in a [copper] pipe, which was perforated so that the fire might get at all of the grains. Then they spread it out in the Temple Court, so that the wind blew over it. Next they put it into a grist mill, and out of it they took a tenth [of an ephah of flour], which was then sifted through thirteen sieves [and was finally offered up].*

*As soon as the omer [of the new harvest] had been offered, they would go out and find the markets of Jerusalem already filled with both flour and parched grain.* [8]

Lock 2-5
Priestly Duties
Page #43

Lock 2-2
Courtyard
Page #42

# JESUS THE SHEAF OF FIRSTFRUITS

The Feast Day of the Sheaf of Firstfruits was prophetic specifically of Jesus' resurrection on the morning after the Sabbath. Jesus Christ fulfilled all the representations of the Sheaf of the Firstfruits as set down by the law. As the firstborn of his mother, he was the foremost and best set aside as a holy offering to the Lord. Jesus the firstborn from the dead among many brothers, was the first representation of the harvest yet to come.

Lock 3-1
Rehearsal
Page #55

*Jesus is called the firstfruit...*
>*But Christ has indeed been raised from the dead, the firstfruits of those who have fallen asleep.*
>*1 Corinthians 15:20*

# PENTECOST

**Before you begin, read:  Exodus 23:16-17, 34:22-23; Leviticus 23:15-21 and Numbers 28:26-31, Deuteronomy 16:9-12.**

Key 3-7
Concluding Day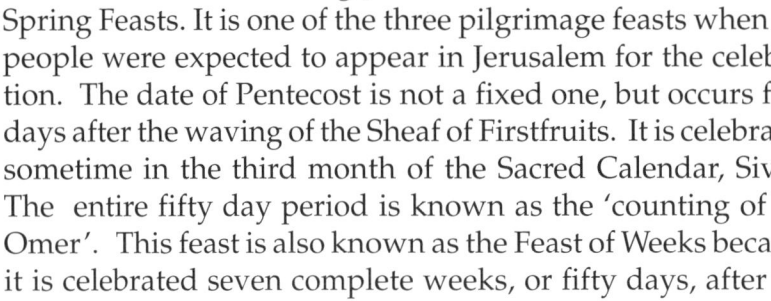

Pentecost is the concluding (Hebrew-*Atzeret*) celebration of the Spring Feasts. It is one of the three pilgrimage feasts when the people were expected to appear in Jerusalem for the celebration.  The date of Pentecost is not a fixed one, but occurs fifty days after the waving of the Sheaf of Firstfruits.  It is celebrated sometime in the third month of the Sacred Calendar, Sivan. The  entire fifty day period is known as the 'counting of the Omer'.  This feast is also known as the Feast of Weeks because it is celebrated seven complete weeks, or fifty days, after the Passover Feast.

Lock 1-3
Sevens
Page #8

Lock 3-1
Rehearsal
Page #57

Unlike Passover and Unleavened Bread, God did not give instructions that this feast was to be celebrated as a memorial to an historical event regarding Israel.  Nevertheless, He declared it a rehearsal.  As a result, varied interpretations developed to satisfy questions of meaning and timing.  Early in Israel's history, this feast was used to commemorate God's promise to Noah that he would never destroy the earth by flood.  Later, many sources claimed that the historical foundation of Pentecost was the giving of the Law at Mount Sinai.  While many interesting speculations can be found, we cannot escape the fact that God chose not to give an explanation.

The establishment of a date for Pentecost also caused a division among the Jewish sects.  Some said the counting was to begin on the day of the waving of the Sheaf of Firstfruits, while others said the counting was to begin with the weekly sabbath. By the first century this confusion had reached a peak.  A new interpretation and end to the confusion was being demanded by the people.

*Firstfruits Offerings. . .*

Lock 2-15
Meal Offering
Page #55

The people of Israel were told to celebrate Pentecost every year with the firstfruits or tithe of their harvest, especially the wheat harvest.  For the public ceremony in the Temple, they were instructed by God to bring two loaves, made from the wheat offering, mixed with yeast. The two loaves were carefully prepared individually, separately kneaded and separately baked. The evening before Pentecost, the Priests baked the loaves in the Temple.

These loaves together with two lambs were offered as a wave offering. This offering was considered one of the most holy offerings of the year (Leviticus 23:20). It was a public peace offering offered at the north side of the altar and eaten only by the officiating priests in the Holy Place. Other public peace offerings were offered on the south side of the altar.

Lock 2-24
Most Holy Sacrifice
Page #47

In practice, the giving of the Firstfruits of the Harvest occurred during the whole period of harvest from Pentecost to the Feast of Tabernacles. Freewill or peace offerings were brought at this time in proportion to the blessing the Lord had given them. This period allowed offerings from towns far away from Jerusalem to be brought to the Temple. Such an account follows:

Lock 2-23
Peace Offering
Page #31

> *"How are the firstfruits taken up [to Jerusalem]? All [the inhabitants of] the towns that make up a lay post assemble in the city of the [head of that] post, but spend the night in its open place without entering any of the houses. Early in the morning, the head of the post says, "Let us arise and go up to Zion, unto the house of the Lord our God" (Jer. 31:6).*

> *Those who live near [Jerusalem] bring fresh figs and grapes, but those from a distance bring dried figs and raisins. Before them walks an ox, its horns overlaid with gold, a crown of olive leaves on its head. A flute strikes the tempo for their procession until they approach Jerusalem. When they arrive close to Jerusalem, they send messengers to announce their coming. Meanwhile, they arrange their firstfruits in an ornamental display. Governors of priests, chiefs of the Levites, and treasurers [of the Temple] go out to meet them. The number of those going out varies in keeping with the number of the entrants. All the skilled artisans of Jerusalem are required to rise up before them and greet them: "Brethren, men of such-and-such a place, peace be upon you in your coming."*

> *The flute continues to strike the tempo before them until they reach the Temple Mount. When they reach the Temple Mount, even King Agrippa places a basket on his shoulder and walks as far as the Temple Court. As they approach the Court, the Levites sing, "I will extol Thee, O Lord, for Thou has raised me up, and hast not suffered mine enemies to rejoice over me" (Ps. 30:2).*

*The turtledoves [tied to] each basket are [offered up as] burnt offerings, but the baskets of firstfruits that the people hold in their hands they present to the priests.*

*While the basket is yet on his shoulder, each man recites the passage beginning: "I profess this day unto the Lord thy God" (Deut. 26:3), until he reaches the end of the passage (Deut. 26:10). Rabbi Judah said: Until he reaches "A wandering Armenian sought to slay my father" (Deut. 26:5). When he reaches these words, he takes the basket off his shoulder and holds it by its rim, and the priest places his hand under it and waves it. Then the Israelite begins to recite "An Armenian sought to slay my father," until he completes the entire passage. He then deposits the basket by the side of the altar, prostrates himself, and departs.*

*Originally, all who knew how to recite the prescribed words [in Hebrew] would recite them, while those unable to do so repeated them after the priest. But when people began to refrain from bringing firstfruits in shame [of their ignorance], it was decided that both those who could as well as those who could not recite them [in Hebrew] should repeat the words after the priest.*

*The rich bring their firstfruits in baskets overlaid with silver and gold, while the poor bring them in wicker baskets made of peeled willow branches and give both baskets and firstfruits to the priests."[9]*

The children are taught from the book of Ruth during this time. They are told the story of Ruth, a Gentile, and her acceptance into the fold of Israel.

Key 3-8
Trumpets

In Jewish tradition three trumpets are given names in connection to the feasts: the First Shofar, the Last Shofar, and the Great Shofar (Hebrew-*Shofar HaGadol*). The First Shofar is associated with the Feast of Pentecost, the Last Shofar with the Day of Trumpets, and the Great Shofar with the Day of Atonement.

# THE HOLY SPIRIT IN PENTECOST

Because Pentecost was tied to no historical event when instituted by the Lord, it continued to be a source of confused meaning among the Jews for many centuries. Interestingly, this confusion had reached a peak during the first century. It was at this time the true meaning and intent was revealed by God. All past celebrations were a rehearsal for the day of the outpouring of the Holy Spirit and the birth of the church.

Lock 3-1
Rehearsal
Page #58

> *When the day of Pentecost came, they were all together in one place. Suddenly a sound like the blowing of a violent wind came from heaven and filled the whole house where they were sitting. They saw what seemed to be tongues of fire that separated and came to rest on each of them. All of them were filled with the Holy Spirit and began to speak in other tongues as the Spirit enabled them. Acts 2:1-4*

Lock 2-17
Fire Kindled
Page #20

Christ spoke of the intimacy that would be experienced with the coming of the Counselor. This Counselor, the Holy Spirit, would dwell within them.

> *And I will ask the Father, and he will give you another Counselor to be with you forever—the Spirit of truth. The world cannot accept him, because it neither sees him nor knows him. But you know him, for he lives with you and will be in you. John 14:16-17*

Paul explained to the Ephesians that this Holy Spirit marked or sealed believers as in Christ, sharing unity with the Father:

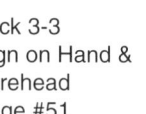

Lock 3-3
Sign on Hand &
Forehead
Page #51

> *I in them and you in me. May they be brought to complete unity to let the world know that you sent me and have loved them even as you have loved me. John 17:23*

Glorious as this intimacy is, Paul explains it is only a deposit on a full inheritance yet to come:

> *Having believed, you were marked in him with a seal, the promised Holy Spirit, who is a deposit guaranteeing our inheritance until the redemption of those who are God's possession—to the praise of his glory. Ephesians 1:13b-14*

Lock 3-7
Concluding Day
Page #58

Pentecost was the concluding day of the Spring Feast—prophetic of Jesus' first coming and appropriately, the Holy Spirit was poured out at the conclusion of Jesus' work.

> *But I tell you the truth: It is for your good that I am going away. Unless I go away, the Counselor will not come to you; but if I go, I will send him to you. John 16:7*

Lock 2-15
Meal Offering
Page #58

God's instructions regarding this feast day reveal to us His further intent—two lambs and two loaves offered uniquely with leaven, revealing the arrival of the kingdom of heaven. For Christ said, *"The kingdom of heaven is near."* (Matthew 10:7) and the kingdom of heaven is like leaven:

> *He told them still another parable: "The kingdom of heaven is like yeast that a woman took and mixed into a large amount of flour until it worked all through the dough." Matthew 13:33*

> *Is God the God of Jews only? Is he not the God of Gentiles too? Yes, of Gentiles too, since there is only one God, who will justify the circumcised by faith and the uncircumcised through that same faith. Romans 3:29-30*

Paul in Romans 11 speaks of the two loaves relating that they represent the Jew and the Gentile. We find this point reinforced by Peter when he relates to the Jewish church the incident of Cornelius the Gentile receiving the Holy Spirit. This confirmed that it was God's intent to include the Gentiles in the gift of the Holy Spirit.

> *He redeemed us in order that the blessing given to Abraham might come to the Gentiles through Christ Jesus, so that by faith we might receive the promise of the Spirit. Galatians 3:14*

> *This mystery is that through the gospel the Gentiles are heirs together with Israel, members together of one body, and sharers together in the promise in Christ Jesus. Ephesians 3:6*

It is interesting that the Book of Ruth is read during this feast for it too, was a message of God's plan of redemption to bring the Gentiles into His household. Ruth, the Moabitess, was part of the genealogy of Jesus.

## Authors' Comment

Perhaps the confusion among the Jews regarding the Feast of Pentecost can be explained by the fact that it ushered in the church age for which they had little reference. The other feasts were tied to the nation of Israel historically. The history of this feast is to be found in the birth of the church.

# THE SUMMER MONTHS

The Spring Feasts have come to an end early in the third month. There is an interval of three and one half months before the Fall Feasts begin in the seventh month. During this time the climate is dry and the harvest is ripening in the fields. The people look forward to the fall harvest and the celebration of thanksgiving that will follow in Jerusalem.

If the Spring Feasts clearly describe the first coming of Jesus and the Fall Feasts are prophetic of His second coming, then this summer season must represent that period of time between these two advents—the time in which we live, referred to as the church age.

Lock 1-7
Redemptive Week
Page #8

## A TIME OF REPENTANCE

Beginning on the first day of the sixth month, a period of repentance is observed. At this time, personal repentance is the focus in preparation for the coming Fall Feasts. It is the custom among some Jewish sects to visit one another and ask forgiveness during this period. These things must be done prior to the Day of Atonement. It is believed that only when their relationships with one another have been appeased may atonement be made for transgressions committed in their relationship with God.

Key 3-9
Personal Repentance

This 30 day period combined with the first 10 days of the seventh month is known as Teshuvah, the time of repentance and return. Regarding this period it is written:

Key 3-10
Repentance from
Adultery

> *"Return, O Israel." Teshuvah [repentance] is dear to the Holy One, blessed be he, for he abrogates his own words for the sake of Teshuvah. How? He wrote in the Torah: "When a man taketh a wife, and marrieth her, then it cometh to pass, if she find no favor in his eyes, because he hath found some unseemly thing in her, that he writeth her a bill of divorcement, and giveth it in her hand, and sendeth her out of his house, and she departeth out of his house, and goeth and becometh another man's wife, and the latter husband hateth her, and writeth her a bill of divorcement, and giveth*

*it in her hand, and sendeth her out of his house; or if the latter husband die, who took her to be his wife; her former husband, who sent her away may not take her again to be his wife, after that she is defiled" (Deut. 24:1-4). But the Holy One, blessed be he, does not do so. Despite the fact that Israel deserted him and served another, "and they forsook the Lord, and served Him not (Judges 10:6), he said to them: Do Teshuvah and come to me and I will accept you. Jeremiah makes it explicit: "If a man put away his wife, and she go from him, and become another man's, may he return unto her again? Will not that land be greatly polluted? But thou hast played the harlot with many lovers; and wouldest thou yet return to Me? Saith the Lord" (Jer. 3:1). Come, and I will accept you. "Return, O Israel, unto the Lord thy God." (Pesikta Rabbati, Shuvah Yisrael)* [10]
[Brackets authors' addition]

Key 3-11
Birthpains

The Jews clearly relate this period of time concluding with the Day of Atonement as a time of judgment. The message of this 40-day period is clearly repent before the great and terrible day is upon you.

# PASSOVER/RESURRECTION CHART

## How to Read

On the facing page we have presented a chart that helps explain the timetable of events of the week of the crucifixion, blending the scriptural accounts. We do not intend to enter the debate surrounding the exact day and hour of Jesus' death. Changes of calendars, calculations of the day, meaning of terms all contribute to varied theories. However, we could not escape the conviction born out of our study that God has a perfect timetable on which his plan of salvation rests.

In the Roman Commissioner's account of the Passover ceremonies he makes this comment, *"For it is considered a great disgrace among the Jews if one does not bring the Pesach offering at the correct time."* Few of those who debate the time of Jesus' death would argue against his representation as the Passover Lamb. Why would he be an offering brought at other than the correct time?

Scripture states that Jesus was resurrected on the first day of the week, Sunday. The day previous would have been Saturday, the Jewish weekly Sabbath. Jesus was in the grave three nights and three days. Counting back from Sunday:

| **Night** | **Day** |
|---|---|
| 1 Saturday | 1 Sunday |
| 2 Friday | 2 Friday |
| 3 Thursday | 3 Thursday |

Passover begins on the 14th day of the first month. Jewish law says that this day can only occur on a Sunday, Tuesday, Thursday or Saturday. The day after, the 15th, is the first day of Unleavened Bread. This day is called a High Sabbath, thus causing two sabbaths to occur during the week.

This dilemma of more than one sabbath appearing in Passover week has been a subject of contention among Jewish sects for generations. The law stated the waving of the Sheaf of Firstfruits is to occur on the day after the sabbath. Which sabbath is meant, the weekly sabbath or the High Sabbath?

Jesus rose from the dead Sunday the day after the weekly sabbath. I Corinthians 15:4-5 indicates to us that Jesus fulfilled the waving of the Sheaf of Firstfruits at his resurrection. Therefore, the waving of the sheaf appears to be intended for the day after the weekly sabbath following the Passover.

Scripture says that the Jews wanted Jesus removed from the cross because the next day was the Sabbath. This sabbath could have been the High Sabbath of the first day of the Feast of Unleavened Bread, the 15th. Therefore, placing his death on the 14th which was Passover, just as the Passover Lamb was offered.

In addition, John 12:1 says that six days before Passover, Jesus arrived in Bethany and in verse 12-19 it says Jesus made his triumphal entry into Jerusalem. Six days before Passover would be the 9th of Nisan, so Jesus entered Jerusalem on the next day, the 10th, a parallel to the entry of the Passover Lamb brought to Jerusalem to be set aside for death.

Jesus beautifully fulfilled the provisions of the sacrifice of Passover week. Not everyone agrees with this accounting, because of varying calendars, but it is not difficult to see that God was not confused about His days and that Jesus fulfilled God's timetable.

Lock 1-1
Time
Page #8

Lock 2-25
Passover Lamb
Page #46

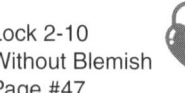

Lock 2-10
Without Blemish
Page #47

# PASSOVER/RESURRECTION CHART
## Exodus 12 & Leviticus 23 detail the Feast of Unleavened Bread (Passover)

*(All Scripture in King James Version)*

**Timeline:**

| 10 | 11 | 12 | 13 | 14 | 15 | 16 | 17 |
|----|----|----|----|----|----|----|----|
| Sunday | Monday | Tuesday | Wednesday | Thursday | Friday | Saturday | Sunday |

Sundown — Sundown — Sundown — Sundown

EVE 1 | DAY 1 | EVE 2 | DAY 2 | EVE 3 | DAY 3 First Day of the Week

HIGH SABBATH — WEEKLY SABBATH

Jewish days are counted from 6 p.m. to 6 a.m. - evening to evening

---

Gen. 1:5 "And God called the light Day and the darkness he called Night. And the evening and the morning were the first day."

Ex. 12: 2 "This month shall be unto you the beginning of months; it shall be the first month of the year to you. *This is the first month of the Jewish Calendar in which Passover begins on the 10th day of the first month.* Ex. 12: 3 ... In the tenth day of this month they shall take to them every man a lamb..."

**JESUS SLAIN:** Luke 22:1, 7, "Now the feast of unleavened bread drew nigh, which is called the Passover. Then came the day of unleavened bread, when the passover must be killed... *Jesus was with his disciples on the Eve of Passover, just prior to his arrest. vs. 66* "And as soon as it was day, the elders of the people and the chief priests and the scribes came together and led him into their council, saying. . ." Luke 23:2 "And they began to accuse him. . . vs. 4 Then said Pilate...I find no fault in this man..." vs. 14 "...I. having examined him before you, have found no fault in this man..." vs. 17 "...release one unto them at the feast..." Luke 23:44 "And it was about the sixth hour, and there was a darkness over all the earth until the ninth hour."

**PASSOVER LAMB SLAIN:** Ex. 12:6 "And ye shall keep it until the fourteenth day of the same month: and the whole assembly of the congregation of Israel shall kill it in the evening."

Luke 23:53-54 "And he took it down and wrapped it in linen and laid it in a sepulchre that was hewn in stone. . . And that day was the preparation and the sabbath drew on." vs. 55-56 "And the women also, which came with him. . . And they returned, and prepared spices and ointments and rested the sabbath day. . ."

---

**APPEARED TO THE ELEVEN DISCIPLES:**
Luke 24:36 "And as they thus spake, Jesus himself stood in the midst of them . . ."
Mark 16:14 "Afterward he appeared unto the eleven as they sat at meat..."
1 Cor. 15:4-5 "And that he was buried, and that he rose again the third day according to the scriptures: And that he was seen of Cephas, then of the twelve:
Acts 1:3 "To whom also he shewed himself alive after his passion by many infallible proofs, being seen of them forty days, and speaking of the things pertaining to the kingdom of God."
Luke 24:15 "And it came to pass that while they communed together and reasoned. Jesus himself drew near and went with them. . ."
**APPEARED TO MARY:** John 20:19 "Then the same day at evening, being the first day of the week, when the doors were shut where the disciples were assembled...came Jesus..."
**PENTECOST:** Acts 2:1 "And when the day of Pentecost was fully come they were all with one accord in one place." (Counts 50 days sabbath)

Luke 24:44 And he said unto them, These are the words which I spake unto you, while I was yet with you, that all things must be fulfilled, which were written in the law of Moses, and in the prophets, and in the psalms, concerning me.

---

**THREE DAYS AND THREE NIGHTS:**
Luke 24:46 "...Christ to suffer, and to rise from the dead the third day."
Matt. 16:21 "...be killed, and be raised again the third day."
Luke 11:29 "...they seek a sign; and there shall no sign be given it, but the sign of Jonas the prophet."
Jonah 1:17 "Now the Lord had prepared a great fish to swallow up Jonah. And Jonah was in the belly of the fish three days and three nights."

**Jesus "RESURRECTION"** - Matt. 28, Mark 16:19, Luke 24:46, Luke 24:1 (first day)
**SHEAF OF FIRSTFRUITS:** 1 Cor. 15: 20-23 Christ the firstfruits; Lev. 23:11 ..."on the morrow after the sabbath...."

**FIRST DAY OF THE WEEK:** Jesus rose early on the first day of the week — Sunday. His body was gone!
Luke 24:1,3 "Now upon the first day of the week, very early in the morning, they came to the sepulchre... And they entered in, and found not the body of the Lord Jesus."
Mark 16:1-6, 9 "And when the sabbath was past, Mary Magdalene, and Mary, the mother of James, and Salome, had bought sweet spices ... And very early in the morning the first day of the week, they came ...Ye seek Jesus ....which was crucified: he is risen..."
John 20:1-5 "The first day of the week..."
Matt. 28:1 "In the end of the sabbath, as it began to dawn toward the first day of the week ... *This was the weekly sabbath.*

-67-

# QUICK REFERENCE
# TO FALL FEASTS

| Month | Day | Name of Feast | Other Names |
|---|---|---|---|
| 6-Elul *(Aug/Sep)* | 1-30 thru Tishri 10 | Time of Repentance | Teshuvah |
| 7-Tishri *(Sep/Oct)* | 1, 2 | Feast Day of Trumpets New Year's Day | Rosh HaShanah |
| | | (Day of Awakening) | Yom HaTeruah |
| | | (Day of Judgment) | Yom HaDin |
| | | (Coronation of Messiah) | HaMelech |
| | | (Day of Remembrance) | Yom HaZikkaron |
| | | (Birthpangs of Messiah) | Chevlai Shel Mashiach |
| | | (The Hidden Day) | Yom Hakeseh |
| | 10 | Day of Atonement | Yom Kippur |
| | 15-21 | Feast of Tabernacles | Sukkot |
| | | | Feast of Booths |
| | | 7th Day of Feast | Hoshana Rabbah |
| | 22 | 8th Day | Shemini Atzeret |
| | 23 | 8th Day continued | Simchat Torah |

# Chapter 4

## THE FALL FEASTS

### OVERVIEW

Our study of the Fall Feasts became more exciting after our new encounters with the prophetic significance of the Spring Feasts and their fulfillment by Jesus, Messiah ben Joseph.

We quickly saw that in studying the Fall Feasts we were observing the prophetic second coming of Christ, Messiah ben David. Hosea likens the appearing of the Messiah as spring and winter rains. Two comings were represented by the Spring and Fall Feasts:

> *"Do you not say, 'Four months more and then the harvest'? I tell you, open your eyes and look at the fields! They are ripe for harvest. Even now the reaper draws his wages, even now he harvests the crop for eternal life, so that the sower and the reaper may be glad together. John 4:35-36*

> *Let us acknowledge the Lord; let us press on to acknowledge him. As surely as the sun rises, he will appear; he will come to us like the winter rains, like the spring rains that water the earth. Hosea 6:3*

This chapter will provide you with some keys to the second coming of the Messiah as they relate to the book of Revelation and armed with these keys we will begin to unlock some of its mysteries.

**Before you begin, read: Leviticus 16:2-34, 23:23-43 ; Deuteronomy 16:13-17; 17:14-20; 31:9; Numbers 29:1-39.**

Lock 3-1
Rehearsal
Page #61

In the fall of the year the Feast of the Seventh Month is celebrated. It is a remembrance of the time that Israel spent living in temporary dwellings in the wilderness and a thanksgiving for the fall harvest. This feast also points prophetically to the second coming of Jesus and His Kingship.

The Feast of the Seventh Month is divided into three parts: Feast Day of Trumpets, the Day of Atonement, and Feast of Tabernacles. It is common practice to include all three parts of this feast in the one name Feast of Tabernacles.

During the time that the Temple stood, all of Israel was to assemble in Jerusalem for this feast. It was considered the greatest feast of the year and was referred to as the Great Feast of the Lord.

## GOD'S INSTRUCTIONS

Just prior to Moses' death, the Lord presented a new covenant to the people of Israel in Moab. We saw in our study of the Feast of Pentecost that Moab was significant in demonstrating the acceptance of the Gentiles into the redemptive plan of God. As Israel was about to enter the promised land we see two covenants in hand: the old made at Sinai (Horeb) and the new made at Moab.

> *These are the terms of the covenant the Lord commanded*
> *Moses to make with the Israelites in Moab, in addition to*
> *the covenant he had made with them at Horeb.*
> *Deuteronomy 29:1*

This Book of the Covenant was to be placed beside the ark of the covenant by the priests who carried it. This covenant contained the moral, civil and ceremonial laws; all the ordinances of the Lord by which Israel could approach Him and the means by which His presence could dwell among them as King.

This Book of the Law was to be opened and read with great ceremony during the time of the Feast of Tabernacles in the fall of the year. The law was read and taught as general teaching throughout the year, but this was a solemn and special reading at this appointed time and place. Illustrations of this historical event can be read in the books of Ezra 3 and Nehemiah 8.

Key 4-1
Book of Covenant

The king was also instructed to make a copy of the Book of the Law that the priests had and keep it in the throne of his kingdom. He was to read it and meditate on it on a daily basis. Therefore, a Book of the Law was kept in the side of the Ark of the Covenant (God's earthly throne) and a copy was kept in the throne of Israel's earthly king.

During the sabbatical year the <u>Mishnah</u> instructs the king to read from the law:

> *After the close of the first Festival-day of the Feast [of Tabernacles], in the eighth year, after the going forth of the Seventh Year, they used to prepare for him in the Temple Court a wooden platform on which he sat, for it is written, At the end of every seven years in the set time . . . . The minister of the synagogue used to take a scroll of the Law and give it to the chief of the synagogue, and the chief of the synagogue gave it to the Prefect, and the Prefect gave it to the High Priest, and the High Priest gave it to the king, and the king received it standing and read it sitting. — Mishnah, Sota 7:8*

Lock 1-3
Sevens
Page #58

When the Book of the Law was found during Josiah's reign, he took his place in the Temple and read from the Law before all the people.

> *The king stood by his pillar and renewed the covenant in the presence of the Lord—to follow the Lord and keep his commands, regulations and decrees with all his heart and all his soul, and to obey the words of the covenant written in this book. II Chronicles 34:31*

> *He [king] went up to the temple of the Lord with the men of Judah, the people of Jerusalem, the priests and the prophets—all the people from the least to the greatest. He read in their hearing all the words of the Book of the Covenant, which had been found in the temple of the Lord. The king stood by the pillar and renewed the covenant in the presence of the Lord—to follow the Lord and keep his commands, regulations and decrees with all his heart and all his soul, thus confirming the words of the covenant written in this book. Then all the people pledged themselves to the covenant. II Kings 23:2-3 [Brackets authors' addition.]*

# FEAST DAY OF TRUMPETS

**Before you begin, read:  Leviticus 23:23-25, Numbers 28:11-15, 29: 1-6, Nehemiah 8; Ezra 3:1-6.**

## New Moon Ceremonies

At the beginning of each lunar month, God established a celebration of the New Moon.  Special sacrifices were made during the New Moon celebrations and blessings were sung.  The blessings consisted of verses such as Psalms 148:1-6 in which the heavenly bodies and all creation were summoned to praise their Creator.

### In the Temple . . .

Lock 2-6
Priest/King & His
Council
Page #16

Lock 1-5
New Moon-One
Long Day
Page #16

The determination of the time for the start of the New Moon celebration consisted of an elaborate system.  Eye witnesses were engaged to report the first appearance of the new moon.  In the Temple, a council of elders and the High Priest awaited the report and in turn proclaimed, "It is sanctified!" at which time the new month officially began.  Because of the time necessary for the sanctification of the month to move throughout the land, two days were actually celebrated to ensure obedience to God's command.  This 48-hour period was known as One Long Day.

### In the Palace . . .

Key 4-2
Homage to the King

The kings of Israel gave banquets for the people during the time of the new moon.  Those invited attended to demonstrate their loyalty and show homage to the king.  It was at this time they received commissions regarding services they could perform for him.  His judgment was also sought on matters of dispute among them.  The story of Jonathan and David in I Samuel 20 refers to such a New Moon festival:

> *So David said, "Look, tomorrow is the New Moon festival, and I am supposed to dine with the king; but let me go and hide in the field until the evening of the day after tomorrow. Vs. 27 But the next day, the second day of the month, David's place was empty again.  Then Saul said to his son*

> *Jonathan, "Why hasn't the son of Jesse come to the meal, either yesterday or today?" I Samuel 20:5, 27*

This tradition of assembling before the king had its fuller meaning in the seventh month. On the new moon of the seventh month, all Israel assembled to acknowledge the kingship and sovereignty of God.

## NEW MOON OF THE SEVENTH MONTH

The New Moon celebration of the seventh month, Tishri, was distinguished from all other new moons as a High Sabbath. A High Sabbath is a sabbath that can occur on other days of the week than the seventh day. The Jewish Sacred calendar is calculated, however, so that this New Moon Feast cannot fall on Sunday, Wednesday, or Friday. This day marks the Jewish New Year on the Civil Calendar and is known in Hebrew as Rosh HaShanah (Rosh means head or chief and Shanah means year).

Lock 1-3
Sevens
Page #71

Lock 1-2
1st of Tishri
Page #4

Lock 1-1
Time
Page #66

During other feasts and new moons, songs of praise and rejoicing (Hallel) were sung. But Jewish tradition explains, *"When the King sits on the chair of judgment and the books of life and death are before him, Israel cannot sing."* (Tractate R.H. 32) Therefore, the Hallel is not sung on the Day of Trumpets or the Day of Atonement.

Lock 3-6
Hallel
Page #44

On all other festival days the moon is either full or near full. On this day the moon is hidden (new moon).

> *The People of Israel is symbolically compared to the moon and is radiant on its Sabbaths and Festivals. On Rosh Hashanah, however, Israel diminishes itself and conceals its greatness in awe of the Day of Judgment. The Almighty, too, places a cover of concealment over His People's sins and accords them forgiveness.[1]*

For this reason Jewish tradition connects the Day of Trumpets with a period of great distress for Israel. For this reason the Torah readings in the Temple on this day are purposed in bringing both God and Israel to remembrance of their relationship, in order that Israel might not be utterly destroyed.

On the first day of the feast the reading is from the account of God's promise to make a great nation of Abraham's seed. This reading also includes Isaac's birth.

On the second day, considered a continuation of the first day, the Torah reading consists of God's testing of Abraham with the commandment to sacrifice Isaac. The rabbis teach at this time that as Abraham and Isaac approached the mountain to sacrifice, Satan turned himself into a wide stream to hinder them. But the Lord rebuked the stream and dried it up so they could continue. (We encourage you to read this complete story in Appendix B at the end of this chapter.)

Lock 1-5
New Moon-One
Long Day
Page #72

The haftarah reading consists of a portion of the book of Jeremiah containing the account of Israel's future redemption. Rachel refuses to be consoled for the exile of her children and God assures her that her hope will be vindicated.

## CORONATION OF MESSIAH THE KING

A major theme of this feast day is the future coronation of Messiah as King. In Hebrew it is called HaMelech. At this time it is believed Messiah ben David will take his throne. In the temple services Psalms 47, a song of coronation, is read seven times on this day.

## THE BOOK OF THE COVENANT

The New Moon of the seventh month is also called Yom HaDin, which in Hebrew means Day of Judgment. It is believed that on this day Messiah ben David as King will assume the throne of judgment. At this time the door to heaven will be opened to receive the righteous.

Key 4-3
Door/Gates Opened

Key 4-4
3 Books

The <u>Mishnah</u> describes this day as one in which three books of judgment are opened:

Key 4-5
Sealing

1. The Book of the Righteous (also called the Book of Life): contains those who are judged at this time to be righteous before the Lord. The righteous dead are believed to be resurrected at this time and gathered to God with the living righteous.

2. The Book of the Wicked includes those immediately inscribed for death, known as vessels fit for destruction.

3. The Book of the Sinners or Average People are those whom God is still dealing with and whose fate is not yet sealed. They are held over from the Feast Day of Trumpets to the Day of Atonement when

their fate is sealed. If they repent they are inscribed in the Book of Life. If they do not repent they are inscribed in the Book of the Wicked.

In connection with the concept of the time of judgment, the New Moon of the seventh month is called in Hebrew, Yom Ha Teruah, the Day of the Awakening Blast or Shout. In the Temple, trumpets are sounded all day long. On other days trumpets are blown but on this day the trumpets are sounded in an alarm blast. The trumpet blown on this day is one of the three trumpets given names in Jewish tradition. This trumpet is known as the Last Shofar. It is the trumpet that heralds the coming of Messiah and the resurrection of the dead. It is in this connection that the day has become most commonly known as the Day of Trumpets.

> *But everything exposed by the light becomes visible, for it is light that makes everything visible. This is why it is said: "Wake up, O sleeper, rise from the dead, and Christ will shine on you."  Ephesians 5:13-14*

Lock 3-8
Trumpets
Page #60

*"The blowing of the shofar on Rosh Hashanah is an ordinance of Scripture [and must therefore be obeyed, if only for that reason].  But it also has a deeper meaning.  It says to us: Awake, ye slumberers, from your slumber, and rouse yourselves from your deep sleep.  Search your deeds and turn ye in repentance.  Remember your Creator, ye who forget truth because of the vanity of the hour, who go astray all through the year in pursuit of trifles which can neither profit nor save.  Let every one of you forsake his wicked path and his evil purpose."* [2]

## BIRTHPAINS OF THE MESSIAH

Another name for the New Moon of the seventh month is in Hebrew, Chevlai Shel Mashiach, meaning Birthpains of the Messiah. Sometimes this term is also referred to as the Time of Jacob's Trouble. These terms have their source in the following scriptures:

> *"God speaks to Abraham, 'When your descendants sin, and they appear before Me for judgment on Rosh Hashanah, let them blow the ram's horn; this will remind Me of the piety of their ancestors and lead Me to forgive them'...*
>
> *Regarding Psalm 89:16, Rabbi Josiah said:  'Do not other peoples know how to sound blasts?  How many kinds of horns and trumpets they possess!  But the verse means: Happy is the people who know how to evoke the favor of their Creator by means of the blast.  For when they blow the shofar, the Holy One (blessed be He!) arises from the throne of judgment and sits upon the throne of mercy; He is filled with compassion for them and transforms His Quality of Justice into the Quality of Mercy.'"* [3]

*Before she goes into labor, she gives birth; before the pains come upon her, she delivers a son. Who has ever heard of such a thing?  Who has ever seen such things?  Can a country be born in a day or a nation be brought forth in a moment?  Yet no sooner is Zion in labor than she gives birth to her children. Isaiah. 66:7, 8*

Lock 3-11
Birthpains
Page #64

*Ask and see: Can a man bear children?  Then why do I see every strong man with his hands on his stomach like a woman in labor, every face turned deathly pale?"  How*

*awful that day will be! None will be like it. It will be a time of trouble for Jacob, but he will be saved out of it. Jeremiah. 30:6-7*

It was this period that was described by Daniel in Chapter 12:

*At that time Michael, the great prince who protects your people will arise. There will be a time of distress such as has not happened from the beginning of nations until then. But at that time your people—everyone whose name is found written in the book—will be delivered. Daniel 12:1*

## DAYS OF AWE

Key 4-6
National Cleansing

The Feast Day of Trumpets is the beginning of a 10-day period often called in Jewish writings Days of Awe (Hebrew -*Yamin Noraim*). Concluding on the Day of Atonement, this season is filled with an awesome fear of God. At this time prayers of repentance are said in a plural form for as each man repents and is forgiven, it is believed all Israel is cleansed.

*". . . So, if one's fellow should sin, it is as though one has sinned oneself; therefore, despite the fact that one has not committed that iniquity, one must confess to it. For when one's fellow has sinned it is as though one has sinned oneself."[4]*

Key 4-7
Door/Gates Closed

This judgment period culminates on the Day of Atonement, seen as the final judgment day, at the end of which the gates of heaven are closed.

During this period Ezekiel 33:1-7 is read speaking to the watchmen to warn the people:

*The word of the Lord came to me: "Son of man, speak to your countrymen and say to them: 'When I bring the sword against a land, and the people of the land choose one of their men and make him their watchman, and he sees the sword coming against the land and blows the trumpet to warn the people, then if anyone hears the trumpet but does not take warning, and the sword comes and takes his life, his blood will be on his own head. If he had taken warning, he would have saved himself. But if the watchman sees the sword coming and does not blow the trumpet to warn the people and the sword comes and takes the life of one of them, that man will be taken away because of his sin, but I will hold the watchman accountable for his blood. Son of man, I have*

*made you a watchman for the house of Israel; so hear the word I speak and give them warning from me."*
*Ezekiel 33:1-7*

Psalms 27 is read which speaks of a time of trouble for Israel and a plea to God to hide her:

*For in the day of trouble he will keep me safe in his dwelling: he will hide me in the shelter of his tabernacle and set me high upon a rock.  Psalms 27:5*

*Rabbi Ishmael said: "God says to Israel. Open to Me a gate of repentance no bigger than the point of a needle, and I will open to you a gate [of forgiveness] wide enough to drive wagons and carts through." Cant. R. 5:2, The Torah, pg. 869*

*Rabbi Ishmael said:  A king's son had traveled a hundred days journey from his father.  His friends advised him to return home, but he said "I cannot, the trip is too long." Then his father sent him word, "Come back as far as your strength permits, and I will go to meet you the rest of the way."  Thus God says to Israel, "Return to Me, and I will return to you."  Pesikta Rabbati, 44, 184b-185a, The Torah, pg. 869*

## AUTHORS' COMMENT

If the Feast Day of Trumpets celebrated for a two-day period known as One Long Day is seen prophetically as the day when the righteous are sealed, then the days that follow would correspond to a period of time when the average people or sinners are given an additional time in which to repent.   This time corresponds perhaps to that referred to by Jesus as the 'beginning of birthpains'.  At the end of the tenth day the Day of Atonement final judgment is completed, all opportunity of repentance is past and the doors of heaven are closed.

Lock 1-5
New Moon-One
Long Day
Page #74

Lock 4-4
3 Books
Page #74

# DAY OF ATONEMENT

**Before you begin, read: Leviticus 16; Numbers 29:7-11; Hebrews 8-10.**

## A DAY OF FASTING AMONG DAYS OF FEASTS

Lock 1-4
10th of Tishri
Page #26

Lock 4-6
National Cleansing
Page #76

Lock 3-9
Personal Repentance
Page #63

The Day of Atonement is celebrated on the 10th day of the seventh month, Tishri. The Jewish calendar is calculated in such a way as to prevent the Day of Atonement, a day of fasting, from occurring on Friday or Sunday because food preparation is forbidden on the Sabbath (Saturday) and this would force a two-day fast. During the 30 days previous to the seventh month, the thrust of repentance was personal. During the first 10 days of the seventh month the repentance was focused on the sins of the nation of Israel. This day is looked upon as a day of national cleansing for Israel and represents forgiveness of sin and a new beginning for the New Year.

*". . . I will remove the sin of this land in a single day." Zechariah 3:9*

Lock 3-8
Trumpets
Page #75

Lock 4-7
Door/Gates Closed
Page #76

Lock 4-5
Sealing
Page #74

Prophetically this day is seen as the final day of the judgment begun on Tishri 1. Because of the awe filled concept of the final judgment it is referred to simply as The Day or That Day. At the end of this day it is believed that the Great Shofar (trumpet) will be blown for those who have become believers during the birthpains and have been inscribed in the Book of Life. Following this the gate of heaven will be closed and no further means of repentance will be available. Those that remain are believed to be inscribed in the Book of the Wicked.

*Much time has been lost, and sailing had already become dangerous because by now it was after the Fast. . . Acts 27:9*

Lock 2-7
White Garments
Page #17

### Preparations of the People . . .

It is the most solemn day of the year. During the Temple period all of Israel fasted, afflicting both flesh and soul. For this reason it was often referred to as The Fast. They did not partake of food or drink, nor did they bathe or anoint their bodies with oil. They did not have marital relations on this day. A sense of moral responsibility, repentance and reconciliation brought weeping among the people. Many wore white garments called garments of the dead, imagining themselves standing before the throne of glory to give a reckoning.

On the eve of the Day of Atonement, called *Kol Nidrey* in Hebrew, each person was obligated to purify himself in a ritual bath and a feast was taken in anticipation of the coming day of fasting. After the meal Psalms 126 was read.

Key 4-8
Ritual Bath

> *When the Lord brought back the captives to Zion, we were like men who dreamed. Our mouths were filled with laughter, our tongues with songs of joy. Then it was said among the nations, "The Lord has done great things for them." The Lord has done great things for us, and we are filled with joy. Psalm 126:1-3*

During the time of the dispersion after the destruction of the Temple in 70 A.D., the Jews were greatly persecuted. Many were forced on threat of death to take an oath of faith in Jesus. In truth, they had no conviction in Jesus as the Messiah, but took the oath to save their lives. This was considered an oath taken not in faith. On the Eve of the Day of Atonement provision was made to renounce these oaths and receive forgiveness before the Day of Atonement.

### Preparation of the High Priest. . .
Seven days prior to the Day of Atonement the High Priest moved from his home to his chamber in the Temple. He alone conducted the services during this week as he offered the daily sacrifices, sprinkled the blood, burned the incense, and tended the lighting of the lampstand. This week was a time of preparation and practice for the coming Day of Atonement when the High Priest could not make any errors during the service. For on this day and no other throughout the year, he was to enter the Holy of Holies into the very presence of God and was to obtain cleansing from sin for all of Israel through sacrifice. He was watched and tutored by the Sanhedrin so he was completely familiar and knowledgeable with the procedures of the service on the actual Day of Atonement.

Lock 2-5
Priestly Duties
Page #56

Lock 2-3
Holy Place
Page #27

Lock 2-4
Holy of Holies
Page #23

On the 10th day the High Priest began with the regular daily sacrifice, he bathed himself and put on the golden garments. After completing the daily service, he bathed again and put on white linen garments symbolizing perfect purity. He bathed five times and washed his hands and feet ten times during the day.

Lock 2-8
Golden Garments
Page #24

Lock 2-7
White Garments
Page #78

### Preparation of the Sacrifices. . .
A young bull was prepared for the sacrifice and stood in the courtyard of the Temple near the Holy Place to the south. The High Priest stood facing the east toward the worshippers, and

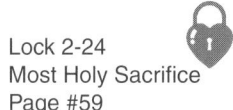

Lock 2-24
Most Holy Sacrifice
Page #59

Lock 2-19
Sin Offering
Page #30

Lock 4-2
Homage to the King
Page #72

the bull was turned to face west toward the sanctuary. The High Priest laid hands on the bull and confessed his sins and the sins of his household. He pronounced the mystic name of God, YHWH, three times in his prayer. During the course of the service he pronounced the sacred name ten times. The worshippers fell prostrate whenever the name of God was pronounced.

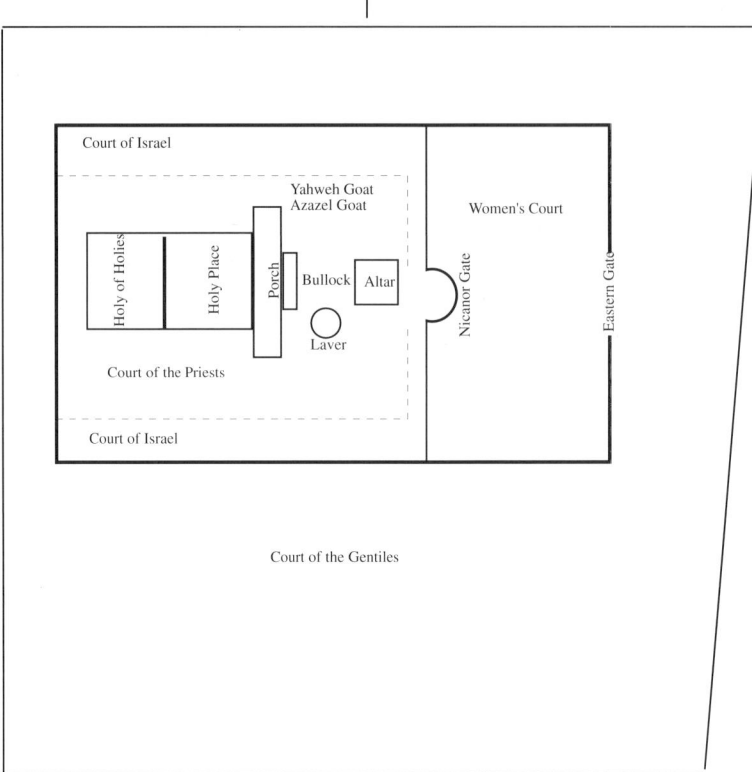

**Herod's Temple—The Second Temple
On The Day of Atonement**

Lock 2-24
Most Holy Sacrifice
Page #79

Additional sacrifices were presented closer to the worshippers on the north side of the altar. Here two goats stood ready with their heads facing in the direction of the sanctuary. Beside them an urn called *Calpi* contained two tablets, used as lots. On one of the tablets was inscribed the name of God YHWH and on the other Azazel. The priest reached into the urn and lifted out the tablets, one in his right hand and the other in his left hand. He placed the appropriate tablets on the head of each goat. A scarlet cloth was tied to the horns of the Azazel goat and it was turned around to face the people. A scarlet cloth was tied around the neck of the goat for YHWH. The Priest declared, "A sin offering for YHWH." The people fell prostrate and answered, "Blessed be the Name, the glory of His kingdom forever and ever." While the goats waited, the third and most solemn part of the service began.

The High Priest returned to the area where the young bull was tethered. He placed his hands on the bull's head for a second time and confessed the sins of the priesthood, "the seed of Aaron, Thy holy people." Once again, all the worshippers prostrated themselves at the pronouncement of the name of God and said, "Blessed be the Name, the glory of His kingdom forever and ever."

Lock 2-2
Courtyard
Page #56

The High Priest killed the bull on the west side of the altar, which is the only sacrifice killed on this side of the altar. The high priest then caught the blood in a vessel. The basin was handed to an assistant, who kept it moving in order to prevent the blood from coagulating.

Lock 2-14
Sacrifices of
Anointing
Page #26

The High Priest then filled a golden censer with burning coals from the Altar of Sacrifice and poured handfuls of incense into a golden ladle. With the censer in his right hand and ladle in his left, he proceeded into the Holy of Holies. Once he began his journey into the Holy of Holies he could not be touched.

> *Jesus said, "Do not hold on to me, for I have not yet returned to the Father. Go instead to my brothers and tell them, 'I am returning to my Father and your Father, to my God and your God.' John 20:17*

## CLEANSING OF THE SANCTUARY

### *Incense Offering . . .*
The following account describes the High Priest in the Holy of Holies as he offers the incense:

Lock 2-4
Holy of Holies
Page #79

Key 4-9
Incense Offering

> *The curtain of the Most Holy Place was folded back, and the high-priest stood alone and separated from all the people in the awful gloom of the Holiest of All, only lit up by the red glow of the coals in the priest's censer. In the first Temple the ark of God had stood there with the 'mercy-seat' overshadowing it; above it, the visible presence of Jehovah in the cloud of the Shechinah, and on either side the outspread wings of the cherubim; and the high priest had placed the censer between the staves of the ark. But in the Temple of Herod there was neither Shechinah nor ark — all was empty; and the high priest rested his censer on a large stone, called the 'foundation stone.' He now most carefully emptied the incense into his hand, and threw it on the coals of the censer, as far from himself as possible, and so waited til the smoke had filled the Most Holy Place. Then, retreating backwards, he prayed outside the veil....[5]*

> *For no one can lay any foundation other than the one already laid, which is Jesus Christ. 1 Corinthians 3:10*

While the incense was being offered in the Holy of Holies, the people worshipped in silence outside.

Key 4-10
Silence

*Blood Sprinkling . . .*

When the High Priest came out he picked up the basin with the blood of the bull and returned to the Holy of Holies. He sprinkled it with his finger once upwards toward the mercy seat and seven times downward at the base of the ark. Just outside the veil he placed the bowl on a stand and went out again into the courtyard.

The goat that had been marked for YHWH was then killed and the blood caught. No hands were laid on this goat as a transference of sins. The High Priest entered the Holy of Holies for the third time and sprinkled the blood once upwards and seven times downwards. The remaining blood was placed outside the veil beside the blood of the bull. The blood of the goat and the bull were then mixed together and sprinkled on each of the four horns of the Golden Altar of Incense and then seven times on the top. The remaining blood was poured out at the base of the Altar of Sacrifice on the west side.

The ceremony for forgiveness of sins committed against the sanctuary in all its parts was now complete. The sacrifices being completed the priests, worshippers and the sanctuary were cleansed.

*Therefore, brothers, since we have confidence to enter the Most Holy Place by the blood of Jesus, by a new and living way opened for us through the curtain, that is, his body, and since we have a great priest over the house of God, let us draw near to God with a sincere heart in full assurance of faith, having our hearts sprinkled to cleanse us from a guilty conscience and having our bodies washed with pure water. Hebrews 10:19-22*

*...there was now again free access for all; or, to put it otherwise, the continuance of typical sacrificial communion with God was once more restored and secured. . . But the consciences were not yet free from a sense of personal guilt and sin. That remained to be done through the 'scapegoat.'* [6]

## THE AZAZEL

Now the symbolic ceremony of transferring the sins of the people to the Azazel began. The High Priest laid his hands on the goat marked for Azazel. As the goat faced the people, they watched as their sins were transferred to him. Now their own personal guilt and sin was removed.

It became a tradition that a fit man be chosen to lead this goat out into the wilderness. He led the goat out through the eastern gate of the Temple to a spot beyond the city where a precipitous cliff overhangs a ravine. The man and goat went to the edge of the cliff. The man removed the red sash and divided it into two parts. One part was attached to the cliff, the

other tied to the horns of the goat and the goat was then pushed over the edge of the cliff. Legend was that when the sacrifice was acceptable to God a miracle occurred. The scarlet cloth tied to the stone turned white symbolizing the promise of Isaiah 1:18:

> *Come now, let us reason together, says the Lord. "Though your sins are like scarlet, they shall be as white as snow; though they are red as crimson, they shall be like wool."*

Interestingly, Jewish history records that this miracle had not been observed for 40 years prior to the destruction of the Temple (70 A.D.). For the believers in Jesus as Messiah this period would mark the time from his death until the destruction of the Temple.

> *Then he adds: "Their sins and lawless acts I will remember no more: And where these have been forgiven, there is no longer any sacrifice for sin. Hebrews 10:17-18*

According to the scriptures, the goat was to be released into the wilderness. However, by the time of the second Temple the tradition of pushing the Azazel goat over the cliff had been instituted. See Appendix C at the end of this chapter for a further discussion of the Azazel.

## THE PRIEST AMONG THE PEOPLE

While the Azazel goat was being led out into the wilderness the High Priest proceeded to cut up the bull and the goat for YHWH. The body, skin, etc. were taken outside the Temple area and burned. The High Priest then joined the congregation in the Court of Women and read two portions of Leviticus 16 and 23:27-32, which are God's instructions regarding the Day of Atonement. He also recited the portion of Numbers 29:7-11 having to do with the sacrifice for the day. Just as on the Day of Trumpets, no joyous songs of praise were sung or Psalms of praise read.

Key 4-12
Priest in Courtyard

Lock 3-6
Hallel
Page #73

*Conclusion. . .*
Washing his hands and feet again, the High Priest removed the white linen garments and put on the golden vestments of the bridegroom. He then completed the regular daily sacrifices. Washing again he put on his linen garments for the last time and entered the Holy of Holies to remove the censer and ladle which he had left there. On his return he washed and took off his linen garments which were never used again. He

Lock 2-8
Golden Garments
Page #79

Lock 2-7
White Garments
Page #79

Lock 4-7
Door/Gate Closed
Page #78

put on his golden garments, tended the lamps and burned the evening incense. The regular evening service was completed and the Temple gates were closed.

His duties of the day having been completed, he put on his ordinary clothing and returned to his home. Many of the other priests and worshippers were invited to his home for a great feast and a joyous evening to end their day of fasting.

## ADDITIONAL POINTS OF INTEREST

### *Maidens and the Bridegroom . . .*
It is said in the <u>Mishnah</u> that on the afternoon of the Day of Atonement the maidens of Jerusalem went in white garments into the vineyards near the city where they danced and sang, hoping to attract a bridegroom.

Lock 2-7
White Garments
Page #83

> *There were no happier days for Israel than the 15th of Ab and the Day of Atonement, for on them the daughters of Jerusalem used to go forth in white raiments; and these were borrowed, that none should be abased which had them not; ...And the daughters of Jerusalem went forth to dance in the vineyards. And what did they say? 'Young man, lift up thine eyes and see what thou wouldest choose for thyself: set not thine eyes on beauty, but set thine eyes on family; for Favour is deceitful and beauty is vain, but a woman that feareth the Lord she shall be praised...* [7]

This brings to mind the parable that Jesus taught of the ten virgins:

> *'At that time the kingdom of heaven will be like ten virgins who took their lamps and went out to meet the bridegroom. Five of them were foolish and five were wise. The foolish ones took their lamps but did not take any oil with them. The wise, however, took oil in jars along with their lamps. The bridegroom was a long time in coming, and they all became drowsy and fell asleep. At midnight the cry rang out: 'Here's the bridegroom! Come out to meet him!' Then all the virgins woke up and trimmed their lamps. The foolish ones said to the wise, 'Give us some of your oil; our lamps are going out.' 'No,' they replied, 'there may not be enough for both us and you. Instead, go to those who sell oil and buy some for yourselves.' 'But while they were on their way to buy the oil, the bridegroom arrived. The virgins who were ready went in with him to the wedding banquet. And the door was shut. Later the others also came. 'Sir! Sir!' they said. 'Open the door for us!' But he replied, 'I tell you the truth, I don't know you.' Therefore keep watch, because you do not know the day or the hour.* Matthew 25:1-13

# FEAST OF TABERNACLES

**Before you begin, read: Leviticus 23:33-44; Numbers 29:12-40; Deuteronomy 16:13-15.**

Having completed a 40-day period of repentance and forgiveness, the people began preparations for the most joyous festival of the year. The Feast of Tabernacles continued for seven days, from the 15th through the 21st of the seventh month. Of all the feasts this one attracted the largest number of people, probably because it was the most joyful and it was at the end of the harvesting season.

God gave three major instructions regarding this feast. First, the feast was to be a time when all Israel lived in temporary dwellings. This was so their descendants would know that He had caused the Israelites to live in temporary dwellings when He delivered them from captivity in Egypt. At this time, God also dwelt among them in a temporary dwelling, the Tabernacle.

> *Then have them make a sanctuary for me, and I will dwell among them. Exodus 25:8*

> *The Word became flesh and made his dwelling among us. We have seen his glory, the glory of the One and Only, who came from the Father, full of grace and truth. John 1:14*

Second, the feast was to be one of thanksgiving for the harvest. At this time of year the fruit of the orchards and vineyards was gathered. This rejoicing in the harvest was to include their sons and daughters, their servants, strangers, the fatherless and widows within their gates. As they rejoiced they acknowledged that all they had was from the Lord.

Third, God gave an elaborate set of instructions regarding the sacrifices to be offered during the seven days of this feast. As in the other feasts, God also indicated that this feast was a rehearsal pointing to an ultimate fulfillment at His appointed time. An example of the celebration of this feast can be seen in Nehemiah 8.

Lock 3-1
Rehearsal
Page #69

### Preparations of the People . . .
Between the Day of Atonement and the 15th were days of preparation in which the people collected many branches from several different kinds of trees and built the booths they would

temporarily live in during the seven days of the feast. The people furnished their booths with furniture and dishes from their home and tried to make it as comfortable and homey as they could. For they would eat and sleep in these booths during the entire feast week. The booth was a shade or a protection, a covering from the heat of the sun as it provided a shadow in which to dwell. The atmosphere of this week was filled with anticipation and joy.

> *Have mercy on me, O God, have mercy on me, for in you my soul takes refuge. I will take refuge in the shadow of your wings until the disaster has passed. Psalms 57:1*

### Special Offering. . .

Special attention needs to be given regarding the sacrifices made during this 7-day period. These sacrifices are listed in the 29th chapter of Numbers beginning with verse 12. Upon close examination it shows that 70 bulls were offered over the 7-day period along with other sacrifices and with a single bull offered on the 8th day. (Refer to Appendix A, Sacrifices and Offering Chart at the end of Chapter 2.)

Key 4-13
Feast of Nations

Lock 2-24
Most Holy Sacrifice
Page #80

The significance of these 70 bulls is explained by Jewish tradition as representative sacrifices for the nations and for this reason the Feast of Tabernacles is sometimes referred to as the Feast of Nations. One interpretation is found in The Book of Our Heritage by Eliyahu Kitov, who describes the offering of the 70 bulls as follows:

> The 70 nations originated from Noah's descendants:
>
> *This is the account of Shem, Ham and Japheth, Noah's sons, who themselves had sons after the flood. . .(From these the maritime peoples spread out into their territories by their clans within their nations, each with its own language.). . .These are the sons of Ham by their clans and languages, in their territories and nations. . .These are the sons of Shem by their clans and languages, in their territories and nations. . .These are the clans of Noah's sons, according to their lines of descent, within their nations. From these the nations spread out of the earth after the flood. Genesis 10: 1, 5, 20, 31, 32*

*Now the children's children of these Patriarchs come; they rejoice on the Festival of Sukot before God, and say to Him: Lord of the Universe! We desire neither houses nor the field's produce; our only desire is for You. On attaining this pure joy, they become a source of blessing for themselves and all the world, and, through their merit, bounty and blessing descend upon all the world for the entire year. The very offerings they themselves bring during Sukot, are not intended in their own behalf, for they offer seventy oxen to attain atonement and blessing for all the seventy nations of the world. [8]*

Rabbi Eleazer gave the following interpretation of the offering of the 70 bulls:

*These seventy oxen corresponded to the seventy original nations of the world who descended from the sons of Noah, and who were the ancestors of all the nations till this day.*

*Israel brought these sacrifices as an atonement for the nations of the world and in prayer for their well-being as well as for universal peace and harmony between them. . .*

*'Rabbi Yehoshua Ben Levi said: If the nations of the world would have known the value of the Temple for them, they would have surrounded it with fortresses in order to protect it. For it was of greater value for them than for Israel.[9]*

## TEMPLE SERVICES

### In the Mornings . . .

During the Feast of Tabernacles all 24 divisions of priests were required to be on duty because of the many ceremonies and duties of the greatest feast of the year. The most intense joy of the daily ceremonies was the offering of the Libation of Water. (Some authorities feel the Libation of Water did not take place on the first day of the ceremonies.) Each morning three groups of priests conducted simultaneous services. The first group of priests conducted the ritual of 'the water pouring' or a 'house of watering', the second group conducted the 'waving of the willows' and the third group prepared and offered the sacrifices.

Lock 2-5
Priestly Duties
Page #79

### Libation of Water . . .

Three groups of priests came together to conduct the ceremony. Joined by a merry crowd from the congregation of worshippers, the High Priest and his assistants lead one procession out of the Temple through the Water Gate down to the spring of Shiloah. There they filled a golden vase with water known as Living Water. They returned to the Temple and waited at the Water Gate for a signal.

Key 4-14
Living Water

In the meantime a second group of priests had also gone out of the Temple by way of the Eastern Gate to the Valley of Motza. There they cut small willow trees at least 25 feet in length. The priests then made a formation standing shoulder to shoulder in several rows approximately 30 feet apart. At a signal, they each stepped forward on their right foot, swinging the willow branches to the left in unison. As they stepped forward on the left foot, the willows were swung to the right. Thus, they proceeded to the Temple. Waving the willows in this manner produced the effect of a rushing wind* approaching the Temple. When they reached the Eastern Gate they also awaited a signal to proceed.

*The Hebrew word for wind is the same word translated for spirit. This portion of the ceremony could, therefore, symbolically be interpreted as the Spirit of God coming into the Temple.*

A trumpet (shofar) was blown announcing that both groups had arrived in position and should proceed. Then a priest stood up and led the procession playing the flute. The flute player was called 'the pierced one'. The 'pierced one' called for the wind and the water to enter the Temple. The procession met at the altar where the priests that formed a third group began to lay the sacrifices upon the altar.

Two containers sat above the altar: one of silver containing wine and the other of gold ready to receive the 'Living Water.' With great ceremony the High Priest poured the water into the receptacle. Each container emptied into a common spout thereby mixing the water and wine as it was poured out on the altar.

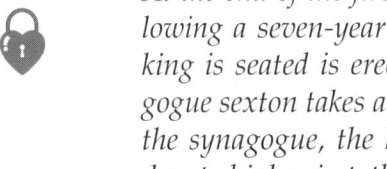

Key 4-15
Lulav

Key 4-16
Hosanna Prayers

As this took place the group with the willows circled the altar seven times and placed the branches upright around the altar forming a covering over the top of the altar. During this circling worshippers who had made a lulav joined the priests who were circling the altar with the willows. The lulav was made up of several kinds of tree branches: palms, myrtle, willow and citron all bound together. They sang Isaiah 12:3, *"With joy you will draw water from the wells of salvation."* Following the songs of praise, the four Hosannah prayers were recited as specified for the day. Each prayer phrase ended with Hosannah.

Lock 4-1
Book of Covenant
Page #70

During the periods of Israel's history when a king sat on the throne, it was the custom for the king to read from the Law at the end of the first day of the Feast of Tabernacles.

Lock 1-3
Sevens
Page #73

> *At the end of the first day of Sukkot in the eighth year following a seven-year cycle, a wooden dais upon which the king is seated is erected in the Temple Court. The synagogue sexton takes a Torah scroll and gives it to the head of the synagogue, the head of the synagogue gives it to the deputy high priest, the deputy high priest gives it to the high priest, and the high priest gives it to the king. The king stands up to receive it and then sits down and reads.*[10]

The reading for the second day of the Feast of Tabernacles is Zechariah 14 and Ezekiel 38: 14-39:16.

> *On that day living water will flow out from Jerusalem, half to the eastern sea and half to the western sea, in summer and in winter. The Lord will be king over the whole earth. On that day there will be one Lord, and his name the only name.. . .Then the survivors from all the nations that have attacked Jerusalem will go up year after year to worship the King, the Lord Almighty, and to celebrate the Feast of Tabernacles. . .Zechariah 14: 8, 16*

*In the afternoons . . .*

During the afternoons of the seven days, the people gathered in the courts of the Temple to hear teachings and debates among the Rabbis.

*In the evenings — Torch Dance. . .*

Those who had witnessed the water libation ceremony gathered together in the Court of the Women in the evening for a great celebration called 'Rejoicing At The Place of The Water-Drawing' or 'Festivity of The Water-Drawing'.

The fire observance and Torch Dance took place at that time. The people crowded into the great Court of the Women for this ceremony was a most interesting and joyous one. The details of this ceremony are in the following account from <u>The Jewish Festivals, History & Observance</u> by Hayyim Schauss:

> *Evening has come. The great Court of the Women is crowded with people, ready for the celebration. Above, on the roof of the colonnades that encircle the court, galleries have been built for the women; below them are the men. In the center of the court burn great golden menorahs, set on bases that are fifty yards high. Each menorah has four branches, which terminate in huge cups into which oil is poured. Four ladders are placed against each menorah and four young priests mount them and pour oil into the cups to keep the wicks burning. (The wicks were made from worn-out garments of the priests.) The light of these menorahs attains such intensity that all Jerusalem is lit up by them.*
>
> *The lights flare up, higher and still higher; the sound of flutes is heard. Men gather in the spacious court, fine men, the choice men of Jerusalem. They bear torches in their hands and they dance, waving the torches, throwing them in the air and catching them again. And again and again! Others stand on tiptoe and bend their heads down to the ground, rising again without getting off their toes. These are dancers! And songs arise. One sings:*
>     *"Blessed be our youth*
>     *That hath not shamed our later years."*
> *Another sings:*
>     *"Blessed be our later years*
>     *That atoned for our youth."*
> *A third sings:*
>     *"Blessed be he who hath not sinned;*
>     *And he who sinned and repented,*
>     *He is forgiven."*

*It is late in the night. The dance goes on. On the fifteen steps that lead from the Court of the Women to the Court of the Laymen stand Levites, bearing harps, cymbals, flutes, trumpets, and other instruments; they play and as they play they sing the Psalms of Ascents (Psalms 120-134).[11]*

### The last day of the Great Feast . . .

Lock 3-6
Hallel
Page #83

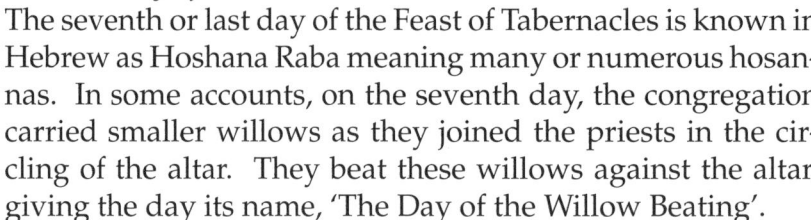

The seventh or last day of the Feast of Tabernacles is known in Hebrew as Hoshana Raba meaning many or numerous hosannas. In some accounts, on the seventh day, the congregation carried smaller willows as they joined the priests in the circling of the altar. They beat these willows against the altar, giving the day its name, 'The Day of the Willow Beating'.

Lock 4-16
Hosanna Prayers
Page #88

Lock 4-4
3 Books
Page #77

Lock 4-5
Sealing
Page #78

Despite the seeming contradiction, Jewish tradition says this last day of the Feast of Tabernacles is the final sealing of judgment which began on the Day of Trumpets. On this day all the world's inhabitants pass in view before the judgment seat. All opportunities for claims of justice and merit are past. This day one can only look to the mercy of his creator. Unlike the Day of Atonement when prayers of repentance are said, at this time there are only prayers for mercy. Each prayer is accompanied by a hosanna or hallel at the end, much as a plea for help. More hosannas are said this day than any other day of the feast. This sealing extends til dawn of the 8th Day. Adjustments were made in the Feast calendar to provide that this day never fell on the weekly Sabbath, causing it always to be a High Sabbath.

Lock 3-7
Concluding Day
Page #62

Once again in God's reluctance to condemn, the gates of heaven are opened and the seal is placed on those who came in the last hour.

Lock 4-3
Door/Gates
Opened
Page #74

*The ancient Sages have also coined a parable on this matter: 'The Kingdom of Heaven is like the kingdom on earth.' And the modes of judgment in both are similar. In the kingdom on earth, when a merciful and just king sits in judgment, he decides it immediately, on finding merit. If not, he suspends judgment till the defender might discover merit for the accused. After a time he issues judgment. If he decides for mercy, he informs the accused immediately; if not — he keeps the decision to himself, lest the accused finds some merit, in which case the decree of judgment could be torn up and transformed to mercy. In the end he hands over his written judgments to his messengers whether for death or life. The messengers then leave to discharge their tasks;*

*whether to dispense harsh judgments or mercy. If the written decisions were merciful, they cannot again change to harsh judgment. If they bespeak judgment, they may still be transformed into mercy at the last moment.*

*How? If a harsh decree went forth against so-and-so who had rebelled against the king, and the king's emissaries arrive to the place of the condemned, and find him happily and loyally fulfilling all the king's decrees, they say: this is not the one against whom such-and-such was decreed; the person who now appears to us is another man! They return to the king, and he also agrees with them. They tear up the royal decree and 'seal' him for a good life.*

*In the Heavenly Kingdom it is also thus. On Rosh Hashanah all the world's inhabitants pass before God: The perfect tsadikim (the just) are immediately inscribed and sealed for life; the intermediate ones are suspended till Yom Kipur and their judgment is sealed on Yom Kipur. The conclusion of their 'sealing,' however, is on Hoshana Raba, and it extends till dawn on Shmini Atzeret. Therefore, there is profuse prayer and supplication on Hashana Raba; and an awakening towards teshuvah and Divine mercy. Even if a harsh decree had already been rendered, it is torn up, and in heaven new 'notes' (of acquittal) are written.* [12]

A prayer was said after the people left their booths for the last time at the end of the feast:

Key 4-17
Leviathan

*'May it be Your will, Lord our God and the God of our fathers, just as I merited and sat in this sukah, so may I merit the coming year, to sit in the sukah of the skin of Leviathan.'* [13]

## ADDITIONAL POINTS OF INTEREST

Jewish tradition offers many and varied meanings for the symbolism of the Feast of Tabernacles ceremonies:

### The Booths . . .
Some biblical scholars contend that the booths also were symbolic of the wedding chamber of the wedding ceremony in which the marriage was consummated.

Key 4-18
Wedding Chamber

### The Lulav . . .
The lulav is said to be shaken in the four directions of the compass to represent victory over the nations. This interpretation is described by Raphael Patai:

*"From a later period, however, that of the Second Temple, we have knowledge of an annual ceremony [Tabernacles] in which the nations of the world were symbolically overcome by the Lulav, shaken toward the four quarters was figuratively and ritually referred to as an "arrow."* [14]

Lock 4-15
Lulav
Page #88

Others say the lulav was shaken in four directions and then up and down to represent God's dominion over all the nations and the heavens and earth. Many interpret the lulav to be a symbol of unity and peace between Israel and the Gentiles.

### The Water Libation Ceremony . . .

Lock 4-14
Living Water
Page #87

For many a marriage ceremony is depicted in the water libation celebration. For others it represents the nations petition before the Lord for the fall rains to come that the land may be fruitful. Those interpreting the water libation ceremony as representing a marriage, compare the torch dance to the celebration of the guests at the announcement of the consummation.

### The Torch Dance . . .

Key 4-19
Tree of Life

The glorious lights are interpreted by some to represent Israel, redeemed on the Day of Atonement, shining forth as the light of the world for another year.

Lock 2-17
Fire Kindled
Page #61

In addition to much being made of the lights, the lampstands themselves carry much symbolism of the tree of life and perhaps the fire kindled confirming the beginning of the king's reign.

### Solomon's Temple . . .

Solomon's temple was dedicated at the time of this feast:

*All the men of Israel came together to King Solomon at the time of the festival in the month of Ethanim, the seventh month. . .So the king and all the Israelites dedicated the temple of the Lord. . .So Solomon observed the festival at that time, and all Israel with him—a vast assembly, people from Lebo Hamath to the Wadi of Egypt.*
*1 Kings 8:2, 63b, 65*

*As for the foreigner who does not belong to your people Israel but has come from a distant land because of your name—for men will hear of your great name and your mighty hand and your outstretched arm—when he comes and prays toward this temple, then hear from heaven, your*

*dwelling place, and do whatever the foreigner asks of you,*
*so that all the peoples of the earth may know your name*
*and fear you, as do your own people Israel, and may know*
*that this house I have built bears your Name.*
*1 Kings 8:41-43*

As we have stated, we like to rely on scriptures for our interpretation of symbolism and only offer these interpretations for your interest.

# JESUS OBSERVES
# THE FEAST OF TABERNACLES

We have already discovered that the things Jesus did and taught during the feasts were very significant. His words and actions shed light on the symbolism and prophetic purpose of the feasts.

The gospel of John records in the seventh chapter curious behavior by Jesus at the time of the Feast of Tabernacles. Jesus, so scrupulous to fulfill every letter of the law, announces to his brothers that he will not join them in going up to the feast.

> *You go to the Feast. I am not yet going up to this Feast, because for me the right time has not yet come. John 7:8*

However, after the feast had already begun, Jesus did go up to the Temple:

**Key 4-20**
**Late to the Banquet**

> *Not until halfway through the Feast did Jesus go up to the temple courts and begin to teach. John 7:14*

In Chapter 6-Kingship, we will see interesting information that will show the significance of Jesus' late arrival.

> *Jesus answered, "Everyone who drinks this water will be thirsty again, but whoever drinks the water I give him will never thirst. Indeed, the water I give him will become to him a spring of water welling up to eternal life." John 4:13-14*

As to the things Jesus taught on the occasion of the feast, we again see his teaching directed to the events of the ceremony. After the morning ceremonies, it was the custom for the people and the teacher to linger in the courtyard of the Temple in small groups for discussion and teaching. It was at such a time that Jesus taught:

**Lock 4-14**
**Living Water**
**Page #92**

> *On the last and greatest day of the Feast, Jesus stood and said in a loud voice, "If anyone is thirsty, let him come to me and drink. Whoever believes in me, as the Scripture has said, streams of living water will flow from within him." John 7:37-38*

# THE 8TH DAY

*Shemini Atzeret. . .*

Just as the day of Pentecost was the closing day of the Spring Feasts, so the 8th Day, Shemini Atzeret, is the close of the Fall Feasts.

Lock 3-7
Concluding Day
Page #90

> *On the eighth day hold an assembly and do no regular work.*
> *Numbers 29:35*

On this day special prayers are said for rain that the earth might be fruitful in the year to come. Though many of the ceremonies of the Feast of Tabernacles can be interpreted as a plea for rain, prayers are not offered until now.

Jewish tradition relates the symbol of rain with the theme of resurrection of the dead. Like the seeds buried in the ground, through the rain they sprout and rise.

There is a note of solemnity attached to this day, for the seven days of sacrifices for the nations have come to an end. Jewish tradition says the final sealing, when all the world's inhabitants pass before the seat of judgment is completed on the dawn of this day.

Lock 4-4
3 Books
Page #90

The sacrifices of this day are like those of the Day of Trumpets and the Day of Atonement: one bull, one ram and seven lambs. The sages taught that these sacrifices comprise the theme of atonement and sealing.

Lock 4-5
Sealing
Page #90

> *And only after having concluded their offerings for all the world's nations, do they bring an offering in their own behalf: 'And on the eighth day, it shall be an assembly unto you' — i.e. between Me and you alone — 'and you shall sacrifice a burnt-offering...one ox...' First make offerings in their behalf, and afterwards in your own behalf! For I have made you shepherds to sustain My entire world with love and compassion.*[15]

Lock 4-13
Feast of Nations
Page #86

We offer the following quote to shed light on Jewish understanding of this day:

*The eighth day is an atzeret (a solemn assembly) for all Israel and they say before God: It is difficult for us to separate ourselves from your commandments. Although the mitzvot of sukah and lulav, the festival sacrifice and the water-libation, are concluded — we linger before you and rejoice in you. Messengers from above then come and find all Israel rejoicing before God with the happiness of Love. And even if there were among them such as had been condemned, harm does not strike them. They are now different people, they love God, and rejoice in Him and His commandments."* [16]

Lock 3-7
Concluding Day
Page #95

Key 4-21
Intimate Communion

Lock 1-1
Time
Page #73

Lock 1-3
Sevens
Page #88

But, this day though solemn is also tender, for *atzeret* is an expression of affection. It is an invitation to tarry with God, to come aside for an intimate time together.

The rabbis interpret God's instructions to mean God asks those who have come for the Feast of Tabernacles to tarry with him an additional day. In Jewish understanding seven being a complete unit of time, the eighth day is considered to mark a day after time.

*It has been mentioned before in the name of the Sages concerning the one ox, which is brought as an offering on Shmini Atzeret [eighth day], that God regarded it as an intimate light meal between Him and His beloved people of Israel alone. . . For the Torah is betrothed to Israel as a wife to her husband and they rejoice with her as a groom rejoices with his bride . . . Now the people of Israel enter within to rejoice with the joy of the Torah which is hidden within the treasure house of God.*[17] [Bracket authors' addition]

During the days when the Temple still stood, this day also marked the end and beginning again of the yearly Torah readings. In dispersion, the end of the year's Torah reading was celebrated on an additional day called Simchat Torah.

Lock 1-5
New Moon - One
Long Day
Page #77

### Simchat Torah . . .
Simchat Torah was celebrated together with Shimini Atzeret as one long day on Tishri 22 and 23. It was a day of rejoicing in the Torah. On this day the yearly reading of the Torah is completed and begun again. In the days of the Second Temple there was a seven year cycle of reading the Law. The Law, Prophets and Writings were each read during years one through three. In year three through six they were repeated. In the seventh year they were read through again.

These readings were done by the priest and even the king on some occasions.  At this time the reader stood on the platform or by the pillar designated for this purpose in the Temple.  The person called to the concluding reading from the Law for this day was a most distinguished person or Rabbi.

Lock 4-1
Book of Covenant
Page #88

> *The person called to this concluding portion of the Torah is called, 'Chatan Torah' (the groom of the Torah), as if the Torah were betrothed to him and he were its groom....After him the 'Chatan Bereishit' (the groom of the beginning of the Torah) is called to a Reading in another scroll, which consists of the first passage of the Torah, from the beginning till, 'which God created and made.'*
>
> *...It is customary for the 'Chatan Torah' to invite the entire congregation to a feast on Simchat Torah.* [18]

# JESUS OBSERVES THE 8TH DAY

**Before you begin, read: John 8.**

Although the inclusion of the account of the woman caught in adultery John 7:53-8:11 is questioned by some authorities, the recorders intent is of interest.

Lock 4-5
Sealing
Page #95

Lock 3-7
Concluding Day
Page #96

You will note the writer establishes that the incident occurred the day after the last day of the Feast of Tabernacles. This 8th Day was known as the Day of Rejoicing in the Torah (Law). The writer even specifies that Jesus appeared in the Temple courts at *dawn*. Remember that a final sealing, one of mercy was believed to take place on the last day of the Feast extending until *dawn* of the 8th Day.

> *Then each went to his own home. But Jesus went to the Mount of Olives. At dawn he appeared again in the temple courts, where all the people gathered around him, and he sat down to teach them. John 7:53-8:2*

The recorder of John tells us a story of a woman, caught in adultery, brought to Jesus. Jesus was instructed that according to the law the woman was to be stoned. But, the Pharisees asked him, "Now *what do you say?*" *John 8:5*. Jesus was questioned about the law on the day known as Rejoicing in the Torah or the Law.

In John 8:6 we are told that Jesus bent down and wrote on the ground. Interestingly, one of the readings from scripture in the previous days of the feast speaks of writing in the dust:

Lock 4-14
Living Water
Page #94

> *O Lord, the hope of Israel, all who forsake you will be put to shame. Those who turn away from you will be written in the dust because they have forsaken the Lord, the spring of living water. Jeremiah 17:13*

Lock 3-10
Repentance from
Adultery
Page #63

The witnesses in the story in John declare the woman guilty, but Jesus forgives her; His judgment one of mercy.

We will also see in the next chapter a discussion on Jewish law concerning an adulterous wife. The Old Testament abounds with accounts of God accusing and judging Israel as an adulteress. The 8th Day of the feast was considered a special time between Israel and her God.

The continuing discussion between Jesus and the Pharisees speaks to the issue of who are the true children of Abraham. Jesus distinguishes them as those who believe in him.

We do not intend to labor this point, but this account seems tied to the theme of the Fall Feasts. For the Day of Atonement is seen as a time of Israel's national cleansing. The dealings of Jesus with the adulteress point to his dealing with his adulteress Israel. Jesus said that not all who claim Abraham as father will be part of the redeemed Israel.

The joy of the evening torch dance and lights was also recent in the peoples experience when Jesus said:

> *When Jesus spoke again to the people, he said, "I am the light of the world. Whoever follows me will never walk in darkness, but will have the light of life." John 8:12*

Again we were thrilled to find new meaning in Jesus' earthly walk when we understood the scriptures from a Jewish perspective.

# APPENDIX B -
# THE BINDING OF ISAAC

The following story is told in the Talmud of the Binding of Isaac:

The Binding of Isaac

45. "And it came to pass after these things that God tried Abraham" (Gen. 22:1). After what things? . . . [Following the feast given] upon the "child's having grown and being weaned" (Gen. 21:8), Satan spoke up to the Holy One, "Master of the universe, out of the entire feast that this old man, upon whom You bestowed fruit of the womb at the age of one hundred—out of the entire feast he prepared, could he not have spared, say, one turtledove, one fledgling, as an offering to You?"

The Holy One replied, "Is it not true that Abraham prepared the feast in honor of his son? Still, if I say to him, 'Sacrifice your son to Me,' he will sacrifice him at once." Satan said, "Try him." At once "God tried Abraham."

"And He said: 'Take, I beg thee (*na*), thy son'" (Gen. 22:2). R. Simeon bar Abba said: The word *na* can imply only entreaty. The matter may be illustrated by the parable of a king of flesh and blood who had to face many wars, in all of which he had one mighty warrior who invariably achieved victory. In the course of time, he faced a war particularly severe. The king said to the mighty warrior, "I beg you, stand to with me in this war, that mortals should not say, 'The earlier wars were of no substance.'"

Likewise, the Holy One said to Abraham, "I have tried you with many tests, and you have stood up to them all. Now, I beg you, stand to with Me in this test, that it not be said, 'The earlier ones were of no substance.'"

"Take now thy son" (Gen. 22:2). . .

"And offer him up there for a burnt offering upon one of the mountains" (Gen. 22:2). Abraham asked, "Which mountain?" God: "Wherever you see My glory standing and waiting for you. . ."

"And Abraham rose up early in the morning" (Gen. 22:3). . . .

"And he [himself] saddled his ass" (Gen. 22:3). . .

"And took two of his young men with him. . ." (Gen. 22:3)

"And rose up, and went" (Gen. 22:3). On the way, Satan ran ahead of Abraham, appeared before him in the guise of an old man, and asked, "Where are you going?" Abraham: "To pray." Satan: "Why should one going to pray have fire and a knife in his hand, and kindling wood on his shoulder?" Abraham: "We may abide there a day or two, and we will have to slaughter an animal, bake bread, and eat." Satan: "Old man, do you think I was not there when the Holy One said to you, 'Take now thy son'? Old man, you are out of your mind. A son who was given you at the age of one hundred—and you are setting out to kill him!" Abraham: "Even so." Satan: "And should He test you even more severely, will you still stand firm?" Abraham: "Yes, even more and more severely." Satan: "But tomorrow He will call you murderer for shedding the blood of your son." Abraham: "Even so."

Seeing that his efforts were in vain, Satan left Abraham and, disguising himself as a young man, stood at Isaac's right and said, "Where are you going?" Isaac: "To study Torah." Satan: "While still alive or after your death?" Isaac: "Is there a man who can study after his death?" Satan: "O hapless son of a hapless mother! How many fasts did your mother fast, how many prayers did she utter until at last you were born! And now this old man has gone mad in his old age and is about to slit your throat." Isaac: "Nevertheless, I shall not deviate from the will of my Maker and from the bidding of my father." Satan: "If so, shall all those fine tunics your mother made [for you] become a legacy for Ishmael, for him who hates your family?" Apparently you give no thought [to what would follow upon your death]." As the proverb has it, "If the whole word does not enter [the listener's mind], half of it does." For Isaac turned to his father and said: "Father, listen to what this one is saying to me!" Abraham replied, "Pay no attention to him!"

When Satan saw that neither Abraham nor Isaac heeded what he had to say, he proceeded to turn himself into a wide stream. At once [having to cross the stream], Abraham went down into the water until it reached to his knees and then said to his lads: Follow me. They went down after him. Halfway across the stream, the water came up to his neck. In that instant, Abraham lifted his eyes heavenward and said: Master of the universe, you chose me. You appeared to me, saying: "I am unique and you are unique. Through you shall My Name become known in My world—so bring your son Isaac before Me as a burnt offering." And I did not hold back. As You see, I am occupied with your bidding. But now "I am come into deep waters" (Ps. 69:3). If either I or Isaac were to drown, who will fulfill Your commands, and by whom will the uniqueness of Your Name be proclaimed? The Holy One replied: As you live! My Name shall be proclaimed in the world through you.

The Holy One rebuked the stream and it dried up, so that they found themselves standing on dry land.

What did Satan do? He said to Abraham, "This is what I heard from behind the [heavenly] curtain: 'A lamb will be the burnt offering—Isaac is not to be the burnt offering.'" But such is the punishment of a liar—even when he tells the truth, no one listens. [Hence Abraham gave Satan no heed.]

"Then on the third day Abraham lifted up his eyes, and saw" (Gen. 22:4). . .

'Abide ye here, people like the ass'" (Gen. 22:5).

"Abraham took the wood of the burnt offering and laid it upon Isaac his son" (Gen. 22:6), as upon one [condemned] who is made to carry the cross upon his shoulder.

"And Isaac said . . . 'Behold, the fire and the wood, but where is the lamb for the burnt offering?' "(Gen. 22:7). In that instant, fear and dread terror fell upon Isaac, when he saw in Abraham's hand nothing at all fit for an offering. So, suspecting what was intended, he asked, "Where is the lamb for the burnt offering?" Abraham replied, "The Holy One has chosen you." Isaac said, "If He has so chosen, my life is given to Him but I grieve for my mother." Nevertheless, "they went both of them together" (Gen. 22:8)—one to bind, the other to be bound; one to slaughter, the other to be slaughtered.

"And they came to the place" (Gen. 22:9)—both carrying stones [for the altar], both carrying the fire, both carrying the wood. For all that, Abraham acted like one making wedding preparations for his son, and Isaac like one making a wedding bower for himself.

Then Isaac said, "Father, hurry, do the will of your Maker, burn me into a fine ash, then take the ash to my mother and leave it with her, and whenever she looks at it she will say, 'This is my son, whom his father has slaughtered.' . . . Father, what will you do in your old age [without me]?" Abraham replied, "My son, we know that we can survive you for but a short time. He who comforted us in the past will comfort us until the day we die."

When Abraham was about to begin the sacrifice, Isaac said, "Father, bind my hands and my feet, for the urge to live is so willful that when I see the knife coming at me, I may flinch involuntarily [causing the knife to cut improperly] and thus disqualify myself as an offering. So I beg you, bind me in such a way that no blemish will befall me." So Abraham "bound his son well" (Gen. 22:9). Then Isaac said to Abraham, "Father, don't tell Mother about this while she is standing over a pit or on a rooftop, for she might throw herself down and be killed."

"And he placed him on the altar" (Gen. 22:9). Abraham's eyes were directed at Isaac's, and Isaac's at the heaven of heavens. Tears were flowing from Abraham's eyes, until his entire body was all but afloat in them. He took the knife in order to cut Isaac's throat deeply enough so that a quarter of a *log* of blood would issue from him. At that instant Satan appeared and shoved Abraham's arm aside, so that the knife fell out of his hand. When he reached out to pick it up, his mouth fell wide open with weeping as a great cry of anguish erupted from him. Then, his eyes blinking frantically, he looked up to the Presence and pleaded in a rising voice, "I lift mine eyes to the mountains; whence will my help come?" (Ps. 121:1). At that, the Holy One appeared above the angels and flung open the firmament. Isaac lifted up his eyes, and, as he beheld the chambers of the chariot, he trembled and shuddered. The ministering angels stood in rows upon rows, crying and weeping, as they said to one another, "Behold, one who is unique is about to slaughter, and one also unique is about to be slaughtered. Master of the universe, the oath 'Thus shall be thy seed' [Gen. 15:5]—what is to become of it?" The Holy One said to the angel Michael, "Why are you standing still? Do not let Abraham go on!" "Then the angel of the Lord called unto him out of heaven, and said: 'Abraham, Abraham,'" (Gen. 22:11), twice, as one who cries out in distress, "What [dreadful] thing are you about to do?"

When Abraham turned his face toward the angel, the angel said again, "What are you about to do? 'Do not lay thy hand upon the lad!'" (Gen. 22:12). Abraham asked, "Who are you?" Michael replied, "I am an angel." Abraham: "When the Holy One told me to offer my son, He Himself spoke to me; so too, if He now wishes something else, He Himself should speak to me."

At once the Holy One flung open the firmament, as well as the thick cloud [covering it], and said, "By Myself I swear" (Gen. 22:16). Abraham replied, "You have sworn, and I too swear that I will not go down from this altar until I say all that I need to say." God: "Say it." Abraham: "Did you not say to me, 'Count the stars . . . so shall thy seed be' (Gen. 15:5)?" The Holy One: "Yes." Abraham: "Out of whom?" God: "Out of Isaac." Abraham: "When You commanded me to sacrifice Isaac, I should have replied: Yesterday You told me, 'In Isaac shall thy seed be called' [Gen. 21:12]; now You say to me, 'Offer him there for a burnt offering' [Gen. 22:2]. Nevertheless, I restrained my impulse and did not reply as I should have done. Even so now [I say to You], When Isaac's children shall sin and find themselves in distress, be You mindful on their behalf of the binding of Isaac; let it be reckoned on their behalf of the binding of Isaac; let it be reckoned in Your presence as though his ash were in fact heaped upon the altar—be then filled with compassion for his children, forgive them, and redeem them from their distress." The Holy One replied, "You had your say, and now I will have Mine. Isaac's descendants will sin in

My very presence, and I will have to judge them on New Year's Day. However, should they implore Me to seek out some merit on their behalf, and to remember on their behalf the binding of Isaac, let them blow in My presence the horn of this creature." Abraham: "The horn of what creature?" God: "Turn around." At once "Abraham lifted up his eyes, and looked, and behold a ram" (Gen. 22:13). . .

Throughout that day, Abraham saw the ram become entangled in a tree, break loose, and go free; become entangled in a bush, break loose, and go free; then again become entangled in a thicket, break loose, and go free. The Holy One said, "Abraham, even so will your children be entangled in many kinds of sin and trapped within successive kingdoms—from Babylon to Media, from Media to Greece, from Greece to Edom." Abraham asked, "Master of the universe, will it be forever thus?" God replied, "In the end they will be redeemed at [the sound of] the horns of this ram, as it said, 'The Lord shall blow the horn [shofar] when He goes forth in the whirlwinds at Teman [Edom]'" (Zech. 9:4).

# APPENDIX C -THE AZAZEL GOAT

In early translations of the scriptures the word 'azazel' was translated as a common noun meaning 'dismissal'. Still others rendered the word 'steep mountain', or 'goat that departs' or understood Azazel to be the name of a place.

Apparently the term 'scapegoat' was coined by William Tyndale, who was the first great English Bible translator. Today we find the term 'scapegoat' is used to describe a person, animal or object that individuals lay blame on when they fall into misfortune, or they can blame for their faults and sins.

The sacrifice that came to be known as the scapegoat was used to transfer the sins of a whole community not just a single individual. We must remember that while we know the common term used today, we are dealing with scriptures written during the time when the term 'scapegoat' was unknown. The Azazel was the goat that the sins of the people were transferred to and was led away into the wilderness or destroyed by sending it over a cliff into a deep ravine.

One Jewish commentary stated that the Azazel was most likely a demonic being that lived in the desert and that its domain was thought to have been an impure place.

Another Jewish commentator states:

> "For Apocryphal Jewish works, composed in the last few centuries before the Christian era, tell of angels who were lured by beautiful women into lust and, ultimately, into rebellion against God. In these writings, Azazel is one of the two leaders of the rebellion. And post-talmudic documents tell a similar story about two rebel angels, Uzza and Azzael— both variations of the name Azazel. These mythological stories, which must have been widely known, seem to confirm the essentially demonic character of the old biblical Azazel."

> "The more responsible Jewish teachers avoided the mythological notion of rebel angels. The Talmud indeed refers frequently to Satan; but he is not, like the Satan of the New Testament, an enemy of God. He serves God as prosecutor, though at times he is overeager to get convictions."
> . . . [1]

# AND TWO WILL BECOME ONE

*For this reason a man will leave his father and mother and be united to his wife, and they will become one flesh.  Genesis 2:24*

The word 'one' in the above scripture, is the same Hebrew word that is used in the common Jewish phrase, "Hear, O Israel:  The Lord our God, the Lord is One."  According to the Young's Concordance, there were several Hebrew words that were translated as the word 'one' in KJV English.  Two of the words that were translated as 'one' are the Hebrew words for man (אִישׁ- ish) and woman (אִשָּׁה- ishshah).  These two words are the masculine and feminine form of the word 'one.' (Hebrew is read from right to left.)

| Hebrew Word | Pronunciation | English Translation | Translated To |
|---|---|---|---|
| יהוה | Yahweh (YHWH) | God | God |
| אִישׁ | ish | Man | One |
| אִשָּׁה | ishshah | Woman | One |

The following is an excerpt from the <u>Midrash</u>:
*If their love merits it, the Sh'chinah, the Divine Presence, dwells with a man and his wife.  If not, fire devours them.  Adam was called Ish and Eve was called Ishah.  If they go in My ways and keep all My precepts, behold, My name is given to them (referring to the Hebrew letters yod and hay that form the first half of the Tetragrammaton)[1].  He shall be called Ish (Man—Ish spelled with a yod) and she shall be called Ishah (Woman— Ishah spelled with a hay).  If they do not walk in My ways I will remove My name (the letters yod and hay) from them and all that will be left will be Aish, a consuming fire.  Each will consume the other.*

The first two Hebrew characters in the Tetragrammaton  for God's name YHWH (יהוה) are : ה and י.  If you remove the characters yod (י ) and hay (ה) from the word for man (אִישׁ ) and the word for woman (אִשָּׁה ), the characters that are left form the word fire (אֵשׁ- esh).

| Character Pronounced | Character |
|---|---|
| *yode or yod* | י |
| *he or hay* | ה |

The <u>Midrash</u> teaches that, a covenant marriage relationship produces love, but without God in it, conflict and devastation (fire) result. So too, at the end of days our Lord will remove himself from those who do not have a covenant relationship with him and they will be consumed by fire.

# Chapter 5

## MARRIAGE & ADULTERY

### OVERVIEW

Because the marriage of the Lamb and his bride is referred to in the book of Revelation, we felt it would be of interest to you to have some background on the Jewish customs and traditions regarding marriage and the wedding ceremony.

As our research developed, we found that the cultural and spiritual implications of these customs shed invaluable light on our understanding of events in John's vision. In a larger sense, they provide keys to the mystery of God's relationship with his people.

Rabbi Samson Raphael Hirsch writes:

*The highest conception of which this people is capable . . . the conception of its relation to God and God's relation to it, is always visualized by it in the form of wedlock . . . . It is the bride of God . . . and . . . the whole varied story of its inner and outer life is nothing but the picture of a married life, with periods of joy and sorrow, of faithfulness and unfaithfulness, of devotion and estrangement, of quarrel and reconciliation, of rejection and reunion, in an eternal blessed covenant. . . . How pure, how elevated must have been the conception of marriage among this people, what striking example of mutual love and esteem, of mutual devotion and sacrifice must Jewish marriage have offered, how fortunate must the husband have felt in his wife and the wife in her husband, that the covenant between God and His people could have been thought of under such a simile.* [2]

What a great concept— *"...and they will become one.." Genesis 2:24.* God instituted marriage between man and woman to demonstrate the relationship that He desired between each of us and Himself. This relationship is intimate and private as well as an economic and political union.

> *The fruit of your womb will be blessed, and the crops of your land and the young of your livestock—the calves of your herds and the lambs of your flocks. Your basket and your kneading trough will be blessed. Deuteronomy 28:4-5*

> *I in them and you in me. May they be brought to complete unity to let the world know that you sent me and have loved them even as you have loved me. John 17:23*

There are a great many scriptures that depict the relationship between Israel and God as that of a bridegroom and bride. We often find that Israel's faithlessness is deplored as adultery against the marriage covenant. The prophets Hosea, Isaiah, Jeremiah, Ezekiel and Malachi often used sexual imagery when warning Israel regarding her faithlessness, referring to her as the adulteress. Therefore, we have also included in this chapter some information on the Jewish laws and tradition regarding adultery and divorce. These customs also shed surprising light on the events of the book of Revelation.

# MARRIAGE

## THE VIRGIN

When in the Western world we hear the word virgin, we most likely think of a person who has never engaged in sexual activity. When the Bible uses the word virgin along with the phrase "who has never known a man", its meaning is primarily of a woman who has never engaged in sexual activity. The Strong's and Young's Concordance render the word virgin as one who is separated, kept in concealment and is unmarried.

However, during ancient times, the word virgin was an aspect of not only a personal relationship, but the political position of a household within a community. The concept of virginity in biblical culture had a broader meaning. In the Bible world promiscuity was not just seen as sexual indiscretion, but as a risk to the lands and reputations of the whole household. This concept was well described by Matthews and Benjamin in their book, <u>Social World of Ancient Israel 1250-587 BCE.</u> They stated that an unmarried woman's virginity was a symbol of the honor and political standing of her father's household. A man's reputation and position in his village was measured by his ability to fulfill his duties to his family. These responsibilities were to provide for the safekeeping of his household, particularly the women. It was understood that if the father was able to shield his women then all the members would be well protected. On the other hand, if the father failed in his duties to his family and harm came to them; the village would expel him and assign his family and land to another.

Key 5-1
Father of Household

The virgin was considered to be the most politically significant woman in the state of Israel in ancient times. Not only was she a symbol of her father's honor, she herself had duties of responsibility. She, too, must provide for and protect the honor of her household by avoiding anything that might be interpreted as promiscuity.

Key 5-2
Virgin

It was also the virgins duty to make a good marriage covenant and abide by it. Her virginity testified that a covenant made with her family and that of the groom would be productive both in land and children. When the marriage was consummated, the evidence of her virginity became a legal guarantee of lands and children for her household.

Political relationships were often marked by competition and violence during Bible times. Rape was not just an act of sexual violence, it was a challenge to the political and social status of the father of the household. Biblical stories that involve sex and violence were not fundamentally lustful in nature, but they described a means of assessing the political status and strength of the households of the men and women involved.

Key 5-3
Assailant

These concepts bring new insight into the scenario of the Garden of Eden. It was not a surprise that Satan approached the woman. This attempt was a hostile takeover bid for the household of God. Eve's action in receiving the temptation from the serpent endangered her household. Because she made no attempt to cry out, she became an accomplice to her assailant's takeover bid. Matthews and Benjamin explain the part a virgin must play in protecting her family's honor, should she be attacked:

> *In the city, a virgin must cry out or be considered an accomplice in her assailant's bid to take over the household to which she is promised. . . "Cry out" is not only a call for help, but also a lawsuit, which begins when the plaintiff stands and cries out for justice at the threshing floor of the village or the gate of the city (2 Sam 15:1-6).*[3]

In the case of a married woman being kidnapped or raped, part of the law regarding marriage provided for her ransom:

Key 5-4
Ransom

> The <u>Mishnah</u> states in Ketuboth 4 . . .*When she is married the husband exceeds the father in that he has the use of her property during her lifetime; and he is liable for her maintenance and for her ransom [if she is captured] and for her burial.*

Acts of sexual violence did not all qualify as challenges to the honor of households. Specific households that were considered honorable, wealthy and worthy of such take over bids were usually the targets. The households of Shechem (Genesis 34), Amnon (2 Samuel 12:1-22), and Absalom (2 Samuel 16:15-22) used rape or defilement as a way to challenge the households of Jacob, Absalom and David. This type of defilement was used to determine who would control the lands and children of different regions. If the challenged household was unable to provide protection for its women, then it was considered to be shamed and was no longer solvent. It was the right of the successful assailant to take the resources of the challenged household. By raping Dinah, Shechem was able to lay claim to her inheritance in Jacob's household. He became the legal guardian of her father's lands and children until negotiations were accomplished.

In order for the shamed household to reestablish its honor and status in the community, it must follow a similar protocol to that used by the assailant. The prince or son of the shamed household must kill the prince of the assailant's household. This act was to be done while the prince of the assailant's household was exercising his authority or power over that which had been seized.

Key 5-5
Prince of
Household

## THE SANCTITY OF MARRIAGE

Jewish tradition looks upon marriage as the consecration (setting apart) of a man and woman in a sacred spiritual bond. This gives special significance to Israel being described as holy (set apart) for God:

> *For you are a people holy to the Lord your God. The Lord your God has chosen you out of all the peoples on the face of the earth to be his people, his treasured possession. Deuteronomy 7:6*

The sages of old said that a prerequisite for experiencing the fullness of the presence of God is perfection or completion. It was their belief that marriage brings a man and woman to this completed state so they may experience a fuller communion with the Lord God. The Hebrew word for bride is *kallah* which means the complete or perfect one. When a husband and wife came together in sexual relations, the presence of God was said to be made manifested because of the completeness (consummation) of the union.

Key 5-6
Consummation

The Zohar teaches:
*A person can be considered one and whole . . . and without defect . . . when he is joined together with the complementary part of him and is thus hallowed by the elevated sanctification of kidushin. [betrothal-holiness]. He who has not married a woman . . . remains but half a person. . . .*

## WEDDING ARRANGEMENTS

Since ancient times Jewish wedding arrangements have included two important parts: the formal betrothal ceremony (*eirusin*), followed about a year later with the second part, the marriage ceremony (*nissuin*). In modern times, the time between the two ceremonies is often shortened.

According to Jewish tradition arranged marriages were the rule. Though most were planned by the fathers, however, the consent of the man and woman was always considered. It was especially important that the bride gave her consent. Sometimes partners were chosen by relatives or a marriage broker and in modern times by the couples themselves.

**Lock 5-1**
**Father of Household**
**Page #109**

*Betrothal Ceremony. . .*
The ceremony for the betrothal was a formal one. According to Jewish custom the young man would go to the home of the bride to propose marriage. He took three items with him:

*I will betroth you to me forever; I will betroth you in righteousness and justice, in love and compassion.*
Hosea 2:19

- Betrothal Contract (*Tenaim*)
  See Appendix D at the end of this section.
- Skin of Wine  (for sealing the contract)
- Bride Price (sum of money)

The groom presented the betrothal contract to the bride's father. The contract included the place of the proposed marriage, financial obligations of both parties, and the dowry to be brought by the bride. If the contract and the price were agreed upon by the bridegroom and the father of the bride, the wine was poured and the young woman was called in. If she agreed to the terms she lifted the glass of wine and drank from it. The betrothal ceremony was complete after the bride and groom had partaken of the wine.

**Key 5-7**
**Bought With A Price**

**Key 5-8**
**Bridegroom**

The groom then made the  statement that he would return to his father's house to begin preparations on a place for his bride.

At this point the betrothal contract having been agreed upon and signed was considered a legal and binding document. It would take a written bill of divorce to dissolve it.

**Lock 5-2**
**Virgin**
**Page #109**

The community looked upon the couple as man and wife, although neither the marriage ceremony nor the consummation had taken place. The bride continued to live at home in her father's house under his care and protection until the actual marriage ceremony. She was considered to be consecrated or set apart for her husband.

Such a betrothal ceremony is described in the betrothal of Rebekah to Isaac with a servant acting as the groom's agent.

*I praised the Lord, the God of my master Abraham, who had led me on the right road to get the granddaughter of my master's brother for his son. Now if you will show kindness and faithfulness to my master, tell me; and if not, tell me, so I may know which way to turn. Laban and Bethuel answered, "This is from the Lord; we can say nothing to you one way or the other. Here is Rebekah; take her and go, and let her become the wife of your master's son, as the Lord has directed." When Abraham's servant heard what they said, he bowed down to the ground before the Lord. Then the servant brought out gold and silver jewelry and articles of clothing and game them to Rebekah; he also gave costly gifts to her brother and to her mother. Then he and the man who were with him ate and drank and spent the night there. . . Then they said, "Let's call the girl and ask her about it."*
*Genesis 24:48b-54, 57*

### The Wedding Chamber . . .

After the betrothal ceremony, the construction began for the *chuppah* or wedding chamber. According to the Talmud, the groom's father had the responsibility for its construction. In ancient tradition, the term *chuppah* seemed to have various meanings. Sometimes it designated the rooms where the bridegroom and bride waited prior to the ceremony. Other times it designated the place where the marriage was consummated and was called the honeymoon bed. In some cases, the couple retired there for the full seven days of celebration following the wedding.

Lock 4-18
Wedding Chamber
Page #91

Originally the *chuppah* was made from cedar and pine taken from trees that had been planted at the birth of the perspective bride and groom. It was decorated beautifully and every comfort was provided in this chamber in which the bride and groom would consummate the marriage and break their fast.

Lock 4-19
Tree of Life
Page #92

Over time the *chuppah* came to be symbolized by a canopy under which the wedding couple stood during the marriage ceremony. This canopy was usually a square cloth made of silk or velvet with eight tassels on each side and was lavishly decorated. Open on four sides, it symbolized the Jewish home filled with acts of love and known for hospitality to strangers. For Rabbi Yasi ben Yohanan had said, "Let your house be wide open". Tradition says the tent of Abraham had entrances on all four sides in which to welcome, from all di-

> Isaiah used the term chuppah to describe a future canopy:
>
> *Then the Lord will create over all of Mount Zion and over those who assemble there a cloud of smoke by day and a glow of flaming fire by night; over all the glory will be a canopy. It will be a shelter and shade from the heat of the day, and a refuge and hiding place from the storm and rain. Isaiah 4:5-6*

Lock 2-4
Holy of Holies
Page #82

rections, travelers and guests. Four poles were used to support it and were held by four men during the marriage ceremony. For some the square measure was symbolic of the foursquare of the Holy of Holies where God met man face to face.

### *The Days Before the Wedding . . .*

Before the wedding ceremony the groom established and built a home for his future bride. He and his father made all the arrangements for the wedding ceremony and the banquet.

Lock 5-1
Father of House-
hold
Page #112

It was the bridegroom's father who decided when the wedding preparations were complete. When the *chuppah* was complete and he was satisfied with all the preparations, he gave permission to announce the time of the wedding. If during the preparation time the bridegroom was asked, *"When will the wedding be?"* he was to reply, *"No man knows except my father."*[4]

Key 5-9
Two Witnesses

Prior to the wedding ceremony, the groom designated two close friends to assist him. They were known as the 'friends of the bridegroom'. They functioned as the two witnesses that are required for all Jewish weddings. One witness was assigned to the bride to assist her and lead her to the ceremony. The second witness was assigned to the groom. His special task was to stand outside the wedding chamber after the ceremony and announce the consummation of the marriage to the guests.

Lock 4-1
Book of Covenant
Page #97

The honor of reading the Law (Torah) in the synagogue on the Sabbath prior to the wedding was given to the groom. He was also chosen to read the Law on the Sabbath following the wedding.

For the bride, the days before the wedding were spent in learning to please her husband. She continued her training in housekeeping and motherhood. The preparations for her part in the wedding ceremony were also made: wedding garments, learning to apply cosmetics, and preparations for the banquet.

## THE MARRIAGE

### *Wedding Date. . .*

Jewish weddings were severely restricted and could not be performed on a Sabbath or during any major Feast. Neither were weddings allowed during a time of national mourning or fasting, such as the Day of Atonement.

The <u>Mishnah</u> states that virgins should marry on Wednesday. The primary reason for choosing Wednesday was that during the Talmudic era the rabbinical courts were in session on Monday and Thursday. First marriage brides were usually assumed to be virgins and were so referred to in the betrothal contract made during the betrothal ceremony. If the groom discovered his bride had been misrepresented to him as a virgin, he had the option to attend court on Thursday. Here he could obtain a *Get*, a written bill of divorce. It was not a common occurrence for the groom to find the need to attend court for such a divorce.

Lock 5-2
Virgin
Page #112

### Spiritual Purification . . .

The night before the wedding ceremony, the bride performed her ritual bath, in Hebrew called *mikvah*. She immersed herself in water as a part of the process of purification and consecration necessary prior to the marriage consummation.

Lock 4-8
Ritual Bath
Page #79

It was also customary for the bride and groom to fast on the day of the their wedding. Fasting was a demonstration that the couple had removed themselves from the purely physical and had repented of their sins. Jewish tradition likens this fast time to the Day of Atonement in which all previous sins are forgiven and life is started anew.

### The Marriage Contract . . .

The *Ketubbah* was the legal marriage contract and can be traced back to the Old Testament. The contract of Ruth and Boaz is recorded thus:

Key 5-10
Marriage Contract

> *I have also acquired Ruth the Moabitess, Mahlon's widow, as my wife, in order to maintain the name of the dead with his property, so that his name will not disappear from among his family or from the town records. Today you are witnesses! Ruth 4:10*

It stated that the bridegroom weds his bride according to the law of Moses and Israel. He promises to please, to respect, to nurture and to provide for the needs of his bride. It is a vital legal instrument to the bride in the case of divorce or death of the husband. It describes the legal means of financial and personal protection for the bride and provision for the return of her dowry. ( See Appendix E at the end of this section.)

Lock 5-1
Father of Household
Page #114

The bridegroom may not cohabit with his bride until the written marriage contract has been signed and the marriage blessings have been given. On the day of the marriage, prior to the ceremony, the *Ketubbah* was presented for signature. As in the

Lock 5-9
Two Witnesses
Page #114

betrothal contract, this contract was signed by the father of the bride and witnessed by the friends of the bridegroom.

*Before the destruction of the Temple, crowns or diadems of gold were worn by the bride and groom as part of the wedding garments. In Talmudic times, the bride's crown was known as the "city of gold" which represented Jerusalem.*

### The Ceremony. . .

Jewish wedding ceremonies have gone through many changes. The customs and traditions varied according to the community from which they originated. We have chosen to describe for you the most prevalent customs and traditions found in resource materials.

The wedding ceremony was a gay and festive event considered to be a major celebration in Jewish communities. According to tradition the wedding of a virgin must continue for a period of seven days.

Lock 2-7
White Garments
Page #84

On the day of the wedding the bride was dressed in white which represented purity. She also wore a headdress and a veil. The veil was usually a gift from the groom. Along with the bridal garments, the bride sometimes adorned herself with jewels or coins,

*Yet you have a few people in Sardis who have not soiled their clothes. They will walk with me, dressed in white, for they are worthy. He who overcomes will, like them, be dressed in white, I will never blot out his name from the book of life, but will acknowledge his name before my Father and his angels. . . . I counsel you to buy from me gold refined in the fire, so you can become rich; and white clothes to wear, so you can cover your shameful nakedness; and salve to put on your eyes, so you can see. Revelation 3:4, 5, 18*

which were part of her dowry. Her preparations complete, the bride was seated on a throne or chair and waited in her room for the groom's appearance.

*I delight greatly in the Lord; my soul rejoices in my God. For he has clothed me with garments of salvation and arrayed me in a robe of righteousness, as a bridegroom adorns his head like a priest, and as a bride adorns herself with her jewels. Isaiah 61:10*

The groom was dressed by his attendants as a king might be. His garments were made of white, which symbolized purity, and he sometimes wore a white linen robe (*kittel*) and a prayer shawl (*tallit*). Tradition says the bride and bridegroom stand pure without spot or blemish as they are united on this one day.

Lock 5-8
Bridegroom
Page #112

The groom was escorted to the bride's waiting room by his father and the bride's father. At that time, the groom let down the veil over the bride's face and returned to his waiting room.

Lock 4-15
Lulav
Page #92

The bride and groom were considered by the community to be as a king and queen on this day. They were placed on thrones and carried to the ceremony. The guests went before them with palm and myrtle branches, throwing grain or money and sometimes singing and dancing.

The custom of carrying candles by those escorting the bride and groom is very old and seems to symbolize lighting the way as they begin their future lives together. In different regions, candles and torches were carried by the mothers and sometimes by the fathers. Another custom was the bridegroom being accompanied by a man carrying a torch with six lights that was similar to the menorah.

Lock 3-4
Processions
Page #46

The groom arrived first to welcome his bride. The bride was customarily escorted by the couple's mothers. They were usually welcomed by the rabbi or the cantor with a blessing: "Blessed is he who comes in the name of the Lord." They circled around the groom seven times (in some traditions the circling is three times). This custom seems to have come from the scripture which states that a woman *"will encircle a man"* (Jeremiah 31:22).

> The mention of "children of the bridechamber" occurring in Matthew 9:15 means "guests" who have been invited to the marriage.

> *For I tell you, you will not see me again until you say, "Blessed is he who comes in the name of the Lord." Matthew 23:39*

Lock 5-8
Bridegroom
Page #116

The blessings were then said and a glass of wine was lifted. After the blessings and drinking of the wine, the ceremony of sanctification *(kiddushin)* was performed. The groom turned to the bride and recited the marriage formula: "Behold! You are consecrated to me with this ring according to the laws of Moses and Israel." A plain band was placed on the forefinger of the bride's right hand.

> *I tell you, I will not drink of this fruit of the vine from now on until that day when I drink it anew with you in my Father's kingdom. Matthew 26:29*

After the completion of the ring ceremony the marriage contract was read aloud to the assembled guests. The contract was then handed to the groom who in turn gave it to the bride. The bride or the bride's mother was expected to keep it safe.

Lock 5-10
Marriage Contract
Page #115

When the reading of the contract was completed the Seven Benedictions were read. Another cup of wine was given to the bride and groom to sip. This completed the marriage ceremony.

### Seclusion. . .

Following the ceremony, the bride and groom made their way to the wedding chamber, while the guests proceeded to the lavishly prepared banquet.

Lock 4-18
Wedding Chamber
Page #113

The bridegroom usually arrived first at the wedding chamber where he welcomed his bride. Here they took their first meal together breaking their fast.

Lock 4-21
Intimate
Communion
Page #96

In ancient times, the marriage was consummated at this time. The witness, a friend of the bridegroom, stood outside the door of the chamber and awaited the news of the consummation. He, in turn, made the announcement to the banqueting guests that the consummation was complete. Great rejoicing broke

Lock 5-6
Consummation
Page #111

Lock 5-8
Bridegroom
Page #116

Lock 5-9
Two Witnesses
Page #115

out among the guests and the festivities continued for seven days.

Lock 5-2
Virgin
Page #115

The bloody sheet from the wedding chamber provided proof of the virginity of the bride. This sheet was given to the mother of the bride for safekeeping, in the event there was ever any question of her virginity.

In some areas the retirement to the wedding chamber developed into a brief seclusion symbolic of the earlier consummation tradition.

## THE BANQUET

Lock 4-20
Late to the Banquet
Page #94

After an appropriate time had lapsed, the couple left the *chuppah* and joined their guests at the wedding banquet. The rejoicing and feasting which had already begun continued. At the end of the wedding feast, the seven blessings were once again repeated. Two cups of wine were drunk, one at the beginning and one at the end of the blessings.

On occasions when the bride and groom did not spend seven days in the wedding chamber, they remained in the community during the next full week. The groom was not allowed to leave his bride to go to work, even with her permission. He could not be called into military service for a one year period following the marriage. The only exception for the groom being called into military service would be for the defense of his country or nation in a national emergency.

## THEY SHALL BECOME ONE

When God created Adam and Eve, He blessed them and instructed them to be fruitful and increase in number in order to fill the earth (Genesis 1:28). After God had created Eve from Adam's rib and given her to him, Adam said:

> *"This is now bone of my bones and flesh of my flesh; she shall be called 'woman,' for she was taken out of man." For this reason a man will leave his father and mother and be united to his wife, and they will become one flesh. Genesis 2:23-24*

The purpose of the sanctified life together is to create a sanctuary in which the couple can fulfill the duties of producing offspring, educating their children, and providing companionship and protection for each other. In speaking of His relationship with Abraham, God said:

> *For I have chosen him so that he will direct his children and his household after him to keep the way of the Lord by doing what is right and just, so that the Lord will bring about for Abraham what he has promised him. Genesis 18:19*

Children were considered to be blessings and assets to a family. The Jewish rituals attached to the birth of children are not only interesting, but insightful to our understanding of the scriptures.

## ADOPTION

In ancient Israel, the birth of a child was accompanied by much ceremony. After the delivery and prior to the washing, anointing, clothing, and adoption, the newborn was considered to be in a time of transition. The baby was very vulnerable as he was not yet legally a part of the household. When a midwife delivered a child, she held it up and invited its adoption. The baby's first cry was considered to be a petition to join the household and become a member of the village.

Key 5-11
Adoption

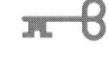

Lock 5-1
Father of
Household
Page #115

To adopt the baby, a father would answer the cry with a hymn or joyful exclamation inviting the household to praise the Creator and accept the child. If the wife of the household was the birth mother she would adopt her own baby. If the birth mother was not the wife, but perhaps a servant, the wife of the household could adopt the child as her own. The parents must officially declare that they had produced a child with the Lord's help. The child would then be introduced by name to the household.

> *In the same way, I tell you, there is rejoicing in the presence of the angels of God over one sinner who repents. Luke 15:10*

If no one claimed the baby for adoption, the midwife would not clean it from the birthing, but would take it to a field and leave it where someone from another household could adopt it or it would die. Such an instance is described in the following:

> *The word of the Lord came to me: "Son of man, confront Jerusalem with her detestable practices and say, 'This is what the Sovereign Lord says to Jerusalem: Your ancestry and birth were in the land of the Canaanites; your father was an Amorite and your mother a Hittite. On the day you were born your cord was not cut, nor were you washed with water to make you clean, nor were you rubbed with*

*salt or wrapped in cloths. No one looked on you with pity or had compassion enough to do any of these things for you. Rather, you were thrown out into the open field, for on the day you were born you were despised. Then I passed by and saw you kicking about in your blood, and as you lay there in your blood I said to you, "Live!" Ezekiel 16:2-5*

It was to this concept of adoption that Paul alluded:

*For he chose us in him before the creation of the world to be holy and blameless in his sight. In love he predestined us to be adopted as his sons through Jesus Christ, in accordance with his pleasure and will. . . Ephesians 1:4-5*

Paul declares that receiving the Spirit begins the adoption process, which is completed at the redemption of our bodies at the resurrection:

Lock 3-11
Birthpains
Page #75

*For you did not receive a spirit that makes you a slave again to fear, but you received the Spirit of sonship. And by him we cry, "Abba, Father." The Spirit himself testifies with our spirit that we are God's children. Now if we are children, then we are heirs—heirs of God and co-heirs with Christ, if indeed we share in his sufferings in order that we may also share in his glory. . . We know that the whole creation has been groaning as in the pains of childbirth right up to the present time. Not only so, but we ourselves, who have the firstfruits of the Spirit, groan inwardly as we wait eagerly for our adoption as sons, the redemption of our bodies. Romans 8:15-17, 22-23*

In Exodus 1:12-22, it is apparent these midwives had a certain amount of authority upon which even monarchs were dependent. The midwife was seen as a negotiator between Pharaoh and the Hebrew childbearers. These midwives could effectively and legally work for or against the monarch by carrying out policies over life and death.

## ADDITIONAL POINTS OF INTEREST

### Samarian Marriage. . .
In Samaria the marriage ceremony was very similar to the Jewish one. Beginning on the Sabbath before the wedding, the family of the bridegroom announced the week for celebrating. The relatives of the groom walked from house to house inviting guests to come and take part in the wedding week.

*Go to the street corners and invite to the banquet anyone you find.  So the servants went  out into the streets and gathered all the people they could find, both good and bad, and the wedding hall was filled with guests... Matthew: 22: 1-14*

### The Marriage at Cana. . .
John 2:1-11 relates the wedding that Jesus and his mother attended at Cana.  According to Jewish tradition a virgin is usually married on Wednesday.  If we look at John 1:19-51 we can see that the days prior help us to set the time for the Cana wedding. The following will help you pick out the days:

| | | |
|---|---|---|
| John 1:19 | Thursday | According to Jewish sources the Sanhedrin met on Thursdays. Therefore, the delegation who went to look into John's activities would have been sent on Thursday. |
| John 1:29 | Friday | "The next day..." would have to be on Friday. |
| John 1:35 | Saturday | "The next day..." again obviously making this day Saturday (the Sabbath). |
| John 1:43 | Sunday | "The next day..." would have been Sunday when Jesus left for Galilee. |
| John 2:1 | Wednesday | "On the third day a wedding took place at Cana in Galilee."  That would have been a Wednesday. |

So, this marriage was not celebrated on a Sabbath or on any of the Feast days which would be according to Jewish tradition and more than likely occurred on Wednesday.

### Friends of the Bridegroom. . .
You may have noticed that there was no mention of the "friends of the bridegroom" in the account of the wedding in Cana.  Groomsmen (friends of the bridegroom) were not customary in Galilee where this wedding took place but they were in Judea.  When we read about the friends of the bridegroom in John 3:29 they are in the locality of Judea.

# JESUS THE BRIDEGROOM

During our study of marriage, we saw that Jesus' teachings often alluded to the state of marriage. Paul's teachings likewise placed emphasis on marriage and its symbolism.

> *Wherefore, my brethren, ye also are become dead to the law by the body of Christ; that ye should be married [NIV-belong] to another, even to him who is raised from the dead, that we should bring forth fruit unto God.*
> *Romans 7:4 (KJV)*

Paul even sees himself in the role of the father, his honor reflected in his ability to present a virgin to her bridegroom.

> *I am jealous for you with a godly jealousy. I promised you to one husband, to Christ, so that I might present you as a pure virgin to him. 2 Corinthians 11:2*

## GOD'S HOUSEHOLD

God, too, describes himself in the role of Father of the household:

Lock 5-11
Adoption
Page #119

> *Consequently, you are no longer foreigners and aliens, but fellow citizens with God's people and members of God's household. . . Ephesians 2:19*

> *. . .he predestined us to be adopted as his sons through Jesus Christ, in accordance with his pleasure and will. . . Ephesians 1:5*

Lock 5-1
Father of
Household
Page #119

As you will recall, the father is the head or ruler of the household and therefore he is responsible for the care and protection of his family and lands. God as the head of His household provides the same for his children.

> *As God has said: "I will live with them and walk among them, and I will be their God, and they will be my people." . . ."I will be a Father to you, and you will be my sons and daughters, says the Lord Almighty." 2 Corinthians 6:16b, 18*

Jesus as the Son of God and the seed of Abraham is the instrument of the covenant God gave to Abraham and his heirs. The promise of children to Abraham as numerous as the stars in the heaven is continually being fulfilled as individuals accept Jesus as Lord and become His heirs. If we are heirs, then we are also members of the family or household of God.

Lock 5-5
Prince of
Household
Page #111

> *I swear by myself, declares the Lord, that because you have done this and have not withheld your son, your only son, I will surely bless you and make your descendants as numerous as the stars in the sky and as the sand on the seashore. Your descendants will take possession of the cities of their enemies, and through your offspring all nations on earth will be blessed, because you have obeyed me. Genesis 22:15-18*

> *You are all sons of God through faith in Christ Jesus, for all of you were baptized into Christ have clothed yourselves with Christ . . .. If you belong to Christ, then you are Abraham's seed, and heirs according to the promise. Galatians 3:26, 29*

> *The Spirit himself testifies with our spirit that we are God's children. Now if we are children, then we are heirs—heirs of God and co-heirs with Christ. . . Romans 8:16-17*

## WEDDING ARRANGEMENTS

*Betrothal Ceremony . . .*
When a betrothal was made the bridegroom went to the father of the prospective bride with three items: a bride price, the wine, and the contract. Jesus is seen in the following scriptures with these items in hand.

Lock 5-8
Bridegroom
Page #117

The price that was paid during the betrothal was the blood of the Bridegroom, Jesus.

Lock 5-7
Bought With a
Price
Page #112

> *Do you not know that your body is a temple of the Holy Spirit, who is in you, whom you have received from God? You are not your own; you were bought at a price... 1 Corinthians 6:19-20*

> *He anointed us, set his seal of ownership on us, and put his Spirit in our hearts as a deposit guaranteeing what is to come. 2 Corinthians 1:21b, 22*

Lock 3-3
Sign on Hand &
Forehead
Page #61

*Having believed, you were marked in him with a seal, the promised Holy Spirit, who is a deposit guaranteeing our inheritance until the redemption of those who are God's possession. . . Ephesians 1:13b, 14*

You might recall that a glass of wine was drunk to seal the betrothal and another to seal the marriage covenant at the end of the wedding ceremony. The cup of wine, that must be drunk by all who would be His betrothed, is His blood.

*Drink from it, all of you. This is my blood of the covenant, which is poured out for many for the forgiveness of sins. I tell you, I will not drink of this fruit of the vine from now on until that day when I drink it anew with you in my Father's kingdom. Matthew 26:27-29*

As he shared the betrothal ceremony with his disciples, he presented it thus:

*And I will do whatever you ask in my name, so that the Son may bring glory to the Father. You may ask me for anything in my name, and I will do it. If you love me, you will obey what I command. And I will ask the Father, and he will give you another Counselor to be with you forever— the Spirit of truth. The world cannot accept him, because it neither sees him nor knows him. But you know him, for he lives with you and will be in you. I will not leave you as orphans; I will come to you. Before long, the world will not see me anymore, but you will see me. Because I live, you also will live. On that day you will realize that I am in my Father, and you are in me, and I am in you. Whoever has my commands and obeys them, he is the one who loves me. He who loves me will be loved by my Father, and I too will love him and show myself to him. John 14:13-21*

The betrothal contract, the new covenant Jesus offered with His blood is recorded throughout the New Testament.

*But the ministry Jesus has received is as superior to theirs as the covenant of which he is mediator is superior to the old one, and it is founded on better promises. . . This is the covenant I will make with the house of Israel. . . I will put my laws in their minds and write them on their hearts. I will be their God, and they will be my people. . . For I will forgive their wickedness and will remember their sins no more. Hebrews 8:6-12*

*This is the covenant I will make with them. . . Then he adds: "Their sins and lawless acts I will remember no more." And where these have been forgiven, there is no longer any sacrifice for sin. Hebrews 10:16-18*

*And God is able to make all grace abound to you so that in all things at all times, having all that you need, you will abound in every good work. . . Now he who supplies seed to the sower and bread for food will also supply and increase your store of seed and will enlarge the harvest of your righteousness. You will be made rich in every way so that you can be generous on every occasion. . .*
*2 Corinthians 8:8, 10-11*

### The Days Before the Wedding . . .

After the betrothal ritual was completed, the bridegroom returned to his father's house. It was during this time that the bridegroom prepared the house that he and his bride would live in.

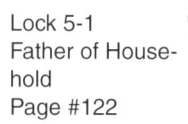

Lock 5-1
Father of House-
hold
Page #122

Lock 5-8
Bridegroom
Page #123

*In my Father's house are many rooms; if it were not so, I would have told you. I am going there to prepare a place for you. And if I go and prepare a place for you, I will come back and take you to be with me that you also may be where I am. John 14:2-3*

The bridegroom also chose his friends that would assist him and be the witnesses at the wedding. Jesus called his disciples his friends in the following scripture:

Lock 5-9
Two Witnesses
Page #117

*You are my friends if you do what I command. I no longer call you servants, because a servant does not know his master's business. Instead I have called you friends, for everything that I learned from my Father I have made known to you. You did not choose me, but I chose you and appointed you to go and bear fruit. . . John 15:14-16a*

John considered himself the friend of the bridegroom in this scripture:

*The bride belongs to the bridegroom. The friend who attends the bridegroom waits and listens for him, and is full of joy when he hears the bridegroom's voice. That joy is mine, and it is now complete. John 3:29*

Abraham was also called a friend in the following scripture:

> *And the scripture was fulfilled that says, "Abraham believed God, and it was credited to him as righteousness, and he was called God's friend. James 2:23*

The days before the wedding were spent in much preparation for the bride. She was learning to please her husband and continued her training in housekeeping and motherhood. She was also preparing wedding garments and making herself a comely bride. As believers we also have to prepare:

> *Do your best to present yourself to God as one approved, a workman who does not need to be ashamed and who correctly handles the word of truth. . . In a large house there are articles not only of gold and silver, but also of wood and clay; some are for noble purposes and some for ignoble. If a man cleanses himself from the latter, he will be an instrument for noble purposes, made holy, useful to the Master and prepared to do any good work. Flee from the evil desires of youth, and pursue righteousness, faith, love and peace, along with those who call on the Lord out of a pure heart. 2 Timothy 2:15, 20-22*

> *Preach the Word; be prepared in season and out of season; correct, rebuke and encourage—with great patience and careful instruction. 2 Timothy 4:2*

**Lock 4-8**
**Ritual Bath**
**Page #115**

> *Let us draw near to God with a sincere heart in full assurance of faith, having our hearts sprinkled to cleanse us from a guilty conscience and having our bodies washed with pure water. Let us hold unswervingly to the hope we profess, for he who promised is faithful. Hebrews 10:22-23*

### *The Wedding Chamber . . .*
The bridegroom's father prepared the *chuppah* and made the arrangements for the wedding and ceremony.

> *The kingdom of heaven is like a king who prepared a wedding banquet for his son. Matthew 22:2*

**Lock 5-1**
**Father of**
**Household**
**Page #125**

You may recall that it was the responsibility of the father of the household to decide when all preparations had been completed and when the wedding would be announced. It was for this reason that Jesus said he did not know the day of his return. When Jesus responded to his disciples when they asked "When will these things happen?" Jesus was speaking as a bridegroom.

*No one knows about that day or hour, not even the angels in heaven, nor the Son, but only the Father...  Mark 13:32*

At Jesus' return, he will receive the greeting of the congregation reserved for the bridegroom and bride:

*For I tell you, you will not see me again until you say, 'Blessed is he who comes in the name of the Lord.' Matthew 23:39*

*The bridegroom was a long time in coming, and they all became drowsy and fell asleep.  At midnight the cry rang out: 'Here's the bridegroom!  Come out to meet him!' ... "Therefore keep watch, because you do not know the day or the hour.  Matthew 25:5-6, 13*

Lock 5-8
Bridegroom
Page #125

*Gather the people, consecrate the assembly; bring together the elders, gather the children, those nursing at the breast.  Let the bridegroom leave his room and the bride her chamber. Joel 2:16*

On the day of the wedding the bride and bridegroom fasted until the ceremony was complete.  Jesus said the time for this fast has not yet come.  The period of time from Jesus' resurrection to today is a time of preparation for the day when Jesus will return for his bride.

*Jesus answered, "Can you make the guests of the bridegroom fast while he is with them?  But the time will come when the bridegroom will be taken from them; in those days they will fast."  Luke 5:34,35*

*Jesus answered, "How can the guests of the bridegroom mourn while he is with them?  The time will come when the bridegroom will be taken from them; then they will fast. Matthew 9:15*

# ADULTERY

The Hebrew name for a document of divorce is a *Get*. Once a betrothal of marriage was entered into, it can only be nullified by this means. It was a requirement that the *Get* be hand delivered to the wife by the bridegroom or his agent. He must announce to her in the presence of two witnesses that he was giving her a bill of divorce.

> *It has been said, 'Anyone who divorces his wife must give her a certificate of divorce.' But I tell you that anyone who divorces his wife, except for marital unfaithfulness, causes her to become an adulteress, and anyone who marries the divorced woman commits adultery.*
> *Matthew 5:31-32*

Upon receiving a notice of divorce, a woman usually returned to her father's house. If there were children from the marriage they remained with the husband. The divorce was considered finalized when she left the home. Divorced women were looked upon with much disfavor and her life was not pleasant.

If a husband suspected his wife of adultery a very specific protocol was outlined. Adultery was defined as sexual relations of ones own freewill with someone other than the spouse.

The <u>Mishnah</u> provides very strict guidelines that the charge of adultery may not be brought frivolously. If a husband suspected his wife of adultery, he was required to have two witnesses to the offense and to warn her that he was aware of the adultery. Only after this was done could a bill of divorce be

Lock 5-9
Two Witnesses
Page #125

given or the test for an unfaithful wife be performed.

> *Go, proclaim this message toward the north: 'Return, faithless Israel,' declares the Lord, 'I will frown on you no longer, for I am merciful,' declares the Lord, 'I will not be angry forever. Only acknowledge your guilt—you have rebelled against the Lord your God, you have scattered your favors to foreign gods under every spreading tree, and have not obeyed me,' declares the Lord.*
> *Jeremiah 3:12-13*

Lock 3-10
Repentance from
Adultery
Page #98

If at any time before the deliverance of the *Get*, either party reconsidered the decision, then everything would stand as before and all marriage obligations were in force.

*The test for an unfaithful wife . . .*
The book of Numbers provides the following description for the test of an unfaithful wife. A betrothed woman could not be administered the bitter water.

*Then the Lord said to Moses, "Speak to the Israelites and say to them: 'If a man's wife goes astray and is unfaithful to him by sleeping with another man, and this is hidden from her husband and her impurity is undetected (since there is no witness against her and she has not been caught in the act), and if feelings of jealousy come over her husband and he suspects his wife and she is impure—or if he is jealous and suspects her even though she is not impure—then he is to take his wife to the priest. He must also take an offering of a tenth of an ephah of barley flour on her behalf. He must not pour oil on it or put incense on it, because it is a grain offering for jealousy, a reminder offering to draw attention to guilt. The priest shall bring her and have her stand before the Lord. Then he shall take some holy water in a clay jar and put some dust from the tabernacle floor into the water. After the priest has had the woman stand before the Lord, he shall loosen her hair, and place in her hands the reminder offering, the grain offering for jealousy, while he himself holds the bitter water that brings a curse. Then the priest shall put the woman under oath and say to her, "If no other man has slept with you and you have not gone astray and become impure while married to your husband, may this bitter water that brings a curse not harm you. But if you have gone astray while married to your husband and you have defiled yourself by sleeping with a man other than your husband"—here the priest is to put the woman under this curse of the oath — "may the Lord cause your people to curse and denounce you when he causes your thigh to waste away\* and your abdomen to swell. . . The priest is to write these curses on a scroll and then wash them off into the bitter water. He shall have the woman drink the bitter water that brings a curse, and this water will enter her and cause bitter suffering. Numbers 5:11-24*

Key 5-12
Ordeal of Jealousy

Lock 2-15
Meal Offering
Page #62

Lock 2-18
Charge to Testify
Page #24

> *I, even I, am he who blots out your transgressions, for my own sake, and remembers your sins no more.*
> Isaiah 43:25
>
> *May they be blotted out of the book of life and not be listed with the righteous.*
> Psalms 69:28

*He did not write on a tablet or on papyrus or on unprepared skin, but only on a [parchment] scroll, as it is written, In a book. (Num. 5:23) And he may not write with gum or copperas or aught that leaves a lasting trace, but only with ink, for it is written, And he shall blot them out; [he must write with] what can be blotted out.[5]*

*\*Your thigh to waste away-meant the loss of childbearing capacity and, if pregnant, the miscarriage of the child.*

God speaks of his relationship with Israel as with an adulterous wife in Hosea and Jeremiah. From these stories we can derive many insights into God's attitude toward Israel, which are instructive regarding the Last Days.

> *Love her as the Lord loves the Israelites, though they turn to other gods and love the sacred raisin cakes. Hosea 3:1b*

> *They consult a wooden idol and are answered by a stick of wood. A spirit of prostitution leads them astray; they are unfaithful to their God. They sacrifice on the mountaintops and burn offerings on the hills, under oak, poplar and tere-*

*binth, where the shade is pleasant. Therefore your daughters turn to prostitution and your daughters-in-law to adultery. Hosea 4:12b-13*

*During the reign of King Josiah, the Lord said to me, "Have you seen what faithless Israel has done? She has gone up on every high hill and under every spreading tree and has committed adultery there. I thought that after she had done all this she would return to me but she did not, and her unfaithful sister Judah saw it. I gave faithless Israel her certificate of divorce and sent her away because of all her adulteries. Yet I saw that her unfaithful sister Judah had no fear; she also went out and committed adultery. Jeremiah 3:6-8*

The writer of Proverbs warns against adultery using symbolisms of water:

*Drink water from your own cistern, running water from your own well. Should your springs overflow in the streets, your streams of water in the public square? Let them be yours alone, never to be shared with strangers. May your fountain be blessed, and may you rejoice in the wife of your youth. Proverbs 5:15-18*

And in Proverbs 9 adultery is compared to stolen water:

*Stolen water is sweet; food eaten in secret is delicious! Proverbs 9:17*

In Chapter 4 of Song of Songs, the Lover speaks of his bride as a fountain:

*You are a garden fountain, a well of flowing water streaming down from Lebanon. Song of Songs 4:15*

Deuteronomy 22 records the punishment for the promiscuous virgin:

*If, however, the charge is true and no proof of the girl's virginity can be found, she shall be brought to the door of her father's house and there the men of her town shall stone her to death. She has done a disgraceful thing in Israel by being promiscuous while still in her father's house. Deuteronomy 22:20-21a*

And likewise the fate of the adulterer:

> *If a man is found sleeping with another man's wife, both the man who slept with her and the woman must die.*
> *Deuteronomy 22:22a*

Ezekiel 16 speaks of the unfaithful wife in the following allegory:

> *I made you grow like a plant of the field. You grew up and developed and became the most beautiful of jewels. Your breasts were formed and your hair grew, you who were naked and bare. Later I passed by, and when I looked at you and saw that you were old enough for love, I spread the corner of my garment over you and covered your nakedness. I gave you my solemn oath and entered into a covenant with you, declares the Sovereign Lord, and you became mine. . . You took some of your garments to make gaudy high places, where you carried on your prostitution . . . I will sentence you to the punishment of women who commit adultery and who shed blood; I will bring upon you the blood vengeance of my wrath and jealous anger. . . This is what the Sovereign Lord says: I will deal with you as you deserve, because you have despised my oath by breaking my covenant. Yet I will remember the covenant I made with you in the days of your youth, and I will establish an everlasting covenant with you. . . Then, when I make atonement for you for all you have done, you will remember and be ashamed and never again open your mouth because of your humiliation, declares the Sovereign Lord.*
> *Ezekiel 16:7-8, 16, 38, 59-60, 63*

Jesus alludes to the unfaithfulness of the church:

*Yet I hold this against you: You have forsaken your first love. Revelation 2:4*

# Appendix D - Betrothal Contract

The following is an example of a form of the Betrothal Contract (Tenaim):

TO GOOD FORTUNE

MAY IT COME UP AND SPROUT FORTH LIKE A GREEN GARDEN.
WHOSO FINDS A WIFE FINDS A GREAT GOOD, AND OBTAINS
FAVOR OF THE GOOD LORD, WHO RATIFIES THIS UNION.

May He who predestinates, bestow a good name and future to the provisions embodied in this agreement, which were agreed upon by the two parties hereto, that is, as party of the first part, Mr. ..., who represents the groom Mr. ..., and as part of the second part, Mr...., who represents the bride Miss ......

Firstly: That the above named groom agrees to take himself as wife the above named bride, through *chuppah* and betrothal, in accordance with the Law of Moses and Israel; that they will neither abstract nor conceal from one another any property whatsoever, but they shall equally have power over their property, pursuant to the established custom.

The above named groom obligates himself to present the bride with gifts according to custom.

The above named bride obligates herself to give as her dowry the sum of ........in cash, and clothes, pillows and linens, as is the custom.

The wedding will take place, if the Almighty so wills it, on the ......day of .......in the year ......or sooner than such date or later if both parties agree thereto.

A fine is to be paid by the party breaking this agreement, to the other party in the fixed sum of ....and also in accordance with the law of the land.

All of the foregoing was done with perfect understanding and due deliberation, and by means of the most effective method, in accordance with the ordinance of the sages, of blessed memory, and in accordance with the law of the land; by means of striking hands, by solemn promises, by true affirmation, by handing over an object (from one contracting party to another), to take effect immediately; and this is not to be regarded as a mere forfeiture without consideration, or as a mere formula of a document. We have followed the legal formality of a symbolic delivery *(kinyan)*, by handing over an object, between the groom and the bride and their representatives, by using a garment legally fit for the purpose, to validate all that is stated above,

AND EVERYTHING IS VALID AND CONFIRMED.

For the further purpose of making this agreement binding and obligatory, the groom and the bride themselves have attached their signatures, hereunto this ....day of....., in the year.....at ....(name of town).

Attested to ....(Groom)
Attested to ....(Bride)

In our presence, the undersigned witnesses, did the above named groom and bride attach their signatures, to affirm all that is stated above, and in our presence did they go through the legal formality of symbolic delivery, by handing over an object from one party to the other *(kinyan)*, that this agreement take effect immediately; and we have verified and affirmed it as is required by law.

In witness whereof, we have hereunto set our hands this ....day of ....in the year...at ....(name of town).

Attested to ....(Witness)
Attested to ....(Witness)

Marriage, Edited by Hayyim Schneid, Jewish Publication Society of America, Philadelphia, Pa.,1973, pg. 97

# Appendix E - Marriage Contract

The following is an example of a form of Marriage Contract (Ketubbah):

On the (first) day of the week, the ....day of the month ...., in the year five thousand, six hundred and ....since the creation of the world, the era according to which we are accustomed to reckon here in the city of (name of city, state and country), how (name of bridegroom), son of (name of father), surnamed (family name), said to this virgin (name of bride), daughter of (name of father), surnamed (family name): "Be thou my wife according to the law of Moses and Israel, and I will cherish, honor, support and maintain thee in accordance with the custom of Jewish husbands who cherish, honor, support and maintain their wives in truth. And I herewith make for thee the settlements of virgins, two hundred silver zuzim, which belongs to thee, according to the law of Moses and Israel; and (I will also give thee) food, clothing and necessaries, and live with thee as husband and wife according to universal custom." And Miss (name of bride), this virgin, consented and became his wife. The wedding outfit that she brought unto him from her father's house, in silver, gold, valuables, wearing apparel, house furniture, and bedclothes, all this (name of bridegroom), the said bridegroom, accepted in the sum of one hundred silver pieces, and (name of bridegroom), the bridegroom, consented to increase this amount from his own property with the sum of one hundred silver pieces, making in all two hundred silver pieces. And thus said (name of bridegroom), the bridegroom: "The responsibility of this marriage contract, of this wedding outfit, and of this additional sum, I take upon myself and my heirs after me, so that they shall be paid from the best part of my property and possession that I have beneath the whole heaven, that which I now possess or may hereafter acquire. All my property, real and personal, even the mantle on my shoulders, shall be mortgaged to secure the payment of this marriage contract, of the wedding outfit, and of the addition made thereto, during my lifetime and after my death, from the present day and forever." (Name of bridegroom), the bridegroom, has taken upon himself the responsibility of this marriage contract, of the wedding outfit and the addition made thereto, according to the restrictive usages of all marriage contracts and the additions thereto made for the daughters of Israel, in accordance with the institution of our sages of blessed memory. It is not to be regarded as a mere forfeiture without consideration or as a mere formula of a document. We have followed the legal formality of symbolic delivery *(kinyan)* between (name of bridegroom), the son of ....the bridegroom, and (name of bride), the daughter of ...., this virgin, and we have used a garment legally fit for the purpose, to strengthen all that is stated above, AND EVERYTHING IS VALID AND CONFIRMED.

Attested to .... (Witness)
Attested to .... (Witness)

Marriage, Edited by Hayyim Schneid, Jewish Publication Society of America, Philadelphia, Pa.,1973, pg. 100

# TABLE OF COMPARISON OF RITES OF ORDINATION , CORONATION & ATONEMENT

| Lev. 9 *The Consecration of Aaron* | | Lev. 16 *The Ritual of VII/10 [Atonement]* | |
|---|---|---|---|
| vv. | | vv. | |
| 2 | A young calf for sin offering | 3 | A young bullock for a sin offering |
| 2 | A ram for burnt offering | 3 | A ram for burnt offering |
| 3 | For Israel: a he-goat for sin offering | 5 | For Israel: two he-goats for sin offering |
| 3 | For Israel: a calf and a lamb for a burnt offering | 5 | For Israel: A ram for a burnt offering |
| 4 | For Israel: an ox and a ram for *shelamim* | | |
| 4 | For Israel: *minha* for oil | | |
| 7 | Moses said to Aaron, "offer thy sin offering and thy burnt offering and atone for thyself" | 6,11 | The priest shall offer his bullock of the sin offering and atone for himself and his house |
| 8 | and for the people . . . Aaron . . . slew . . . | | |
| 9 | Aaron dipped his finger in the blood of the calf of sin offering and put it upon the horns of the altar and poured out the blood at the bottom of the altar | 14 | The priest shall take of the blood of the bullock of sin offering and sprinkle it with his finger upon the mercy seat {kapporet} eastward; and before the mercy seat [i.e., on the ground] he shall sprinkle of the blood seven times |
| 12 | He slew the burnt offering and sprinkled its blood around about the altar | 15 | The same rite to be repeated once with the blood of the he-goat of sin offering within the Veil |
| 15 | The people's offering: ditto | | |
| 18 | The ox and the ram: ditto | 18 | He shall take of the blood of both the bullock and the he-goat, put it upon the horns of the altar round about, and shall sprinkle of |
| | | 19 | the blood upon the altar with his finger seven times[368] |
| 10 | The fat and other parts of the sin offering are burnt upon the altar | 25 | The fat of the sin offering he shall burn upon the altar |
| 19-20 | The fat of the ox and the ram, etc.: ditto | | |
| 11 | The flesh and the hide of the calf of sin offering he burnt with fire without the camp | 27 | The bullock and the he-goat of sin offering shall burn in the fire, their skins and their flesh and their dung without the camp |
| 23 | Moses and Aaron entered the tabernacle with censers on which they burned incense | 12-13 | A censer with incense shall be brought by the priest before God within the Veil |
| 23 | The glory of God appeared to all the people (cf.4:6) | 13,17 | Not even the officiating priest might see the "mercy seat" |
| 21 | The waving | | |
| | | 7-10, 21-22, 26 | The scapegoat |
| 22-23 | The blessing of the people | | |
| 7 | *Purpose of the ritual:* to atone for Aaron and the people | 11,16,20, 24,30, 32-34 | *Purpose of the ritual:* an annual atonement for the sanctuary, the priests, and the people |

"The conclusion that the annual atonement ritual was patterned after the ritual of the priestly consecration and the dedication of the tabernacles closes the circles of both our argument and our present investigation. For in this conclusion, the final proof may be seen of our contention that the pre-exilic New Year's ritual also was modeled after the installation ritual of kings."*

*The above chart of comparison was compiled in "Hebrew Installation Rites." (*Hebrew Union College Annual 20 (1947): 158-159*)

# *Chapter 6*

## KINGSHIP

### OVERVIEW

When we became aware that one of the main themes of the Fall Feasts was Messiah the King's coronation, we were interested to know more about the coronation ceremonies. Old Testament coronations of kings provided only segmented accounts.

As other sources emerged much available information centered around the traditions of kingdoms and coronations in countries other than Israel. Having researched the subject of covenants in the past, we had found insights from other nations can be very enlightening. When Israel asked for an earthly monarch to rule over them, they drew from experiences known to them from outside their borders:

> *". . . We want a king over us. Then we will be like all the other nations, with a king to lead us and to go out before us and fight our battles." I Samuel 8:19b-20*

Just as in the Feasts, we discovered the Coronations of Israel's kings provided a type of prophetic rehearsal for the Coronation of Messiah the King. We hope you will be as excited as we were to discover the kingdom principles and traditions revealed here. Like marriage, they have many applications to understanding God's relationship with His people.

# CORONATION CEREMONIES

The installation ceremonies enacted when a king assumed his reign did not consist of a single day of programs. On the contrary, they often extended over a lengthy period, providing opportunity for the king to gain the loyalty and trust of his subjects and allies. To this end, a monarch submitted himself to numerous rituals and ceremonies. These numerous consecrations symbolized for the king an increase in his status as monarch.

Lock 2-14
Sacrifices of Anointing
Page #82

In Israel the coronation ceremonies had many similarities to the consecration of the High Priest and the events of the Day of Atonement. On page 134, the Table of Comparison of Rites of Ordination, Coronation & Atonement shows the similarity of the sacrifices offered. The following presentation of the coronation ceremony is not intended to describe a strict chronological order. It is a collection of elements found common to many nations.

## SELECTION OF A KING

### Divine Revelation. . .

Lock 2-9
Selection by Divine
Revelation
Page #21

In most of the countries studied, a claim was made that the king was chosen by divine revelation. Often this was through a religious leader or prophet. This divine choice or appointment was often demonstrated publicly by a method such as the casting of lots.

In Israel it was recorded that God revealed His choice of Saul and David through the prophet Samuel. According to Jewish tradition the choice of Saul was confirmed by the use of Urim and Thummin.

When God appointed Saul he first told Samuel:

> *This is the man I spoke to you about; he will govern my people. I Samuel 9:17*

Then Samuel demonstrated this before the people:

> *When Samuel brought all the tribes of Israel near, the tribe of Benjamin was chosen. Then he brought forward the tribe of Benjamin, clan by clan, and Matri's clan was chosen. Finally Saul son of Kish was chosen.* I Samuel 10: 20-21a

In the case of David, God again instructed Samuel of His choice:

> *I am sending you to Jesse of Bethlehem. I have chosen one of his sons to be king.* I Samuel 16:1

And the choice of David was confirmed before his family when Samuel visited. (See I Samuel 16)

In similar fashion was the divine choice of Aaron as High Priest was revealed:

> *Have Aaron your brother brought to you from among the Israelites, along with his sons Nadab and Abihu, Eleazar and Ithamar, so they may serve me as priests. Make sacred garments for your brother Aaron, to give him dignity and honor.* Exodus 28:1-2

Before the people, God's choice was confirmed by the budding of Aaron's staff. (See Numbers 17)

### *Physical Attributes . . .*
One of the most basic and consistent concepts among nations was that the welfare of the nation and its people was tied with the kings well-being. For this reason it was held that a king must not only be divinely chosen but 'perfect' regarding his physical attributes. It was necessary he be without bodily blemish or infirmity. As we learned, this was also required of those serving in the priesthood in Israel.

Lock 2-10
Without Blemish
Page #66

The physical attributes of Saul were recorded:

> *He had a son named Saul, an impressive young man without equal among the Israelites—a head taller than any of the others."* I Samuel 9:2

And in the case of David, he was described as:

> *He was ruddy, with a fine appearance and handsome features. Then the Lord said, Rise and anoint him; he is the one.* I Samuel 16:12b

## FIRST INSTALLATION

### *Baptism/Anointing . . .*

The ceremony of baptism was commonly recognized among nations as a symbol of death and rebirth. In the case of the king, this symbolized rebirth to a new life as a son of the gods. Consequently, it was believed that the spirit of god entered the new king during this portion of his consecration. In ancient Israel a similar belief was held regarding the Davidic rulers.

> *I have installed my King on Zion, my holy hill. I will proclaim the decree of the Lord: He said to me, "You are my Son; today I have become your Father. . . Psalms 2:6, 7*

*Jewish tradition states that the oil of kings was applied to their heads in a circle, while in the case of the priest it was applied in the form of a Greek "X." It was said that the same oil was used to consecrate the Tabernacle and its vessels, Aaron and his sons, and the High Priest.*

The baptism and anointing of the king at a spring of water was believed to ensure his reign would be long. In such a manner Solomon was anointed and probably baptized at Gihon (1 Kings 1:45). Solomon's rival, Adonijah, wished to be acknowledged as king and underwent a similar ceremony at the spring of Rogel. This anointing was sometimes repeated in later ceremonies.

Lock 2-11
Anointed of God
Page #22

God instructed that the kings of Israel be anointed with oil much as Aaron and his sons had been anointed as priests. The king, thereafter was called the Anointed of God, as was the High Priest.

One account of Saul's anointing is seen in:

> *Samuel took a flask of oil and poured it on Saul's head and kissed him, saying, 'Has not the Lord anointed you leader over his inheritance?' I Samuel 10:1*

In like manner, David was anointed by Samuel:

> *. . .Then the Lord said, 'Rise and anoint him; he is the one.' So Samuel took the horn of oil and anointed him in the presence of his brothers, and from that day on the Spirit of the Lord came upon David in power. I Samuel 16:12b-13*

### *Sacrifices of Anointing/Communal Meal . . .*

Lock 2-6
Priest/King & His
Council
Page #72

Closely connected with the anointing of the king-elect was a meal he shared with a small group of trusted guests. This group was often formed from among the leadership of the people or they were chosen from among the king's trusted friends. These men later served as counselors and attendants to the king.

This communal meal seems to have symbolic connections with the meal taken by the priests from the fellowship offering and ram of ordination. Such a meal was also enjoyed by the bridegroom among friends before his wedding (Judges 14:10-11).

Lock 2-3
Holy Place
Page #82

Among the countries studied, this communal meal had striking similarities. The religious leader ordered the preparation of a sacrificial meal and invited a small group of selected guests. Only after the meal was prepared and the guests had assembled did the king-elect arrive. This may have seemed coincidental in the accounts of Saul and David, if it had not been common in the coronations of other nations, indicating a set ritual was taking place. The occasion of such a meal may be repeated during the king's reign.

Lock 4-20
Late to the Banquet
Page #118

During the meal, portions of the sacrificial animal were reserved to be served to the king: the leg or thigh and sometimes an additional tail portion. This leg portion was also mentioned in the priests' ordination, but was reserved unto God as a burnt offering.

Lock 2-14
Sacrifices of
Anointing
Page #136

The account of such a meal ordered by Samuel to be prepared for Saul, is seen in the following:

> Samuel said to the cook, "Bring the piece of meat I gave you, the one I told you to lay aside." So the cook took up the leg with what was on it and set it in front of Saul. Samuel said, "Here is what has been kept for you. Eat, because it was set aside for you for this occasion, from the time I said, 'have invited guests.'" And Saul dined with Samuel that day. I Samuel 9:23-24

### Hiddenness . . .
A period of semi-official existence commonly followed the first official installation ceremonies. The king often returned to his family and tended to domestic affairs or went about among the people.

Key 6-1
Hiddenness

### Humiliation among the people . . .
Surprisingly, it was common for the king to experience humiliation and ridicule during some period of his installation process. Saul was despised by the sons of Belial at this time; David fled before Absalom; and even Aaron as High Priest bore a similar rebuff from the people.

This period of hiddenness and humiliation was a common thread among nations during the continuing installation ceremonies of their kings. When such abasement was endured

Key 6-2
Humiliation

with patience and without defense, it was seen as a demonstration of good character.

### Processions . . .

On occasion the king went out among the people riding upon a mule or colt of a mule and the people paid him homage. At this time they greeted him with a shout, "Blessed is he who comes in the name of the Lord!" This was also the greeting given a bride and bridegroom as they arrived at the wedding ceremony. Zechariah spoke of such a procession:

> *Rejoice greatly, O Daughter of Zion! Shout, Daughter of Jerusalem! See, your king comes to you, righteous and having salvation, gentle and riding on a donkey, on a colt, the foal of a donkey. Zechariah 9:9*

Lock 3-4
Processions
Page #117

Lock 5-8
Bridegroom
Page #127

### Battles with Enemies. . .

Key 6-3
Battles with
Enemies

Often during this time of retirement from ceremonial duties the newly consecrated king confronted his enemies. The welfare of the people depended on the king's ability to protect and provide for them. Demonstrating his victories whether in ritual combat or in a real battle confirmed his fitness to rule. Saul engaged in battle with the Ammonites after his first consecration as king. David demonstrated repeated victories in battle between his first anointing and his second installation.

Key 6-4
Names of
the King

As the king struck alliances and treaties among neighboring peoples, names were added to his. In this way a king came to have many names describing his varied attributes and dominions. Such practices have often caused confusion when studying genealogies and the succession of kings.

## SECOND INSTALLATION

The period we have titled Second Installation of the king is made up of two portions: one, a set of ceremonies celebrated in the religious temple of the nation and two, consisting of the king's assumption to his throne of government in the palace.

A description of the crowning of Joash son of Ahaziah describes these two ceremonies:

> *The guards, each with his weapon in his hand, stationed themselves around the king—near the altar and the temple, from the south side to the north side of the temple. Jehoiada brought out the king's son and put the crown on him; he presented him with a copy of the covenant and proclaimed*

*him king. They anointed him, and the people clapped their hands and shouted, "Long live the king!" When Athaliah heard the noise made by the guards and the people, she went to the people at the temple of the Lord. She looked and there was the king, standing by the pillar, as the custom was. The officers and the trumpeters were beside the king, and all the people of the land were rejoicing and blowing trumpets. II Kings 11:11-13a*

*Jehoiada then made a covenant between the Lord and the king and people that they would be the Lord's people. He also made a covenant between the king and the people. All the people of the land went to the temple of Baal and tore it down. They smashed the altars and idols to pieces and killed Mattan the priest of Baal in front of the altars. Then Jehoiada the priest posted guards at the temple of the Lord. He took with him the commanders of hundreds, the Carites, the guards and all the people of the land, and together they brought the king down from the temple of the Lord and went into the palace, entering by way of the gate of the guards. The king then took his place on the royal throne, and all the people of the land rejoiced. II Kings 11:17-20a*

### In the Temple . . .

In the Temple of Israel, just outside the Holy Place, a platform and/or 'pillar' was erected from which the king participated in the Temple services (See II Chronicles 6:12-13). At this location the ceremonies of coronation took place, as did the consecration of the priesthood. It was here the king received the symbols of his authority: the crown, the royal robe, a scepter or rod and a signet ring or bracelet containing the king's seal.

Key 6-5
Temple Ceremony

Lock 2-16
Days of
Ordination
Page #19

The king's covenant was presented to him as a part of this portion of the ceremony. This covenant contained: the laws of the land by which the king must abide; the covenant of God with the king assuring divine protection for his reign; and the promise of the king to care for and rule his people with provision and justice. In some cases this testimony or covenant was said to contain a prophetic account of the king's reign. In II Samuel 7:8-16, we see God's covenant with David at his coronation.

Lock 4-1
Book of Covenant
Page #114

*Now then, tell my servant David, 'This is what the Lord Almighty says: I took you from the pasture and from following the flock to be ruler over my people Israel. I have been with you wherever you have gone, and I have cut off all your enemies from before you. Now I will make your name great, like the names of the greatest men of the earth. And I will provide a place for my people Israel and will plant them so that they can have a home of their own and no longer be disturbed. Wicked people will not oppress them anymore, as they did at the beginning and have done ever since the time I appointed leaders over my people Israel. I will also give you rest from all your enemies. The Lord declares to you that the Lord himself will establish a house for you: When your days are over and you rest with your fathers, I will raise up your offspring to succeed you, who will come from your own body, and I will establish his kingdom. He is the one who will build a house for my Name, and I will establish the throne of his kingdom forever. I will be his father, and he will be my son. When he does wrong, I will punish him with the rod of men, with floggings inflicted by men. But my love will never be taken away from him, as I took it away from Saul, whom I removed from before you. Your house and your kingdom will endure forever before me; your throne will be established forever. II Samuel 7:8-16*

The tradition of many nations indicate the belief that the orderly function of nature and the welfare of the people depended on the person of the king and his obedience and faithfulness to the above mentioned covenants. That the nation of Israel also held these beliefs is attested to by the many accounts in the Old Testament. Here stories abound of kings who served or rejected God to the blessing or destruction of the nation.

Key 6-6
Acclamation

During the Temple ceremony, the king was often anointed once again before the whole congregation. They, in turn, shouted the acclamation, "Long live the king!" The ceremonies were often concluded with songs relating to the praises of the king. Many of the Psalms of the Old Testament are Coronation Psalms.

Key 6-7
Coronation Songs

*And all the people went up after him, playing flutes and rejoicing greatly, so that the ground shook with the sound. I Kings 1:40*

### In the palace . . .

Lock 3-4
Processions
Page #140

After the Temple ceremony the king was led to the royal palace followed by the people. There he sat on the throne from which he would govern his people.

Key 6-8
Palace Ceremony

In many cases it was at this time that those swearing allegiances to the king, appeared before him. They did homage by bowing their faces to the ground. They presented gifts to him, often symbols of their authority such as shields bearing their insignias. These were kept in the king's treasury and were displayed as a part of the yearly commemoration of the king's coronation.

In Israel on the New Moon Feast of each month, those loyal to the king presented themselves before him as a demonstration of their allegiance. It was such an occasion when David fled from Saul:

Lock 4-2
Homage to the King
Page #80

> *So David hid in the field, and when the New Moon festival came, the king sat down to eat. He sat in his customary place by the wall, opposite Jonathan, and Abner sat next to Saul, but David's place was empty. I Samuel 20:24-25*

In many nations, a yearly festival, usually at the beginning of the New Year, reenacted both the king's humiliations and his victories over his enemies. These New Year celebrations usually occurred in the Fall of the year, corresponding roughly to the New Year of the Hebrew Civil Calendar. Many of the rituals were reenactments of the king's coronation ceremonies. At the time of these New Year festivities, those loyal to the king renewed their allegiance to him and acknowledged him as the choice of god. One means of symbolizing the king's victories involved the shooting of four arrows in the four directions of the compass, to represent his victories over the nations.

Lock 1-2
1st of Tishri
Page #73

> *In the case of Joash, it is true, we hear of the shooting of one arrow only, against Syria, which lies east of Israel, the direction in which the arrow was shot. From a later period, however, that of the Second Temple, we have knowledge of an annual ceremony in which the nations of the world were symbolically overcome by the Lulav, shaken towards the four quarters, and figuratively—ritually referred to as an "arrow." [1]*

Lock 4-15
Lulav
Page #116

It was common for a symbol representing the life of the king to be erected at the time the king assumed his throne. This symbol was sometimes a pillar or structure with symbols representative of the king. Two common symbols used in the Near East were a tree and a sacred fire.

### Tree of Life . . .

At the beginning of the king's reign, a tree was often planted that represented the life and reign of the king. Such a symbol was seen in the dream of Nebuchadnezzar in Daniel 4. The symbolism of such a tree can also be seen in Genesis and Revelation.

Lock 4-19
Tree of Life
Page #113

*Enter through the narrow gate. For wide is the gate and broad is the road that leads to destruction, and many enter through it. But small is the gate and narrow the road that leads to life, and only a few find it. "Watch out for false prophets. They come to you in sheep's clothing, but inwardly they are ferocious wolves. By their fruit you will recognize them. Do people pick grapes from thornbushes, or figs from thistles? Likewise every good tree bears good fruit, but a bad tree bears bad fruit. A good tree cannot bear bad fruit, and a bad tree cannot bear good fruit Every tree that does not bear good fruit is cut down and thrown into the fire. Thus, by their fruit you will recognize them. Matthew 7:13-20*

*The tree you saw, which grew large and strong, with its top touching the sky, visible to the whole earth, with beautiful leaves and abundant fruit, providing food for all, giving shelter to the beasts of the field, and having nesting places in its branches for the birds of the air—you, O king are that tree. You have become great and strong; your greatness has grown until it reaches the sky, and your dominion extends to distant parts of the earth. Daniel 4:20-22*

*Sacred Fire . . .*

Like the tree of life, in some countries it was the custom to light a fire at the king's coronation. From this new fire were all the fires in the country to be rekindled. This fire was to be kept going as long as the king lived.

Lock 2-17
Fire Kindled
Page #92

Perhaps this gives insight into the conditions God established regarding the Tabernacle fire. God lit the fire that consumed the first sacrifices and from that point the fire was to be kept by the priesthood. The sons of Aaron were killed for attempting to use 'strange fire', that which was not of the original source.

This custom also gives interesting dimension to the account of another fire; a new fire from which all the fires of a kingdom were to be kindled:

*They saw what seemed to be tongues of fire that separated and came to rest on each of them. Acts 2:3*

# THE KINGDOM

*Marriage of the king . . .*

The coronation of the king often included or was closely followed by a wedding.  Because the welfare of the nation was believed to be tied to the person of the king, his marriage union was seen as a symbol of the relationship of the nation with its allies.

It was important the king's bride be a virgin, for this was a testimony to the stability of the household from which she came.  It indicated that a covenant made between her household and that of her husband would be productive both politically and economically.  It was the duty of the king and his bride to see that the stipulations of the covenant between their states, symbolized by their marriage, were fulfilled.  The physical relationship of the couple was a symbol of the unification of their two states and the fertility of their union was representative of the resultant health and prosperity of the covenanting nations.

Lock 5-2
Virgin
Page #118

Lock 5-10
Marriage Contract
Page #117

Lock 5-6
Consummation
Page #117

A midwife was a symbol in Israel applied to a monarch.  Her role was a model for the duties of the king.  It was the work of the king to attend the birth of the nation, drawing it out of chaos into order, much like a midwife delivering a child.

Lock 5-11
Adoption
Page #122

Just as the stability of a household was represented by its ability to protect its women, so was the stability of the nation symbolized in the king's ability to protect his wife.  When a king took the throne of another, either by inheritance or war, it was customary for him to marry the wife or widow of the previous king.

Lock 5-1
Father of Household
Page #126

This brings to mind the account of Absalom's attempt to usurp David's throne.  He pitched a tent on the roof to 'lay with' David's concubines.  This was not an act of lust, but a representation of his political takeover bid.  In taking the women of David's household, he was demonstrating David's inability to protect his household and symbolically Israel.

Lock 5-3
Assailant
Page #110

Lock 5-10
Marriage Contract
Page #145

*Treaties and Covenants . . .*

Much like the covenant represented by his marriage, it was the king's duty to provide for his nation through other treaties. These treaties might represent alliances of protection or agreements that increased the nation's borders. He was also expected to bring goods and services to the nation through trade commitments.

A formal treaty followed a traditional outline which can be recognized in covenants recorded in scripture:

1.  The document opened with the credentials of the covenanting parties and often a historical review of their relationship.
2.  The terms of the agreement were stated.
3.  A litany of curses for treaty violation and blessings for treaty compliance was given.
4.  A list of witnesses confirmed the agreement.
5.  Provisions were made to record and publish the agreement abroad.

*Responsibilities of the King . . .*

God warned Israel, through the prophet Samuel, what an earthly king would mean to their nation:

> *He said, "This is what the king who will reign over you will do: He will take your sons and make them serve with his chariots and horses, and they will run in front of his chariots. Some he will assign to be commanders of thousands and commanders of fifties, and others to plow his ground and reap his harvest, and still others to make weapons of war and equipment for his chariots. He will take your daughters to be perfumers and cooks and bakers. He will take the best of your fields and vineyards and olive groves and give them to his attendants. He will take a tenth of your grain and of your vintage and give it to his officials and attendants. Your menservants and maidservants and the best of your cattle and donkeys he will take for his own use. He will take a tenth of your flocks, and you yourselves will become his slaves. I Samuel 8:11-17*

This gives us some insight into what was expected of a king in terms of serving his nation.

1.  The code of laws by which the nation was governed was administered by the king and his agents.

2. It was the king's responsibility to maintain order among the population and to raise an army to protect the nation from its enemies. It was the duty of the army to serve within the borders of allied nations to preserve the treaties.
3. The king's duty to protect the welfare of and provide for his people was carried out in many ways. He negotiated trade agreements, collected taxes and managed the production and distribution of goods.

The king, in most cases, managed all the nations resources which enabled him to provide for an army, commission teachers and build roads and other public conveniences. These were considered symbols of the king's provision and protection of his people.

Another symbol of the king's power and status was the erection of buildings and exotic symbols such as statues. Buildings such as temples in which annual ceremonies were held, offered the people opportunity to demonstrate their loyalty and acknowledge the king's protection and care.

Lock 4-2
Homage to
the King
Page #143

# JESUS THE KING

## THE SOVEREIGN KING AND HIS KINGDOM

From the very outset our study of kingship gave us new perspective on the Bible as a record of the reign of the King of all creation. In Genesis all provision was made for His subjects in the garden. The Tree of Life was planted representing the life of the King. Laws were established and an administrator in the form of Adam was provided.

Lock 5-3
Assailant
Page #145

Lock 5-2
Virgin
Page #145

Lock 5-5
Prince of
Household
Page #123

Lock 6-4
Names of the King
Page #140

An assailant came to the garden and attempted a takeover of the kingdom by violating the virgin of the household. The woman was guilty for she did not cry out. The king placed His army to protect His borders from further assault. Covenants were agreed upon between the King and those who had become aliens. The King's names reflect these alliances.

Laws were enacted to provide for the distribution of goods. Officials were appointed to manage these 'tithes'. Buildings were ordered erected from these resources as symbols of the King's power and presence. Feasts and special days were celebrated in these buildings to remind the people of the King's provision and to give opportunity for them to renew their loyalty.

A very vital kingdom is at work, a kingdom under siege. The Prince of the household was commissioned to recover the inheritance that was stolen. To accomplish this purpose he is given authority as Messiah the King.

> *The Spirit of the Sovereign Lord is on me, because the Lord has anointed me to preach good news to the poor. He has sent me to bind up the brokenhearted, to proclaim freedom for the captives and release from darkness for the prisoners, to proclaim the year of the Lord's favor and the day of vengeance of our God, to comfort all who mourn..*
> *Isaiah 61:1-2*

> *Therefore, just as sin entered the world through one man, and death through sin, and in this way death came to all*

*men, because all sinned. . .Nevertheless, death reigned from the time of Adam to the time of Moses, even over those who did not sin by breaking a command, as did Adam, who was a pattern of the one to come. . . . Consequently, just as the result of one trespass was condemnation for all men, so also the result of one act of righteousness was justification that brings life for all men. For just as through the disobedience of the one man the many were made sinners, so also through the obedience of the one man the many will be made righteous. Romans 5:12, 14, 18-19*

## SELECTION OF THE KING

### Divine Revelation. . .

Just as Saul and David were revealed as God's chosen ones, so in like manner was Jesus. The Prophet, John the Baptist, was given the revelation:

Lock 2-9
Selection By
Divine Revelation
Page #136

*Then John gave this testimony: "I saw the Spirit come down from heaven as a dove and remain on him. I would not have known him, except that the one who sent me to baptize with water told me, 'The man on whom you see the Spirit come down and remain is he who will baptize with the Holy Spirit.' I have seen and I testify that this is the Son of God." John 1: 32-34*

### Physical Attributes . . .

As for the unblemished nature of the king, Jesus was found to be spotless:

Lock 2-10
Without Blemish
Page #137

*...but the precious blood of Christ, a lamb without blemish or defect. I Peter 1:19b*

## FIRST INSTALLATION

### Baptism/Anointing . . .

Jesus was baptized, anointed by the Spirit, and proclaimed the Son of God:

Lock 2-11
Anointed of God
Page #138

*As soon as Jesus was baptized, he went up out of the water. At that moment heaven was opened, and he saw the Spirit of God descending like a dove and lighting on him. And a voice from heaven said, "This is my Son, whom I love; with him I am well pleased." Matthew 3:16-17*

*The next day the great crowd that had come for the Feast heard that Jesus was on his way to Jerusalem. They took*

Lock 5-8
Bridegroom
Page #140

Lock 3-4
Processions
Page #142

*palm branches and went out to meet him, shouting, "Hosanna!" "Blessed is he who comes in the name of the Lord!" "Blessed is the King of Israel!" Jesus found a young donkey and sat upon it, as it is written, "Do not be afraid, O Daughter of Zion; see, your king is coming seated on a donkey's colt." John 12:12-15*

### Sacrifices of Anointing/Communal Meal . . .

Jesus, too, shared an intimate meal with a small group of trusted friends. At this time he provided for a ritual of remembrance.

Lock 2-6
Priest/King & His
Council
Page #138

*When the hour came, Jesus and his apostles reclined at the table. And he said to them, "I have eagerly desired to eat this Passover with you before I suffer. For I tell you, I will not eat it again until it finds fulfillment in the kingdom of God." After taking the cup, he gave thanks and said, "Take this and divide it among you. For I tell you I will not drink again of the fruit of the vine until the kingdom of God comes." And he took bread, gave thanks and broke it, and gave it to them, saying, "This is my body given for you; do this in remembrance of me." Luke 22:14-19*

The Father God himself, consecrated Jesus as King:

*And again, when God brings his firstborn into the world, he says, "Let all God's angels worship him." In speaking of the angels he says, "He makes his angels winds, his servants flames of fire." But about the Son he says, "Your throne, O God, will last for ever and ever, and righteousness will be the scepter of your kingdom. You have loved righteousness and hated wickedness; therefore God, your God, has set you above your companions by anointing you with the oil of joy." Hebrews 1:6-9*

### Humiliation among the people . . .

Following His confirmation and first anointing, just as Saul and David, Jesus goes among the people and suffers humiliation.

Lock 6-2
Humiliation
page #139

*Then the governor's soldiers took Jesus into the Praetorium and gathered the whole company of soldiers around him. They stripped him and put a scarlet robe on him, and then twisted together a crown of thorns and set it on his head. They put a staff in his right hand and knelt in front of him and mocked him. "Hail, king of the Jews!" they said. They spit on him, and took the staff and struck him on the head again and again. After they had mocked him, they took off the robe and put his own clothes on him. Then they led him away to crucify him. Matthew 27:27-31*

## Hiddenness . . .

Following his crucifixion Jesus retires to a place of hiddenness until the second installation ceremony begins at his second coming.

Lock 6-1
Hiddenness
Page #139

> *My children, I will be with you only a little longer. You will look for me, and just as I told the Jews, so I tell you now: Where I am going you cannot come. John 13:33*

> Pilate then went back inside the palace, summoned Jesus and asked him, "Are you the king of the Jews?"
>
> Jesus said, "My kingdom is not of this world. If it were, my servants would fight to prevent my arrest by the Jews. But now my kingdom is from another place." You are a king, then!" said Pilate. Jesus answered, "You are right in saying I am a king. In fact, for this reason I was born, and for this I came into the world, to testify to the truth. Everyone on the side of truth listens to me." John 18: 33, 36-37

During this time of hiddenness Jesus tends to 'domestic affairs'.

> *In my Father's house are many rooms: if it were not so, I would have told you. I am going there to prepare a place for you. And if I go and prepare a place for you, I will come back and take you to be with me that you also may be where I am. John 14:2-3*

> *Who is he that condemns? Christ Jesus, who died—more than that, who was raised to life—is at the right hand of God and is also interceding for us. Romans 8:34*

## Battles With Enemies. . .

The king demonstrates his fitness to rule and protect his people by defeating the enemies of the kingdom:

Lock 6-3
Battles with
Enemies
Page #140

> *And having disarmed the powers and authorities, he made a public spectacle of them, triumphing over them by the cross. Colossians 2:15*

## SECOND INSTALLATION

The coronation ceremonies will resume again as Jesus prepares to reclaim his inheritance. At this time he will be recognized King of All Righteousness. Abundance, peace and prosperity will reign. The enemy of the kingdom will be made his footstool. And the Son will take His bride.

## AUTHORS' COMMENTS

Jesus, during his earthly walk spent much of his teaching time opening the mysteries of the Kingdom. Many of his parables shed light on this subject.

# Diagram for the Book of Revelation

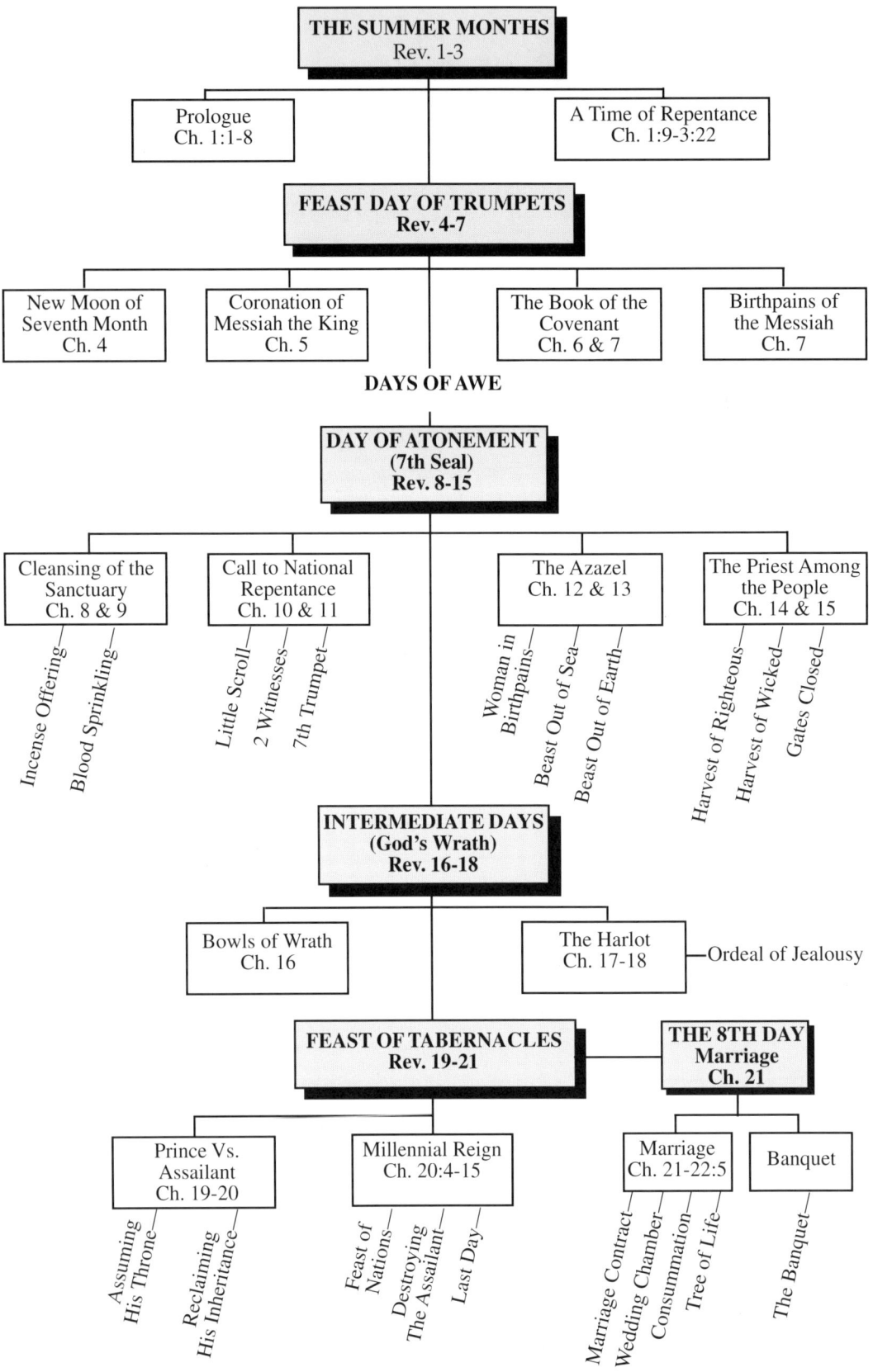

**THE SUMMER MONTHS**
Rev. 1-3

Prologue
Ch. 1:1-8

A Time of Repentance
Ch. 1:9-3:22

**FEAST DAY OF TRUMPETS**
Rev. 4-7

New Moon of
Seventh Month
Ch. 4

Coronation of
Messiah the King
Ch. 5

The Book of the
Covenant
Ch. 6 & 7

Birthpains of
the Messiah
Ch. 7

**DAYS OF AWE**

**DAY OF ATONEMENT**
(7th Seal)
Rev. 8-15

Cleansing of the
Sanctuary
Ch. 8 & 9

Call to National
Repentance
Ch. 10 & 11

The Azazel
Ch. 12 & 13

The Priest Among
the People
Ch. 14 & 15

Incense Offering
Blood Sprinkling

Little Scroll
2 Witnesses
7th Trumpet

Woman in Birthpains
Beast Out of Sea
Beast Out of Earth

Harvest of Righteous
Harvest of Wicked
Gates Closed

**INTERMEDIATE DAYS**
(God's Wrath)
Rev. 16-18

Bowls of Wrath
Ch. 16

The Harlot
Ch. 17-18

Ordeal of Jealousy

**FEAST OF TABERNACLES**
Rev. 19-21

**THE 8TH DAY**
Marriage
Ch. 21

Prince Vs.
Assailant
Ch. 19-20

Millennial Reign
Ch. 20:4-15

Marriage
Ch. 21-22:5

Banquet

Assuming His Throne
Reclaiming His Inheritance

Feast of Nations
Destroying The Assailant
Last Day

Marriage Contract
Wedding Chamber
Consummation
Tree of Life

The Banquet

# Chapter 7

## REVELATION

OVERVIEW

### OVERVIEW

One of the unexpected assets we, the authors, brought to this study was a complete lack of predetermined ideas regarding the pre-, mid- or post-tribulation 'rapture' of believers. Late in our research we began to recognize the drawbacks that can be created by a tendency to hold to such preconceived opinions.

This is not to infer that such positions are without scriptural basis. Indeed, it is the fact that each stance has scriptural foundation which has fueled the seemingly unresolvable debate.

For the serious biblical scholar, holding to a studied notion of chronology based on a pre-, mid- or post-tribulation concept, the sequence of events presented in the book of Revelation is problematic, making interpretation strained.

To the casual reader, the grotesque pictures of beasts and the magnitude of destruction cause the stomach to lurch, all the while the head buzzes with angels flying about.

We feel the prophetic implications of the Feasts of the Lord bring clarity to these varied ways of seeing. However, it is not important that you take the information presented and apply it as we have to the book of Revelation. If our text provides insights from which you confidently go forward with your own research, our purpose is accomplished.

On page 152, we have divided the scenes of John's vision into the chronological sequence suggested by the Fall Feasts. It is by this course we will complete our presentation.

As we enter the mysteries of the book of Revelation, it would be difficult for us to restate those insights from previous chapters that culminate here. We must rely heavily on you to use the references provided to refresh your memory and trace related concepts. If you do not understand an interpretation being presented refer back to the key indicated by the lock in the margin. It was for this purpose the method of keys and locks was conceived.

*A bit more information before we continue . . .*
It is commonly agreed that the writer of the gospel of John was also the Apostle John the recorder of Revelation. John, more than any other gospel writer, emphasized the Feasts in shaping a time frame for Jesus' earthly walk.

John recorded this revelation about twenty years after the destruction of the Second Temple. He wrote in a literary style called apocalyptic which was commonly used to record prophetic insights. Characteristically, apocalyptic writings dealt with end times prophecy and involved a vision or dream delivered to the writer by a messenger or angel. The writings contained imagery and symbolism well known and understood by the common people during that period. While researching we came upon many conflicting interpretations of apocalyptic symbols, so we have found it best to rely upon the scriptures themselves to interpret symbolic meanings.

Lock 1-3
Sevens
Page #96

You will notice the repetition of the number seven in the book of Revelation: seven churches, seven spirits, seven lampstands, seven seals, seven trumpets, and seven bowls. Based upon the Genesis account of creation, Jewish understanding is that seven is a perfect number signifying a complete unit of time. How appropriate that as the vision of the end of the age unfolds it is full of the seven symbolism.

## A PROMISE FROM THE LORD TO YOU

*Blessed is the one who reads the words of this prophecy, and blessed are those who hear it and take to heart what is written in it, because the time is near. Revelation 1:3*

*Jerusalem is quiet, it is the time of the summer months when no feasts are scheduled in the Sacred Calendar. In the fields the harvest is ripening in the summer sun.*

*Israel waits.*

*By the manner of Daniel's 70 weeks for Israel, the last week has not yet begun.*

*By the reckoning of the redemption week, it is the period of the church age.*

*In the context of the prophetic aspect of the Feasts of the Lord, it is the time between the first and second advent of the Messiah.*

# THE SUMMER MONTHS

**Before you begin, read: Revelation 1:1-8.**

## Prologue

> *The revelation of Jesus Christ, which God gave him to show*
> *his servants what must soon take place. Revelation 1:1a*

In the first verse John describes for us the source, means and purpose of the account he is about to record. A revelation God has given to Jesus Christ to show to His servants things which will soon come to pass that His servants might be prepared. This inspires confidence as we look at this revelation, for it implies that this message is not meant to be a mystery. It is meant to prepare us for what is to come.

The first portion of the message, that addressed directly to the seven churches, Jesus delivers himself. However, as John's vision continues we will see Jesus has sent His angel to John to further open His revelation.

> *He made it known by sending his angel to his servant John,*
> *Revelation 1:1b*

As we saw previously, Jesus often taught the people in the context of the Feasts. Here in His message to the churches, He again provides instruction which will relate to John's vision of the prophetic fulfillment of the Fall Feasts. Angels will also provide commentary on the events as they unfold much as the priests of the earthly Temple opened the Law to the congregation.

What John sees will be presented to us from three vantage points: The first, events seen in the heavenlies; the second, those things seen occurring on the earth; and third, instructive commentaries.

**Before you begin, read: Revelation 1:9-3:22.**

## A TIME OF REPENTANCE

Various scholars have suggested a threefold nature to the messages to the seven churches. First, these churches were in existence at the time when John wrote the messages and spoke directly to them. Secondly, the message alluded to the dispensational unfolding of the church age and lastly, the revelation was for the church in the end times. Jesus himself spoke of this threefold key when he said:

> *Write, therefore, what you have seen, what is now and what will take place later. Revelation 1:19*

The beginning chapters of the book of Revelation describe Jesus' call of repentance to the churches. This seems appropriate as we look to the prophetic nature of the Fall Feasts regarding the Second Coming of Jesus, for the Summer Months of the Sacred Calendar concluded with a period of repentance.

Lock 3-9
Personal
Repentance
Page #78

We will not be discussing these messages to the churches, though many of Jesus' references have connecting points to our study. We will note these at appropriate times in our text. For our purposes, it is important to note that the thrust of Jesus' message is a call to repentance.

Lock 1-7
Redemptive Week
Page #63

### *The Heavenly Temple . . .*

As Jesus speaks, John describes Him as walking among the golden lampstands. This is our first indication that we are seeing a scene in the heavenly Temple. This heavenly Temple was the pattern from which the earthly Tabernacle was taken. Throughout John's vision, we will be seeing activities occurring in the heavenly Temple. Furnishings such as a throne, a sea of glass (laver), the altar of sacrifice, the golden censer, and the golden altar of incense, will bring to our remembrance the furnishings of the earthly Temple. The interpretation of the symbolism for the lampstands and stars is provided for us:

Lock 2-3
Holy Place
Page #139

Lock 2-4
Holy of Holies
Page #113

Lock 2-2
Courtyard
Page #81

Lock 2-1
Heavenly Pattern
Page #23

> *The mystery of the seven stars that you saw in my right hand and of the seven golden lampstands is this: The seven stars are the angels of the seven churches, and the seven lampstands are the seven churches. Revelation 1:20*

As the events of John's vision unfold, we will note not only the furnishings, but also the activities of the angels. Frankly, in our early studies we spent a lot of time overlooking the angels.

We treated them as something to be gotten out of the way of important things. As the concept of the Feasts emerged, however, we began to see these angels serving in the heavenly Temple with duties much like the priests of the earthly Temple: a mighty angel (perhaps a guard), angels ministering in worship before the throne, angels as musicians sounding the trumpets during the sacrifices, an angel offering incense, another opens a little scroll and tends the fire of the altar.

> *The point of what we are saying is this: We do have such a high priest, who sat down at the right hand of the throne of the Majesty in heaven, and who serves in the sanctuary, the true tabernacle set up by the Lord, not by man. Hebrews 8:1-2*

Lock 2-5
Priestly Duties
Page #87

We are going to look at the book of Revelation from a heavenly perspective. Rather than focusing on the events occurring on the earth, we will join John in the heavenlies and become a part of the Feast days being celebrated there.

In the heavenly Temple the season of the fall harvest has come. It is the year of Jubilee, the time of release. All the divisions of priests are present in the Temple to receive the offerings which the Son, our High Priest, has prepared.

The coronation of Messiah the King, for which all previous Fall Feasts have been a rehearsal, will now continue. The King will receive the symbols of monarchy—crowns and garments have been prepared. The Covenant of His authority has been recorded.

The gates of the heavenly Temple are opened, the Father God assumes His throne on the platform erected for the King outside the Holy Place. The 'mighty men' loyal to the King are beside him. The council confirms the New Moon—the fullness of time has come.

The Father takes the scroll in his hand—the book to be read at Jubilee—the Book of the Covenant and responsibilities of the King's reign, the prophetic book of the King and His acts, and the books of judgment.

The Lion of Judah, the Prince of the Household, approaches the throne and takes the book. . .

# THE FEAST DAY OF TRUMPETS

**Before you begin, read: Revelation 4.**

## NEW MOON OF THE SEVENTH MONTH

Lock 1-5
New Moon-One
Long Day
Page #96

Lock 1-2
1st of Tishri
Page #143

Lock 4-3
Door/Gate Opened
Page #90

Lock 1-1
Time
Page #96

Lock 2-6
Priest/King & His
Council
Page #150

Let's review some of the elements of this Feast day. The Feast of Trumpets was celebrated at the time of the New Moon of the Seventh Month. The arrival of the New Moon was sanctified by the High Priest and his council of 24 elders, which made up a court of judgment. This day was also New Year's day on the Civil Calendar. Messiah the King is the main theme and focus of this Feast day. Jewish tradition says on this day He will take His place upon the throne of judgment and the door of heaven will be opened to receive the righteous.

> I know your deeds, See, I have placed before you an open door that no one can shut. I know that you have little strength, yet you have kept my word and have not denied my name. *Revelation 3:8*

As John's vision opens we observe several familiar aspects of the New Moon ceremonies. The heavenly throne and its assembly bears similarities to the High Priest and his council who declare the appearance of the New Moon. It is also much like the gathering before the earthly kings at the time of the monthly New Moon; for the heavenly assembly declares their loyalty and pays homage to the King.

> As I looked, thrones were set in place, and the Ancient of Days took his seat. His clothing was as white as snow; the hair of his head was white like wool. His throne was flaming with fire, and its wheels were all ablaze. A river of fire was flowing, coming out from before him. Thousands upon thousands attended him: ten thousand times ten thousand stood before him. The court was seated, and the books were opened. *Daniel 7:9-10*

> *After this I looked, and there before me was a door standing open in heaven. And the voice I had first heard speaking to me like a trumpet said, "Come up here, and I will show you what must take place after this." At once I was in the Spirit, and there before me was a throne in heaven with someone sitting on it... Surrounding the thrones, and seated on them were twenty-four elders. They were dressed in white and had crowns of gold on their heads... Each of the four living creatures had six wings and was covered with eyes all around, even under his wings. Day and night they never stop saying: "Holy, holy,*

*holy is the Lord God Almighty, who was, and is, and is to come." Whenever the living creatures give glory, honor and thanks to him who sits on the throne and who lives for ever and ever, the twenty-four elders fall down before him who sits on the throne, and worship him who lives for ever and ever. They lay their crowns before the throne and say: "You are worthy, our Lord and God, to receive glory and honor and power, for you created all things, and by your will they were created and have their being."*
*Revelation 4:1, 2, 4, 8-11*

Lock 4-2
Homage to the
King
Page #147

Lock 6-6
Acclamation
Page #142

As a picture of the throne of God emerges, there are also familiar images from our study of the Tabernacle and Temple: seven lamps and a sea of glass similar to the lampstands and laver. We are surely seeing the heavenly Temple from which the earthly Temple was patterned.

Lock 2-1
Heavenly Pattern
Page #157

**Before you begin, read: Revelation 5.**

## THE CORONATION OF MESSIAH THE KING

The main theme of the Feast Day of Trumpets in the earthly Temple was a rehearsal of the coronation of Messiah the King. From John's description, we see the actual coronation to which all the rehearsals have pointed. The Messiah approaches the throne and the coronation ceremony *resumes*. We use the word *resumes* because as we have seen, this is a continuation of a coronation that has already begun.

Lock 3-1
Rehearsal
Page #85

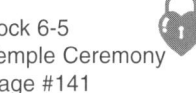

Lock 6-5
Temple Ceremony
Page #141

In the right hand of Him who sat on the throne is a scroll or book sealed with seven seals. The book in the hand of the King indicates to us it is a sabbatical or jubilee year. One who is worthy is sought to open the book. This reference to the Root of David shows us that a king is being sought as a worthy one. The Lion of Judah has prevailed to open the book. He has won the battle over any who would dispute his right to inherit the kingship.

Lock 4-1
Book of Covenant
Page #141

Lock 5-5
Prince of
Household
Page #148

*Then I saw in the right hand of him who sat on the throne a scroll with writing on both sides and sealed with seven seals. And I saw a mighty angel proclaiming in a loud voice "Who is worthy to break the seals and open the scroll?" But no one in heaven or on earth or under the earth could open the scroll or even look inside it. I wept and wept because no one was found who was worthy to open the scroll or look inside. Then one of the elders said to me, "Do not weep! See the Lion of the tribe of Judah, the Root of David, has*

Lock 1-6
Jubilee
Page #7

Lock 6-3
Battles with
Enemy
Page #151

*triumphed. He is able to open the scroll and its seven seals."*
*Revelation 5:1-5*

Lock 6-7
Coronation Song
Page #142

As the Lamb takes the scroll, the four beasts and elders offer incense and homage to the King. They sing a coronation song to honor the King.

> *And they sang a new song:*
> *"You are worthy to take the scroll and to open its seals, because you were slain, and with your blood you purchased men for God from every tribe and language and people and nation. You have made them to be a kingdom and priests to serve our God, and they will reign on the earth."*
> *Revelation 5:9-10*

Lock 5-7
Bought With A
Price
Page #123

Lock 4-13
Feast of Nations
Page #95

In like manner, the congregation sings a coronation psalm in honor of their King.

Lock 4-2
Homage to the
King
Page #161

> *Then I looked and heard the voice of many angels, numbering thousands upon thousands, and ten thousand times ten thousand. They encircled the throne and the living creatures and the elders. In a loud voice they sang: Worthy is the Lamb, who was slain, to receive power and wealth and wisdom and strength and honor and glory and praise! Revelation 5:11-12*

> *Praise the Lord. Praise the Lord from the heavens, praise him in the heights above. Praise him, all his angels, praise him, all his heavenly hosts. Praise him sun and moon, praise him, all you shining stars. Praise him you highest heavens and you waters above the skies. Let them praise the name of the Lord, for he commanded and they were created. He set them in place for ever and ever; he gave a decree that will never pass away.*
> *Psalm 148:1-6*

At the time of the New Moon celebrations in the earthly Temple, all creation was summoned to do homage to their Creator. In the heavenly Temple all creation proclaimed their creator King:

Lock 6-6
Acclamation
Page #161

> *Then I heard every creature in heaven and on earth and under the earth and on the sea, and all that is in them, singing: "To him who sits on the throne and to the Lamb be praise and honor and glory and power, for ever and ever!" Revelation 5:13*

**Before you begin, read: Revelation 6 & 7.**

## THE BOOK OF THE COVENANT

Lock 4-1
Book of Covenant
Page #161

In the previous chapters we discussed three important concepts which will provide us with insight into the Lamb's book which is about to be opened.

First, during the ceremonies in the earthly Temple appropriate scripture readings were assigned to the day. A worthy one was chosen to read scriptures taken from the Law. On Feast days additional scriptures were read describing the appropriate sacrifices for the day and a reading from a smaller scroll, the Prophets. On a Sabbatical Year or Jubilee Year, the king presented the readings.

Lock 1-6
Jubilee
Page #161

Second, a covenant was presented at the time of an earthly king's coronation. This record was variously described as the book of the law by which the king was to govern, the covenant of the king with his God and his people, and a prophetic prediction regarding the period of the king's reign.

Thirdly, Jewish tradition stated that on the Day of Judgment three books of judgment are opened: the book of the righteous, the book of sinners or average people, and the book of the wicked.

Lock 4-4
3 Books
Page #95

All these elements will be seen in the book now to be opened. The King will read from the book for it is the Year of Release. The contents of the book will describe the appropriate sacrifices and prophecies for the day. Secondly, it will confirm the King's authority and describe the events of his reign: His victory over the assailant, His reign upon the earth and finally, His marriage to His bride. Thirdly, we will see the King's judgment.

> *He who overcomes will, like them, be dressed in white, I will never blot out his name from the book of life, but will acknowledge his name before my Father and his angels. Revelation 3:5*

### Seals/Beginning of Birthpains . . .

As the first four seals of the scroll are broken, four horsemen are commissioned to go forth upon the earth. The first of the four horsemen represents a conqueror, the second symbolizes war, the third represents famine, and the fourth brings death to a quarter of the earth.

> *I know your afflictions and your poverty—yet you are rich! I know the slander of those who say they are Jews and are not, but are a synagogue of Satan. Do not be afraid of what you are about to suffer. I tell you, the devil will put some of you in prison to test you, and you will suffer persecution for ten days. Be faithful, even to the point of death, and I will give you the crown of life. Revelation 2:9-10*

As the fifth seal is broken the Altar of Sacrifice is seen in the heavenly Temple and those slain as a burnt offering unto the Lord.

> *When he opened the fifth seal, I saw under the altar the souls of those who had been slain because of the word of God and the testimony they had maintained.*
> *Revelation 6:9*

You will recall, the Altar of Sacrifice was located in the courtyard. This was where the burnt offerings were wholly consumed and the ashes were laid on the ground to be carried out of the Temple area. The burnt offering was considered a sweet savor unto the Lord and was the only offering that a non-Isra-

Lock 2-22
Burnt Offering
Page #31

Lock 2-2
Courtyard
Page #157

Lock 2-24
Most Holy Sacrifice
Page #86

Lock 4-5
Sealing
Page #98

*And do not grieve the Holy Spirit of God, with whom you were sealed for the day of redemption. Ephesians 4:30*

Lock 3-3
Sign on Hand &
Forehead
Page #123

Lock 2-7
White Garments
Page #116

Lock 6-6
Acclamation
Page #162

Lock 4-8
Ritual Bath
Page #126

elite could offer. The souls of the slain seen under the altar are as the ashes that were placed beside the altar. Those slain were given white robes and told to wait as there would be others added to their number. A persecution of believers is yet to follow.

The sixth seal is broken and great distress is seen on the earth with cosmic disturbances in the heavens. We are told these events introduce the day of His wrath.

> *For the great day of their wrath has come, and who can stand? Revelation 6:17*

Before the last seal is broken a sealing of the righteous is ordered. This would seem to correspond to those described in the Jewish tradition as those found written in the Book of the Righteous (Book of Life) on the Day of Trumpets judgment.

> *Then I saw another angel coming up from the east, having the seal of the living God. He called out in a loud voice to the four angels who had been given power to harm the land and the sea. "Do not harm the land or the sea or the trees until we put a seal on the foreheads of the servants of our God." Revelation 7:2-3*

When the angels who seal the righteous have completed their assignment, a great multitude of the righteous are seen before the throne. Those loyal to the earthly king assembled at the New Moon to demonstrate their loyalty and give homage to the king. So in the heavenlies, it is a day to bring homage to the King and proclaim Him sovereign.

> *After this I looked and there before me was a great multitude that no one could count, from every nation, tribe, people and language standing before the throne and in front of the Lamb. They were wearing white robes and were holding palm branches in their hands. ...All the angels were standing around the throne and around the elders and the four living creatures. They fell down on their faces before the throne and worshiped God, saying: "Amen! Praise and glory and wisdom and thanks and honor and power and strength be to our God for ever and ever. Amen!" ...Then one of the elders asked me, "These in white robes — who are they, and where did they come from?" I answered, "Sir, you know." And he said, "These are they who have come out of the great tribulation; they have washed their robes and made them white in the blood of the Lamb." Revelation 7:9, 11-12, 13-14*

At this time, just as in the earthly congregation that gathers before the king at the New Moon, the loyal ones come before the King in the heavenlies to receive their commission to serve him.

> *Therefore, "they are before the throne of God and serve him day and night in his temple; and he who sits on the throne will spread his tent over them. . . Revelation 7:15*

It is also a day for the King to confirm His covenant with His people. The Lamb, the Bridegroom, affirms that he will soon lead them to the wedding chamber he has prepared.

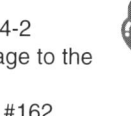

Lock 4-2
Homage to the King
Page #162

> *Never again will they hunger; never again will they thirst. The sun will not beat upon them, nor any scorching heat. For the Lamb at the center of the throne will be their shepherd; he will lead them to springs of living water. And God will wipe away every tear from their eyes. Revelation 7:16-17*

Lock 4-1
Book of Covenant
Page #162

## BIRTHPAINS OF THE MESSIAH

The Day of Trumpets is connected in the Jewish mind with a period known as the Birthpains of the Messiah. When Jesus was asked about his return, he told his disciples of events that would mark the 'beginning of birthpains'. To their Jewish minds this was a term immediately familiar.

In the comparison table on the next page, we have compared the sequence of events described by Jesus with those recorded by John in his vision. It is this sequence that convinced us that the events that John described are presented in a straight forward chronology. John did not write in a complicated manner designed to be understood by an elect few. And Jesus, who taught with such simplicity in his earthly walk, did not bring a 'revelation' veiled in undecipherable complexity. Much like Matthew 24, the seals provide us with a sequence of events that herald the Second Coming of Jesus as King.

# SEQUENTIAL DIAGRAM
## COMPARING MATTHEW 24 WITH SEALS IN REVELATION

| Sequence of Events | Matthew 24 | Revelation Seals |
|---|---|---|
| **Beginning of Birthpains**<br><br>•False Christs | *As Jesus was sitting on the Mount of Olives, the disciples came to him privately. "Tell us," they said, "when will this happen, and what will be the sign of your coming and of the end of the age?" Jesus answered: "Watch out that no one deceives you. For many will come in my name, <u>claiming, 'I am the Christ,'</u> and will deceive many.* | 1. A conqueror on a white horse having a bow and a crown who is bent on conquest. Although this description of the conqueror is similar to the description of Jesus in Revelation 19:11, it is not the same person. (False Christ) |
| •Wars | *You will hear of <u>wars and rumors of wars,</u> but see to it that you are not alarmed. Such things must happen, but the end is still to come. Nation will rise up against nation and kingdom against kingdom.* | 2. A rider on a red horse holding a sword and given power to take peace from the earth and make men slay each other. |
| •Famines<br>•Earthquakes | *There will be <u>famines and earthquakes</u> in various places.* ***All these are the beginning of birthpains.*** | 3. A rider on a black horse holding a pair of scales (commonly interpreted as a sign of famine.) |
| **Persecution/Death**<br>•Deception of many<br>•False Prophets | *Then you will be handed over to be <u>persecuted and put to death</u>, and you will be hated by all nations because of me. At that time <u>many will turn away from the faith</u> and will betray and hate each other, and many <u>false prophets</u> will appear and deceive many people. Because of the increase of wickedness, the love of most will grow cold, but he who stands firm to the end will be saved.* | 4. A rider on a pale horse whose name is Death. Hades was following him. They are given power to kill by famine, sword, plague, and wild beasts. |
| •Testimony to all Nations<br><br>•Abomination of Desolation<br><br>•Judea hides<br><br>•Great Distress | *And this gospel of the kingdom will be <u>preached in the whole world</u> as a testimony to all nations, and then the end will come. So when you see standing in the holy place '<u>the abomination</u> that causes desolation,' spoken of through the prophet Daniel—let the reader understand—then let those who are in <u>Judea flee to the mountains</u>. . .*<br><br>*For then there will be <u>great distress,</u> unequaled from the beginning of the world until now—and never to be equaled again. If those days had not been cut short, no one would survive, but for the sake of the elect those days will be shortened. At that time if anyone says to you, 'Look, here is the Christ!' or, 'There he is!' do not believe it. For false Christs and false prophets will appear and perform great signs and miracles to deceive even the elect—if that were possible. See, I have told you ahead of time. . .* | 5. Those slain for the testimony of Jesus fulfill the symbolism of the burnt offering. They are told that there will be more added to their numbers before His avenging judgment. They are given white robes and told to wait a little longer. |
| **Cosmic Disturbances**<br>•sun darkened<br>•moon darkened<br>•stars fall<br><br>•Son of Man on clouds<br>•Gathering of elect<br><br><br><br>•Wrath of God | *Immediately after the distress of those days 'the <u>sun will be darkened</u>, and the <u>moon will not give its light;</u> the <u>stars will fall</u> from the sky, and the <u>heavenly bodies will be shaken.</u>'*<br><br>*At that time the sign of the Son of Man will appear in the sky, and all the nations of the earth will mourn. They will see the Son of Man coming on the clouds of the sky, with power and great glory. And he will send his angels with a loud trumpet call, and they will gather his elect from the four winds, from one end of the heavens to the other.*<br><br>*The master of that servant will come on a day when he does not expect him and at an hour he is not aware of. He will come like a thief. He will cut him to pieces and assign him a place with the hypocrites, where there will be weeping and gnashing of teeth. [Emphasis Authors']* | 6. Great earthquake, sun blackened, moon turned red, and stars fell from sky. Sky receded like a scroll and every mountain moved from its place (Revelation 6:12-17). The great day of His wrath has come.<br><br>*I will show wonders in the heavens and on the earth, blood and fire and billows of smoke. The sun will be turned to darkness and the moon to blood before the coming of the great and dreadful day of the Lord. Joel 2:30-31* |

The days of the King's ordination have come to completion. The ceremonies at the entrance of the Tent of Meeting move into the Holy of Holies of the Heavenly Temple. Here the incense and blood are offered for the cleansing of the Temple as the congregation waits outside in silence.

This day the King completes the judgment begun on the Feast Day of Trumpets. All will be inscribed in either the Book of Life or the Book of the Wicked.

For those inscribed for life, it is a time of great joy, a day when the year of Jubilee is consecrated. Those who have been in bondage will enter into the completion of their redemption, their inheritance is restored and all debts cancelled. All guilt is washed away for the Accuser is cast out. She who has been blind will give birth to the knowledge of her Messiah.

When the ceremonies are complete, all opportunity for repentance will end. At the blowing of the Great Shofar the gates of the Temple will be closed.

# DAY OF ATONEMENT

Let's review some of the rehearsals in the earthly Temple that have pointed to this Day of Atonement. As we saw in the previous chapters, many similarities existed between the ceremonial events of the ordination of the High Priest, the Day of Atonement, and the Coronation of the kings of Israel.

While we were not able to show a specific period listed as 'seven days of ordination' for the kings of Israel, such a provision was definitely instituted by God for the ordination of the High Priest.

Lock 2-12
Sanctuary
Cleansing
Page #82

Lock 2-17
Fire Kindled
Page #144

Lock 3-1
Rehearsal
Page #161

At the time of the ordination of Aaron, the sanctuary was cleansed and fire from the Lord came down at the close of the ordination period. A fire was also lit to mark the beginning of a king's reign. On the Day of Atonement during the sanctuary cleansing, similar sacrifices for the ordination of priests and the coronation of kings, cleansed the sanctuary. For these reasons these institutions became for us intricately linked as prophetic rehearsals.

Lock 2-16
Days of Ordination
Page #141

Lock 1-5
New Moon - One
Long Day
Page #160

Lock 1-4
10th of Tishri
Page #78

These events coupled with the days that made up the Fall Feasts caused us to place the seven days of ordination and consecration of the King of Kings during the period between the Day of Trumpets and the Day of Atonement. For if the Day of Trumpets began on Tishri 1 and constituted 'one long day', it included Tishri 2. Seven days of tarrying before the Tent of the Meeting would then bring us to the 10th of Tishri the Day of Atonement, the day of entering into the Holy of Holies.

**Before you begin, read: Revelation 8 & 9.**

## CLEANSING OF THE SANCTUARY

Lock 2-19
Sin Offering
Page #80

Lock 2-14
Sacrifices of
Anointing
Page #139

On the Day of Atonement after the regular daily service was complete sacrifices were prepared as specified for the feast day: A bull for the sins of the High Priest and his household and two goats for the sins of the people. Next began the ministry in the Holy of Holies: the offering of incense and blood of the sacrifices.

These same elements are seen in the ceremonies in the heavenly Temple as the seventh seal is broken.

Lock 2-24
Most Holy Sacrifices
Page #164

Lock 4-10
Silence
Page #81

> *When he opened the seventh seal, there was silence in heaven for about half an hour. Revelation 8:1*

### Incense offering. .

The rituals of the incense offering presented here are parallel to those offered on the Day of Atonement in the Temple in Jerusalem. The incense was offered by the High Priest in the Holy of Holies. The Day of Atonement was the only time during the year that the High Priest entered into the Holy of Holies with the censer of incense to make an offering. You will remember that the congregation waited outside in silence as the incense offering was presented. This same offering is being made in the Holy of Holies of the heavenly Temple, as the congregation waits in silence. There the priest casts the incense from his hand onto the censer lit from the altar fire.

Lock 4-9
Incense Offering
Page #81

Lock 2-4
Holy of Holies
Page #157

> *Another angel, who had a golden censer, came and stood at the altar. He was given much incense to offer, with the prayers of all the saints on the golden altar before the throne. The smoke of the incense together with the prayers of the saints went up before God from the angel's hand. Then the angel took the censer, filled it with fire from the altar, and hurled it on the earth; and there came peals of thunder, rumblings, flashes of lightning and an earthquake. Revelation 8:3-5*

### Blood Sprinkling . . .

After the incense was offered in the earthly Temple, the blood of the bull and the goat were each sprinkled separately in the Holy of Holies. It was sprinkled once on top of the Ark and seven times downward at the base of the Ark.

Lock 2-19
Sin Offering
Page #168

Lock 2-21
Blood Sprinkling
Page #82

In the scene of the heavenly Temple, after the incense is offered, seven trumpets are blown. The results down on the earth are death and destruction. This appears to be a similar act of downward blood sprinkling such as was seen with the blood of the bull and goat in the earthly Temple. The cosmic disturbances that began with the sixth seal continue with the blowing of these trumpets and the sprinkling of blood.

Lock 2-5
Priestly Duties
Page #158

> *Also at your times of rejoicing—your appointed feasts and New Moon festivals—you are to sound the trumpets over your burnt offerings and fellowship offerings, and they will be a memorial for you before your God. I am the Lord your God. Numbers 10:10*

During the account of the fifth trumpet, a plague of locust come down upon the earth. We are told that there is still a remnant of the sealed on the earth at this time.

Lock 3-3
Sign on Hand &
Forehead
Page #164

> *They were told not to harm the grass of the earth or any plant or tree, but only those people who did not have the seal of God on their foreheads. Revelation 9:4*

Lock 2-12
Sanctuary Cleansing
Page #168

After the blood of the bull and goat was sprinkled in the earthly Temple, the two were mixed together and sprinkled on each of the four horns of the golden altar and then seven times on top of it. This completed the cleansing of the sanctuary and access to the Lord was again established. As the sixth trumpet is sounded, we see the horns of the altar in the heavenly Temple:

Lock 2-13
Horns of the Altar
Page #82

> *The sixth angel sounded his trumpet, and I heard a voice coming from the horns of the golden altar that is before God. Revelation 9:13*

Now we know there are a lot of things going on that affect the earth with the blowing of these trumpets. However, remember we have joined John in the heavenly Temple ceremony, so let's continue to focus on those events.

**Before you begin, read: Revelation 10 & 11.**

## CALL TO NATIONAL REPENTANCE

Before the seventh angel sounds his trumpet a 'mighty' angel delivers a message that there will be no more delay; the mystery of God will be accomplished.

> *. . .There will be no more delay! But in the days when the seventh angel is about to sound his trumpet, the mystery of God will be accomplished, just as he announced to his servants the prophets. Revelation 10:6b-7*

Lock 1-3
Sevens
Page #154

Of what delay does the angel speak? The delay in Israel's clock between the 69th and 70th week of Daniel's prophecy has been complete (Daniel 9).

What is the mystery of God that is to be accomplished in the days when the seventh angel is about to sound?

> *I do not want you to be ignorant of this mystery, brothers, so that you may not be conceited: Israel has experienced a hardening in part until the full number of the Gentiles has*

*come in. And so all Israel will be saved, as it is written: The deliverer will come from Zion; he will turn godlessness away from Jacob. And this is my covenant with them when I take away their sins. Hebrews 11:25-27*

Appropriate to the Day of Atonement it is the time of Israel's redemption. To this end we will see that the events of John's vision will now center around the city of Jerusalem.

Lock 4-6
National Cleansing
Page #78

We will see two contrasted Jerusalems—a repentant one who accepts her Messiah, and an unrepentant one condemned as a harlot.

### Little Scroll. . .
John is given a little scroll from the hand of the mighty angel. This little scroll reminds us of scriptures read during the Temple services from the Prophets, a smaller scroll than that of the Law.

*I do not want you to be ignorant of this mystery, brothers, so that you may not be conceited: Israel has experienced a hardening in part until the full number of the Gentiles has come in. And so all Israel will be saved, as it is written: "The deliverer will come from Zion; he will turn godlessness away from Jacob. And this is my covenant with them when I take away their sins." As far as the gospel is concerned, they are enemies on your account; but as far as election is concerned, they are loved on account of the patriarchs, for God's gifts and his call are irrevocable. Romans 11:25-29*

*Then the voice that I had heard from heaven spoke to me once more; "Go, take the scroll that lies open in the hand of the angel who is standing on the sea and on the land." So I went to the angel and asked him to give me the little scroll. He said to me, "Take it and eat it. It will turn your stomach sour, but in your mouth it will be as sweet as honey." I took the little scroll from the angel's hand and ate it. It tasted as sweet as honey in my mouth, but when I had eaten it, my stomach turned sour. Revelation 10:8-10*

In just such a manner Ezekiel was commissioned to deliver a prophetic message to Israel:

*Then I looked, and I saw a hand stretched out to me. In it was a scroll, which he unrolled before me. On both sides of it were written words of lament and mourning and woe. And he said to me, "Son of man, eat what is before you, eat this scroll; then go and speak to the house of Israel." So I opened my mouth, and he gave me the scroll to eat. Then he said to me, "Son of man, eat this scroll I am giving you and fill your stomach with it." So I ate it, and it tasted as sweet as honey in my mouth." Ezekiel 2:9-3:3*

The instructions to John indicate that the call to repentance has shifted from the individual to the nations, just as the Day of Atonement focused on national repentance.

*Then I was told, "You must prophesy again about many peoples, nations, languages and kings." Revelation 10:11*

### Two Witnesses . . .

Lock 5-9
Two Witnesses
Page #128

In Revelation 11, John is instructed to measure the Jerusalem Temple and the altar, as well as to count the worshippers. The instrument of measurement he is given is a rod of judgment.

> *I will punish their sin with the rod, their iniquity with flogging; but I will not take my love from him, nor will I ever betray my faithfulness. I will not violate my covenant or alter what my lips have uttered. Psalms 89:32-34*

*But exclude the outer court; do not measure it, because it has been given to the Gentiles. They will trample on the holy city for 42 months. And I will give power to my two witnesses, and they will prophesy for 1,260 days, clothed in sackcloth. Revelation 11:2-3*

Lock 5-12
Ordeal of Jealousy
Page #129

Notice that during the time Jerusalem is tread under foot by the Gentiles it is figuratively called Sodom and Egypt. This analogy parallels closely to the condition of a defiled woman.

> *Their bodies will lie in the street of the great city, which is figuratively called Sodom and Egypt, where also their Lord was crucified. Revelation 11:8*

Jesus, true to the law in all respects, will not abandon his covenant except for the cause of adultery. Mercifully he has sent a warning by two witnesses to Jerusalem. When the witnesses have completed their testimony the beast out of the bottomless pit makes war on them and kills them.

> *For three and a half days men from every people, tribe, language and nation will gaze on their bodies and refuse them burial. The inhabitants of the earth will gloat over them and will celebrate by sending each other gifts, because these two prophets had tormented those who live on the earth. Revelation 11:9-10*

Three and one half days the bodies of the witnesses will lie in Jerusalem, but they will come to life. At that hour an earthquake will cause a tenth of the city to collapse and seven thousand people will be killed.

It is at this point that we have our first indication of a response to the two witnesses' warning. The remnant remaining recognized that the witnesses were from God:

Lock 4-5
Sealing
Page #164

> *At that very hour there was a severe earthquake and a tenth of the city collapsed. Seven thousand people were killed in*

*the earthquake, and the survivors were terrified and gave glory to the God of heaven. Revelation 11:13b*

### The Seventh Trumpet . . .

As the seventh trumpet, the Great Shofar, is blown the announcement goes forth: the nations held captive by the assailant are now ransomed by the Son.

> *The seventh angel sounded his trumpet, and there were loud voices in heaven, which said: "The kingdom of the world has become the kingdom of our Lord and of his Christ, and he will reign for ever and ever." And the twenty-four elders, who were seated on their thrones before God fell on their faces and worshiped God, saying: We give thanks to you, Lord God Almighty, the One who is and who was, because you have taken your great power and have begun to reign. Revelation 11:15-17*

All the yearly rehearsals of a day of national cleansing pointed to this day of fulfillment. The incense and blood have been offered in the heavenly Temple, completing the ceremonies of cleansing. The way is open to free access for all nations to communion with God. The year of Jubilee is sanctified.

> *Then God's temple in heaven was opened, and within his temple was seen the ark of his covenant. And there came flashes of lightning, rumblings, peals of thunder, an earthquake and a great hailstorm. Revelation 11:19*

This in no way implies that the work of Jesus did not provide this access as Paul explained in Hebrews 10:19-22. But, remember the ceremonies of the Temple were to instruct and call to remembrance.

> *Therefore, brothers, since we have confidence to enter the Most Holy Place by the blood of Jesus, by a new and living way opened for us through the curtain, that is, his body, and since we have a great priest over the house of God, let us draw near to God with a sincere heart in full assurance of faith, having our hearts sprinkled to cleanse us from a guilty conscience and having our bodies washed with pure water. Hebrews 10:19-22*

Lock 3-8
Trumpets
Page #78

Lock 4-2
Homage to King
Page #165

Lock 4-6
National
Cleansing
Page #171

Lock 2-12
Sanctuary
Cleansing
Page #170

Lock 4-3
Door/Gates
Opened
Page #160

Lock 1-6
Jubilee
Page #163

**Before you begin, read: Revelation 12.**

## THE AZAZEL

Following the ministry of the High Priest in the Holy of Holies, the next portion of the earthly Temple ceremony for the Day of Atonement centered around the Azazel goat. For this reason, in the heavenly vision before us we will first focus on the *dragon* in the vision of the Woman and the Dragon. The dragon symbolism is interpreted for us as Satan who was cast down from the heavenlies to the earth.

> *At that time Michael, the great prince who protects your people, will arise. There will be a time of distress such as has not happened from the beginning of nations until then. But at that time your people—everyone whose name is found written in the book—will be delivered. Daniel 12:1*

*And there was war in heaven, Michael and his angels fought against the dragon, and the dragon and his angels fought back. But he was not strong enough and they lost their place in heaven. The great dragon was hurled down — that ancient serpent called the devil or Satan, who leads the whole world astray. He was hurled to the earth, and his angels with him. Revelation 12:7-9*

 Lock 4-11
Azazel
Page #82

This is reminiscent of the Azazel sacrifice that was hurled down the cliff on the Day of Atonement. It's sacrifice was concerned with the *sense of guilt* of the people. Note that after the dragon was hurled down, rejoicing broke out in heaven because the *accuser* of the brothers was cast down.

> *. . . For the accuser of our brothers, who accuses them before our God day and night, has been hurled down. Revelation 12:10*

We can hardly avoid remembering the scene of the goat being pushed over the cliff in the wilderness outside the earthly Temple. It's true that the scriptures did not instruct the people to push the goat over the cliff, he was to be led out into the wilderness and let go. But the fact is at the time that John wrote, the practice was to push the goat over the cliff. (Refer to Appendix C.)

### *Woman in Birthpains. . .*

Lock 3-10
Repentance from
Adultery
Page #128

Some writers have drawn comparisons between the description of the woman and pagan goddesses. Others would interpret this to be a vision of the birth of Jesus out of Israel. However, let's look at the context and other scriptures for our interpretation.

> *A great and wondrous sign appeared in heaven: a woman clothed with the sun, with the moon under her feet and a crown of twelve stars on her head. Revelation 12: 1*

Similar symbols are seen in the dream of Joseph in which he sees the sun, moon and stars bow down to him. His father, Jacob, interprets the dream for him comparing the sun and moon to Jacob (Israel) and his wife and the stars to his twelve sons (twelve Tribes of Israel).

> *Then he had another dream, and he told it to his brothers. "Listen," he said, "I had another dream, and this time the sun and moon and eleven stars were bowing down to me." When he told his father as well as his brothers, his father rebuked him and said, "What is this dream you had? Will your mother and I and your brothers actually come and bow down to the ground before you?" Genesis 37: 9-10*

The woman now identified as Israel or more specifically Jerusalem, delivers a male child, who is destined to rule the nations with an iron scepter. This child is identified for us as the Christ in the following scriptures:

> *..he will rule all the nations with an iron scepter. And her child was snatched up to God and to his throne. Revelation 12:5*

> *Out of his mouth comes a sharp sword with which to strike down the nations, "He will rule them with an iron scepter." He treads the winepress of the fury of the wrath of God Almighty. On his robe and on his thigh he has this name written: King of Kings and Lord of Lords. Revelation 19:15-16*

> *For to us a child is born, to us a son is given, and the government will be on his shoulders. And he will be called Wonderful Counselor, Mighty God, Everlasting Father, Prince of Peace. Of the increase of his government and peace there will be no end. He will reign on David's throne and over his kingdom, establishing and upholding it with justice and righteousness from that time on and forever. The zeal of the Lord Almighty will accomplish this. Isaiah 9:6-7*

> *Therefore Israel will be abandoned until the time when she who is in labor gives birth and the rest of his brothers return to join the Israelites. Micah 5:3*

If this woman symbolizes Israel and she is giving birth to the Messiah, the first thought is a picture of the time of Jesus' birth. But if this were so it is totally out of sequence. After the birth of Jesus Israel's history has never fit the description of being hidden and protected from the serpent, that evil one.

The prophets foretold of the day when Israel would repent of her adulteries. The woman in birthpains is Jerusalem who repented at the warning of the witnesses and accepted Jesus as Messiah.

> *Sing, O barren woman, you who never bore a child; burst into song, shout for joy, you who were never in labor; because more are the children of the desolate woman than of her who has a husband, says the Lord. Enlarge the place of your tent, stretch your tent curtains wide, do not hold back; lengthen your cords, strengthen your stakes. For you will*

Lock 3-11
Birthpains
Page #120

Lock 4-6
National Cleansing
Page #173

Lock 1-4
10th of Tishri
Page #168

Lock 5-9
Two Witnesses
Page #172

Lock 3-10
Repentance from
Adultery
Page #174

Lock 5-2
Virgin
Page #148

*Why do you now cry aloud—have you no king? Has your counselor perished, that pain seizes you like that of a woman in labor? Writhe in agony, O Daughter of Zion, like a woman in labor, for now you must leave the city to camp in the open field. You will go to Babylon; there you will be rescued. There the Lord will redeem you out of the hand of your enemies. Micah 4:9-10*

Lock 5-4
Ransom
Page #110

Lock 4-1
Book of Covenant
Page #165

*spread out to the right and to the left; your descendants will dispossess nations and settle in their desolate cities. Do not be afraid; you will not suffer shame. <u>Do not fear disgrace;</u> you will not be humiliated. You will forget the shame of your youth and remember no more the reproach of your widowhood. For your Maker is your husband—the Lord Almighty is his name—the Holy One of Israel is your Redeemer; he is called the God of all the earth. The Lord will <u>call you back</u> as if you were a <u>wife deserted</u> and distressed in spirit—a wife who married young, only to be rejected, says your God. For a brief moment I abandoned you, but with deep compassion I will bring you back. In a surge of anger I hid my face from you for a moment, but with everlasting kindness I will have compassion on you, says the Lord your Redeemer. To me this is like the days of Noah, when I swore that the waters of Noah would never again cover the earth. So now I have sworn not to be angry with you, never to rebuke you again. Though the mountains be shaken and the hills be removed, yet my unfailing love for you will not be shaken <u>nor my covenant of peace</u> be removed, says the Lord, who has compassion on you. O <u>afflicted city,</u> lashed by storms and not comforted, I <u>will build you with stones of turquoise, your foundations with sapphires.</u> I will make your battlements of rubies, your gates of sparkling jewels and all your walls of precious stones. All your sons will be taught by the Lord, and great will be your children's peace. In righteousness you will be estab-*

*What do you think? If a man owns a hundred sheep, and one of them wanders away, will he not leave the ninety-nine on the hills and go to look for the one that wandered off? And if he finds it, I tell you the truth, he is happier about that one sheep than about the ninety-nine that did not wander off. In the same way your Father in heaven is not willing that any of these little ones should be lost. Matthew 18:12-14*

*lished: Tyranny will be far from you: you will have nothing to fear. Terror will be far removed; it will not come near you. If anyone does attack you, it will not be my doing; whoever attacks you will surrender to you. See, it is I who created the blacksmith who fans the coals into flame and forges a weapon fit for its work. And it is I who have created the destroyer to work havoc; no weapon forged against you will prevail, and you will refute every tongue that accuses you. This is the heritage of the servants of the Lord, and this is their vindication from me, declares the Lord. Isaiah 54 [Emphasis Authors']*

Lock 3-11
Birthpains
Page #175

In the context that Israel began her birthpains at the Feast of Trumpets, it is entirely in order that she is now giving birth to the knowledge that Jesus is the long awaited Messiah, on the Day of Atonement. Joseph Good in <u>Rosh HaShanah</u> and <u>the Messianic Kingdom to Come,</u> speaks of this scene in Revelation, saying:

> *Understand that it is not the Messiah who is born, but rather Israel as a corporate nation that is accepting her Messiah, i.e., being born anew spiritually.[1]*

When the child is delivered it is taken up into heaven. God has accepted Israel's repentance. If the newborn child had not been adopted or 'snatched up' by God (Greek means to take for oneself), then the child would have been in what is called the transition time. This made the child vulnerable because it would have been set out in a field for death or possibly to be adopted by another. Satan was standing before the woman waiting for the opportunity to devour this child to adopt it as his own. But, God has accepted Israel's birthing of the knowledge of her Messiah. The woman flees into the desert:

> *The woman fled into the desert to a place prepared for her by God where she might be taken care of for 1,260 days. . . The woman was given the two wings of a great eagle so that she might fly to the place prepared for her in the desert, where she would be taken care of for a time, times and half a time, out of the serpent's reach. Then from his mouth the serpent spewed water like a river, to overtake the woman and sweep her away with the torrent. But the earth helped the woman by opening its mouth and swallowing the river that the dragon had spewed out of his mouth.*
> *Revelation 12: 6, 14-16*

The eagle which helps the woman to flee may be a king such as that seen in the allegory of Ezekiel 17. At this point, the dragon is hurled from heaven.

Notice that the dragon pursues the woman and spews water like a river to destroy her, but the earth helps her and swallows up the river. We are reminded of the testing of Abraham and the Jewish legend in Appendix B regarding Satan's attempt to stop the offering of Isaac by spewing out a river before him.

> *When Satan saw that neither Abraham nor Isaac heeded what he had to say, he proceeded to turn himself into a wide stream. . . the Holy One rebuked the stream and it dried up. . .[2]*

*I am talking to you Gentiles. Inasmuch as I am the apostle to the Gentiles, I make much of my ministry in the hope that I may somehow arouse my own people to envy and save some of them. For if their rejection is the reconciliation of the world, what will their acceptance be but life from the dead? Romans 11:13-15*

Lock 5-11
Adoption
Page #145

*So when you see standing in the holy place the abomination that causes desolation, spoken of through the prophet Daniel—let the reader understand—then let those who are in Judea flee to the mountains. Matthew 24: 15-16*

*You yourselves have seen what I did to Egypt, and how I carried you on eagles' wings and brought you to myself. Exodus 19:4*

**Before you begin, read Revelation 13.**

Now the dragon goes to make war on the rest of the offspring of the woman, those who hold to the testimony of Jesus. Again we see a remnant of believers still remaining on the earth. This would indicate to us that the Day of Atonement is not yet complete, because at the end of its ceremonies the gates of heaven are closed. To accomplish his purpose, the dragon empowers another, the beast to persecute the believers:

> *The dragon gave the beast his power and his throne and great authority. . .Men worshiped the dragon because he had given authority to the beast, and they also worshiped the beast and asked, "Who is like the beast? Who can make war against him?" Revelation 13:2b, 4*

John has left the heavenly Temple ceremony and finds himself on the earth observing events there. You will note that the continued focus of the Day of Atonement is one of the judgment of nations.

*The Beast Out of the Sea. . .*
The beast out of the sea and the beast out of the earth are reminiscent of descriptions typically apocalyptic in their symbolism.

Combining the information given we can conclude that this beast is a political leader having ten horns with crowns on them and seven heads each with a blasphemous name. Just as kings have names describing their attributes and conquests, so this king.

He is also said to resemble a leopard, a bear and a lion. Letting scripture interpret this symbolism for us, we see in Revelation 17, that the seven heads are seven hills and also seven kings. The ten horns are ten kings that will have authority together with the beast. The symbols of the leopard, bear and lion are also used in Daniel 7 where they represent the attributes of kingdoms that will arise on the earth.

When we make the comparison, we will notice that the beast upon which the harlot (Revelation 17 & 18) sits is the same as that which is described as the beast out of the sea. The sea is also much like the waters on which the harlot sits. We will discuss the harlot in the next section. The symbolism of the waters is interpreted for us as: *". . .peoples, multitudes, nations and languages." Revelation 17:15b*

In keeping with Satan's tactics of counterfeiting what God does, he simulates the death and resurrection of Jesus in this beast.

> *One of the heads of the beast seemed to have had a fatal wound, but the fatal wound had been healed. The whole world was astonished and followed the beast.*
> *Revelation 13:3*

### The Beast Out of the Earth . . .

The description of the beast out of the earth is that of a religious leader who supports the political leader, the beast out of the sea. And in Revelation 19 he is identified as a false prophet.

> *. . . and with him the false prophet who had performed the miraculous signs on his behalf. With these signs he had deluded those who had received the mark of the beast and worshiped his image. Revelation 19:20*

Lock 3-3
Sign on Hand and
Forehead
Page #170

Previously, we saw the angels sent out to seal God's own. Again we see Satan counterfeiting what God does. In Revelation 13, the beast out of the earth also orders a seal of ownership:

Lock 4-5
Sealing
Page #172

> *.....he forced everyone. . .to receive a mark on his right hand or on his forehead... Revelation 13:16*

**Before you begin, read: Revelation 14 & 15.**

## THE PRIEST AMONG THE PEOPLE

Lest we become caught up in the things of the earth, before the completion of this beast story our attention is again turned toward the heavenlies. In the earthly Temple, when the High Priest concluded his duties regarding the sacrifices on the Day of Atonement, he walked out into the courtyard near the congregation. There he read and taught the people from the appropriate scriptures for the day. These scriptures would have included portions from the Law, the sacrifices of the day, and the Prophets. Just so, from the heavenly Temple, Christ the High Priest stands on heavenly Mt. Zion among the congregation and the angels proclaim the appropriate message of the day.

Lock 4-12
Priest in Courtyard
Page #83

This also bears resemblance to the completion of the coronation ceremonies in the Temple when the king comes forth from the Temple together with a small group of faithful followers and proceeds to the palace to assume his throne of government.

Lock 6-5
Temple Ceremony
Page #161

### Harvest of the Righteous. . .

At this time a final judgment of the 'average people' takes place on the Day of Atonement and they are sealed as righteous or placed in the Book of the Wicked. The reaping of the earth is ordered:

> *I looked, and there before me was a white cloud, and seated on the cloud was one "like a son of man" with a crown of gold on his head and a sharp sickle in his hand. Then another angel came out of the temple and called in a loud voice to him who was sitting on the cloud, "Take your sickle and reap, because the time to reap has come, for the harvest of the earth is ripe." So he that was seated on the cloud swung his sickle over the earth, and the earth was harvested."* Revelation 14:14-16.

### Harvest of the Wicked. . .

Another angel with a sharp sickle completes the harvest of the earth. Interestingly, this angel comes out from the altar and has power over the fire. Jesus spoke of a similar harvest:

> *Jesus told them another parable: "The kingdom of heaven is like a man who sowed good seed in his field. But while everyone was sleeping, his enemy came and sowed weeds among the wheat, and went away. When the wheat sprouted and formed heads, then the weeds also appeared. The owner's servants came to him and said, 'Sir, didn't you sow good seed in your field? Where then did the weeds come from?' An enemy did this, he replied. The servants asked him, 'Do you want us to go and pull them up?' No, he answered, 'because while you are pulling the weeds, you may root up the wheat with them. Let both grow together until the harvest. At that time I will tell the harvesters: First collect the weeds and tie them in bundles to be burned; then gather the wheat and bring it into my barn.' "* Matthew 13:24-30

This harvest of the wicked is thrown into the winepress of God's wrath. The judgment is complete. All have been inscribed in either the Book of Life or the Book of the Wicked.

 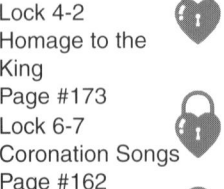
Before God's wrath is poured forth, we see those who have come through the beasts' persecution victoriously singing the coronation songs and paying homage to the King just as those who went before them. With the coronation Temple services concluded, the King's fire is kindled.

> *And I saw what looked like a sea of glass mixed with fire and, standing beside the sea, those who had been victorious*

*over the beast and his image and over the number of his name. They held harps given them by God and sang the song of Moses the servant of God and the song of the Lamb. Revelation 15:2-3*

The seven angels with the seven plagues are commissioned to go forth and complete God's wrath.

*I saw in heaven another great and marvelous sign: seven angels with the seven last plagues — last, because with them God's wrath is completed. . . .Out of the temple came the seven angels with the seven plagues. They were dressed in clean, shining linen and wore golden sashes around their chests. Then one of the four living creatures gave to the seven angels seven golden bowls filled with the wrath of God, who lives for ever and ever. Revelation 15:1,6-7*

### The gates are closed . . .

The heavenly Temple is closed and the Day of Atonement is ended. The wrath of God remains for those "vessels fit for destruction" found written in the Book of the Wicked.

*The virgins who were ready went in with him to the wedding banquet. And the door was shut. Matthew 25:10b*

*And the temple was filled with smoke from the glory of God and from his power, and no one could enter the temple until the seven plagues of the seven angels were completed. Revelation 15:8*

*Go, my people, enter your rooms and shut the doors behind you; hide yourselves for a little while until his wrath has passed by. See, the Lord is coming out of his dwelling to punish the people of the earth for their sins. Isaiah 26:20-21a*

Lock 4-7
Door/Gate Closed
Page #84

## AUTHORS' COMMENTS

### Days of Awe. . .

You will remember, the whole period beginning with the Day of Trumpets and concluding at the closing of the Temple gates on the Day of Atonement is seen as a judgment period. The vision of John would seem to confirm an inscribing of believers occurred on the Day of Trumpets and a final harvest at the end of the activities of the Day of Atonement.

*Since you have kept my command to endure patiently, I will also keep you from the hour of trial that is going to come upon the whole world to test those who live on the earth. Revelation 3:10*

### Mt. Zion . . .

We highly recommend a study of the term Mt. Zion. It is a complex idea extending beyond a geographical location. It is our opinion that in the context of the events described in Revelation 14, Jesus on Mt. Zion is taking his position as Monarch as he concludes that portion of his coronation ceremony that took place in the heavenly Temple.

Lock 6-5
Temple Ceremony
Page #179

Lock 6-8
Palace Ceremony
Page #142

In the heavenly Temple the smoke of the glory and power of God prevents anyone from entering. There will be no more ceremonies here until the Feast of Tabernacles. The congregation goes forth to make preparations for the most joyous feast of the year.

On the earth, the wrath of the King's judgment is poured forth on the wicked. Those who have sworn loyalty to the assailant, lifted up in their pride, gather together against the Prince. The adulteress, who has denied her fornication, will drink the cup of jealousy.

# THE INTERMEDIATE DAYS

In the chronology of the Feast Calendar, we have come to that period of inactivity in the Temple between the Day of Atonement and the Feast of Tabernacles. While these ceremonies are suspended, we see no further visions of the activities in the heavenlies. We do know that during this period in ancient Israel the people enjoyed the peace of knowing their sins were forgiven. Joyously they prepared for the Great Feast to come. Filled with the anticipation of the forthcoming celebration, they erected and decorated their booths with festive array. Perhaps these are the activities being enjoyed by the righteous in the heavenlies as John's vision focuses on the earth.

**Before you begin, read Revelation 16.**

## BOWLS OF WRATH

No longer does the call to repentance go forth upon the earth. Those who remain have been inscribed in the Book of the Wicked: the ones who have worshipped the beast and accepted his mark, the harlot who has refused to repent of her adulteries, the beasts and Satan whom they served. Let's look at their judgement.

The first bowl is poured out upon those with the mark of the beast and those who have worshipped his image and they are plagued with ugly and painful sores.

The second and third bowls turn the sea and waters to blood. The heavenly priest in charge of the waters provides commentary:

> Then I heard the angel in charge of the waters say: "You are just in these judgments, you who are and who were, the Holy One, because you have so judged; for they have shed the blood of your saints and prophets, and you have given them blood to drink as they deserve." Revelation 16:5-6

The fourth bowl is poured out and it is confirmed: there is no repentance in the heart of the wicked.

*They were seared by the intense heat and they cursed the name of God, who had control over these plagues, but they refused to repent and glorify him. Revelation 16:9*

The sixth bowl is poured out and the call goes out to gather for the final battle at Armageddon. And a warning for those of us reading this prophecy:

> *Therefore keep watch, because you do not know on what day your Lord will come. But understand this: If the owner of the house had known at what time of night the thief was coming, he would have kept watch and would not have let his house be broken into. So you also must be ready, because the Son of Man will come at an hour when you do not expect him. Matthew 24:42-44*

*"Behold, I come like a thief! Blessed is he who stays awake and keeps his clothes with him, so that he may not go naked and be shamefully exposed." Revelation 16:15*

Perhaps this alludes to the guards of the earthly Temple who served in the night watch. The head of the guards went about checking to see if each guard was awake. If he was found asleep, his garments were set on fire.

Paul, too, provides a warning:

> *But you, brothers, are not in darkness so that this day should surprise you like a thief. You are all sons of the light and sons of the day. We do not belong to the night or to the darkness. So then, let us not be like others, who are asleep, but let us be alert and self-controlled. For those who sleep, sleep at night, and those who get drunk, get drunk at night. But since we belong to the day, let us be self-controlled, putting on faith and love as a breastplate, and the hope of salvation as a helmet. For God did not appoint us to suffer wrath but to receive salvation through our Lord Jesus Christ. 1 Thessalonians 5:4-9*

As the seventh bowl is poured out it is declared, just as the priest declared at the completion of the sacrifice in the earthly Temple, *"It is done"*. With the pouring of the seventh bowl, the wrath of God will come to completion (Revelation 16:17b).

**Before you begin, read: Revelation 17-18.**

## THE HARLOT

Volumes have been written speculating on the identity of the Harlot. Our study has brought light to some of this mystery for as we saw in Revelation 11 she is a symbol of those who have not responded to the warning of the witnesses. She has not acknowledged her sin or her Messiah.

Let's look at the description of the Harlot or great prostitute:

A woman dressed in purple and scarlet, glittering with gold and precious jewels. On her forehead a title MYSTERY BABYLON THE GREAT THE MOTHER OF PROSTITUTES AND OF THE ABOMINATIONS OF THE EARTH. The interpretation of the symbolism is provided for us in the scripture:

> *The woman you saw is the great city that rules over the kings of the earth. Revelation 17:18*

The Harlot sits on a scarlet beast covered with blasphemous names having seven heads and ten horns. The symbolism of the beast is explained for us in Revelation 17:8-14 fulfilling the symbolism of the Beast out of the Sea as we saw earlier. The beast and the ten horns hate the prostitute and God will put it in their hearts to bring her to ruin.

In contrast to the woman, Jerusalem, who responds to the warning of the witnesses and embraces Jesus as Messiah, is the unrepentant Harlot, Jerusalem under the dominion of the Gentiles. She refuses to leave her adulteries. John is invited to see the details of her judgment at the pouring out of the seventh bowl.

### *Ordeal of Jealousy . . .*

A woman accused of adultery, who denies her guilt, is taken before the priest. In like manner, the Harlot in the book of Revelation is brought for judgment.

The cup of ordeal is given to her:

> *She held a golden cup in her hand, filled with abominable things and the filth of her adulteries. . . I saw that the woman was drunk with the blood of the saints, the blood of those who bore testimony to Jesus. When I saw her, I was greatly astonished. Revelation 17:4b,6*

The charges of adultery are read:

> *She has become a home for demons and a haunt for every evil spirit, a haunt for every unclean and detestable bird. For all the nations have drunk the maddening wine of her adulteries. The kings of the earth committed adultery with*

> *Nevertheless, I have this against you: You tolerate that woman Jezebel, who calls herself a prophetess. By her teaching she misleads my servants into sexual immorality and the eating of food sacrificed to idols. I have given her time to repent of her immorality, but she is unwilling. So I will cast her on a bed of suffering, and I will make those who commit adultery with her suffer intensely, unless they repent of her ways.*
> *Revelation 2:20-22*

Lock 5-3
Assailant
Page #148

> *See how the faithful city has become a harlot! She once was full of justice; righteousness used to dwell in her—but now murderers! Isaiah 1:21*

Lock 3-10
Repentance from
Adultery
Page #175

Lock 5-12
Ordeal of Jealousy
Page #172

Lock 2-18
Charge to Testify
Page #129

*her, and the merchants of the earth grew rich from her excessive luxuries. Revelation 18:2b-3*

She denies the charges:

> *In her heart she boasts, 'I sit as queen; I am not a widow, and I will never mourn.' Revelation 18:7b*

Her sentence is declared:

> *Give back to her as she has given; pay her back double for what she has done. Mix her a double portion from her own cup. Give her as much torture and grief as the glory and luxury she gave herself. Therefore in one day her plagues will overtake her: death, mourning and famine. She will be consumed by fire, for mighty is the Lord God who judges her. Revelation 18:6-7a, 8*

A mighty angel demonstrates that her destruction is much like the violence of the adulteress that is stoned:

> *Woe! Woe, O great city, where all who had ships on the sea became rich through her wealth! In one hour she has been brought to ruin! Revelation 18:19b*

> *Then a mighty angel picked up a boulder the size of a large millstone and threw it into the sea, and said: "With such violence the great city of Babylon will be thrown down, never to be found again. Revelation 18:21*

And a warning for those of us reading this prophecy:

> *Then I heard another voice from heaven say: "Come out of her, my people, so that you will not share in her sins, so that you will not receive any of her plagues; ... Revelation 18:4*

*You say, 'I am rich; I have acquired wealth and do not need a thing.' But you do not realize that you are wretched, pitiful, poor, blind and naked. Revelation 3:17*

The last harvest of the year has been gathered. It is a bountiful one for the King's judgments are true and righteous. A great multitude has assembled in the heavenly Temple to celebrate the final and most joyous feast of the year.

The Temple ceremonies of the coronation are completed. The Prince of the Household has been baptized, anointed and acknowledged as perfect. He has endured humili-ation among His people and a time of hiddenness.

Now a great multitude send Him forth amid shouts of praise to claim His kingdom by defeating those who have risen against Him. He will temporarily take His throne of government and administer His duties among the nations. They will appear before Him and the King will nourish and instruct them.

The usurper will be released to test those who have come to know the King, that they might choose whom they will serve.

Assuming His throne of judgement for the last time, all creation will pass before Him.

# THE FEAST OF TABERNACLES

**Before you begin, read:  Revelation 19-20:3.**

Lock 3-6
Hallel
Page #90

At the completion of the judgment of the Harlot, we are again returned to the heavenly Temple where a great multitude are shouting Hallelujahs.  This would indicate to us that the Feast of Tabernacles has begun, for such Hallelujahs were not a part of the Day of Trumpets or the Day of Atonement.

Lock 4-16
Hosanna Prayers
Page #90

The Hallelujahs are followed by an announcement that the wedding preparations are complete.  The bride has made herself ready:

> *Husbands, love your wives, just as Christ loved the church and gave himself up for her to make her holy, cleansing her by the washing with water through the word, and to present her to himself as a radiant church, without stain or wrinkle or any other blemish, but holy and blameless. Ephesians 5:25-27*

*Let us rejoice and be glad and give him glory!  For the wedding of the Lamb has come, and his bride has made herself ready.  Fine linen, bright and clean, was given her to wear." (Fine linen stands for the righteous acts of the saints.)  Revelation 19:7-8*

The invitations to come to the wedding supper are written:

> *Then the angel said to me, "Write: 'Blessed are those who are invited to the wedding supper of the Lamb!'  And he added, "These are the true words of God." Revelation 19:9*

## PRINCE VS ASSAILANT

*For I tell you, you will not see me again until you say, 'Blessed is he who comes in the name of the Lord.' Matthew 23:39*

### *Assuming the Throne . . .*
As Messiah, the King and Bridegroom ride forth from the heavenly Temple, He bears the symbols of His authority:  crowns, a kingly robe, a sword, and a scepter.  Beside Him are His armies who have sworn their allegiance.  He bears many names which attest to His attributes, authority and conquests.  The coronation ceremonies begun in the heavenly Temple now move to the Palace.  At this time the King takes His place to govern the people.

Lock 6-8
Palace Ceremony
Page #181

> *I saw heaven standing open and there before me was a white horse whose rider is called Faithful and True.  With justice*

*he judges and makes war. His eyes are like blazing fire, and on his head are many crowns. He has a name written on him that no one knows but he himself. He is dressed in a robe dipped in blood, and his name is the Word of God. The armies of heaven were following him, riding on white horses and dressed in fine linen, white and clean. Out of his mouth comes a sharp sword with which to strike down the nations. He will rule them with an iron scepter. He treads the winepress of the fury of the wrath of God Almighty. On his robe and on his thigh he has this name written: KING OF KINGS AND LORD OF LORDS. Revelation 19:11-16*

Lock 2-7
White Garments
Page #164

Lock 6-4
Names of the King
Page #148

Lock 3-4
Processions
Page #150

Lock 5-3
Assailant
Page #185

### Reclaiming His Inheritance . . .

Previously, we laid out the principles by which a household or kingdom could be usurped by an assailant. In Isaiah, God describes Satan as one who covets the rule of God's Kingdom.

*How you have fallen from heaven, O morning star, son of the dawn! You have been cast down to the earth, you who once laid low the nations! You said in your heart, "I will ascend to heaven; I will raise my throne above the stars of God: I will sit enthroned on the mount of assembly on the utmost heights of the sacred mountain. I will ascend above the tops of the clouds; I will make myself like the Most High." Isaiah 14:12-14*

Certain protocol governed the means by which the son of the household could challenge the assailant and regain his inheritance. Before the Prince can take His throne, He must face those gathered for battle who have challenged His kingship.

Lock 5-5
Prince of the
Household
Page #161

*And I saw an angel standing in the sun, who cried in a loud voice to all the birds flying in midair, "Come, gather together for the great supper of God, so that you may eat the flesh of kings, generals, and mighty men, of horses and their riders, and the flesh of all people, free and slave, small and great." Then I saw the beast and the kings of the earth and their armies gathered together to make war against the rider on the horse and his army. Revelation 19:17-19*

> *But that day belongs to the Lord, the Lord Almighty—a day of vengeance for vengeance on his foes. The sword will devour till it is satisfied, till it has quenched its thirst with blood. For the Lord, the Lord Almighty, will offer sacrifice in the land of the north by the River Euphrates. Jeremiah 46:10*

Ezekiel offers us insights into this battle:

*Son of man, this is what the Sovereign Lord says: Call out to every kind of bird, and all the wild animals: 'Assemble and come together from all around to the sacrifice I am preparing for you, the great sacrifice on the mountains of Israel. There you will eat flesh and drink blood. You will eat the flesh of mighty men and drink the blood of the princes of the earth as if they were rams and lambs, goats and bulls—all of them fattened animals from Bashan. At the sacrifice I am preparing for you, you will eat fat till you are glutted and drink blood till you are drunk. Ezekiel 39:17-19*

Lock 6-3
Battles with
Enemies
Page #161

The battle is a quick and decisive victory, the King has proved His ability and right to reign. The 'sons of the assailant' are destroyed and the assailant (Satan) imprisoned.

Lock 5-4
Ransom
Page #176

*But the beast was captured, and with him the false prophet who had performed the miraculous signs on his behalf. With these signs he had deluded those who had worshiped his image. The two of them were thrown alive into the fiery lake of burning sulfur. The rest of them were killed with the sword that came out of the mouth of the rider on the horse, and all the birds gorged themselves on their flesh. And I saw an angel coming down out of heaven, having the key to the Abyss and holding in his hand a great chain. He seized the dragon, that ancient serpent, who is the devil, or Satan, and bound him for a thousand years. Revelation 19:20-20:2*

Lock 5-5
Prince of
Household
Page #161

By means of this battle, the Prince of the household reclaims the inheritance. He has demonstrated his ability to rule. He assumes a temporary throne to reign a thousand years among the nations.

*There remains, then, a Sabbath-rest for the people of God; Hebrews 4:9*

**Before you begin, read: Revelation 20:4-15.**

Lock 1-7
Redemptive Week
Page #189

## THE MILLENNIAL REIGN

### Feast of Nations . . .

In a few short verses a period known as the Millennial Age is described. Those who have not worshipped the beast and have died because of the testimony of Jesus come to life to reign with him and serve as priests. This is the first resurrection.

> To him who overcomes and does my will to the end, I will give authority over the nations—'He will rule them with an iron scepter; he will dash them to pieces like pottery'—just as I have received authority from my Father. Revelation 2:26-27
>
> To him who overcomes, I will give the right to sit with me on my throne, just as I overcame and sat down with my Father on his throne. Revelation 3:21

*I saw thrones on which were seated those who had been given authority to judge. And I saw the souls of those who had*

*been beheaded because of their testimony for Jesus and because of the word of God. They had not worshipped the beast or his image and had not received his mark on their foreheads or their hands. They came to life and reigned with Christ a thousand years. (The rest of the dead did not come to life until the thousand years were ended.) This is the first resurrection. Blessed and holy are those who have part in the first resurrection. The second death has no power over them, but they will be priests of God and of Christ and will reign with him for a thousand years.*
*Revelation 20:4-6*

Lock 5-11
Adoption
Page #177

The awe filled days of judgment and wrath behind, the King begins His reign of peace and joy. Much like a midwife, it is the king's duty to draw the kingdom from chaos into order. To this end He will take up residence among His subjects, a temporary dwelling place, as the new heaven and earth is awaited.

This period will be a time of rest, a rejoicing in the harvest that has been gathered. Zechariah provides us with insight into the period of this millennial reign of Jesus:

Lock 1-7
Redemptive Week
Page #190

> *Then the survivors from all the nations that have attacked Jerusalem will go up year after year to worship the King, the Lord Almighty, and to celebrate the Feast of Tabernacles. If any of the peoples of the earth do not go up to Jerusalem to worship the King, the Lord Almighty, they will have no rain. If the Egyptian people do not go up and take part, they will have no rain. The Lord will bring on them the plague he inflicts on the nations that do not go up to celebrate the Feast of Tabernacles. Zechariah 14:16-18*

Isaiah describes the Messianic Age as a time when " . . . *the earth will be full of the knowledge of the Lord as the waters cover the sea." Isaiah 11:9b*

If the course of this millennial celebration of the Feast of Tabernacles is like that established in the earlier Temples of Jerusalem, it will be full of instruction for the nations that go up to celebrate there. For the sacrifices of this feast will demonstrate to them that atonement for them was a part of God's plan of redemption from the beginning. Through the shaking of the lulav they will acknowledge His victory over them and His right to reign. The King will instruct them from the Word as was the custom in a sabbatical year. The symbolic elements of the Feast of Tabernacles ceremonies will point them to the hope of the Wedding of the Lamb yet to be fulfilled.

Lock 3-1
Rehearsal
Page #168

Lock 4-15
Lulav
Page #143

Lock 4-1
Book of Covenant
Page #176

Lock 4-13
Feast of Nations
Page #162

Isaiah speaks of the Lord instructing the people in the Law during His millennial reign:

*And this gospel of the kingdom will be preached in the whole world as a testimony to all nations, and then the end will come. Matthew 24:14*

> *In the last days the mountain of the Lord's temple will be established as chief among the mountains; it will be raised above the hills, and all nations will stream to it. Many peoples will come and say, "Come, let us go up to the mountain of the Lord, to the house of the God of Jacob. He will teach us his ways, so that we may walk in his paths." The law will go out from Zion, the word of the Lord from Jerusalem. He will judge between the nations and will settle disputes for many peoples. They will beat their swords into plowshares and their spears into pruning hooks. Nation will not take up sword against nation, nor will they train for war anymore. Isaiah 2:2-4*

Given this knowledge of God's purpose, the nations are given an opportunity to accept or reject their Bridegroom and King.

> *Jesus spoke to them again in parables, saying: The kingdom of heaven is like a king who prepared a wedding banquet for his son. He sent his servants to those who had been invited to the banquet to tell them to come, but they refused to come. Then he sent some more servants and said, 'Tell those who have been invited that I have prepared my dinner: My oxen and fattened cattle have been butchered, and everything is ready. Come to the wedding banquet.' But they paid no attention and went off—one to his field, another to his business. The rest seized his servants, mistreated them and killed them. The king was enraged. He sent his army and destroyed those murderers and burned their city. Then he said to his servants, 'The wedding banquet is ready, but those I invited did not deserve to come. Go to the street corners and invite to the banquet anyone you find.' So the servants went out into the streets and gathered all the people they could find, both good and bad, and the wedding hall was filled with guests. But when the king came in to see the guests, he noticed a man there who was not wearing wedding clothes. 'Friend,' he asked, 'how did you get in here without wedding clothes?' The man was speechless. Then the king told the attendants, 'Tie him hand and foot, and throw him outside, into the darkness, where there will be weeping and gnashing of teeth.' For many are invited, but few are chosen. Matthew 22:1-14*

### Destroying the Assailant . . .
It is not so strange in the light of our study to see, at the end of

the thousand years, Satan released again to deceive the nations. The protocol of the assailant and son of the household provides that the son must kill the assailant while the usurper is in the act of exercising his power over his seized dominion.

Lock 5-3
Assailant
Page #189

Lock 6-3
Battles With
Enemies
Page #190

> *When the thousand years are over, Satan will be released from his prison and will go out to deceive the nations in the four corners of the earth—Gog and Magog—to gather them for battle. In number they are like the sand on the seashore. They marched across the breadth of the earth and surrounded the camp of God's people, the city he loves. Revelation 20:7-9a*

The Prince of the Household, the King of Kings, completes His victory destroying the assailant and the final enemy 'death'.

> *I will ransom them from the power of the grave; I redeem them from death. Where, O death, are your plagues? Where, O grave, is your destruction? Hosea 13:14*

### The Last Day. . .
According to Jewish tradition, the last day of the Feast of Tabernacles represents the final judgment when all the world's inhabitants pass before the judgment seat. Any sealing unto salvation which occurs now is an act of the Lord's mercy. In John's account we see this final sealing.

Lock 4-4
3 Books
Page #180

The Father's kingdom purged of all enemies, the King assumes His throne to make final judgment. For the last time the books are opened. The resurrection begun at the opening of the Millennial Age will now be completed.

Lock 5-5
Prince of the
Household
Page #190

Lock 3-7
Concluding Day
Page #98

Lock 4-3
Door/Gates
Opened
Page #173

> *Then I saw a great white throne and him who was seated on it. Earth and sky fled from his presence, and there was no place for them. And I saw the dead, great and small, standing before the throne, and books were opened. Another book was opened, which is the book of life. The dead were judged according to what they had done as recorded in the books. The sea gave up the dead that were in it, and death and Hades gave up the dead that were in them, and each person was judged according to what he had done. Then death and Hades were thrown into the lake of fire. The lake of fire is the second death. If anyone's name was not found written in the book of life he was thrown into the lake of fire. Revelation 20:11-15*

> *When the Son of Man comes in his glory, and all the angels with him, he will sit on his throne in heavenly glory. All the nations will be gathered before him, and he will separate the people one from another as a shepherd separates the sheep from the goats. He will put the sheep on his right and the goats on his left. Matthew 25:31-33*

This concept of a continued harvest can also be confirmed in the prophetic symbolism of the Feast rituals regarding the Firstfruits. The Law provides that the offerings of the harvest could be brought during the whole period from Pentecost through the Feast of Tabernacles.

Jesus may have also offered a parable that sheds light on this thinking, that the Lord's mercy is offered until the last hour:

> *For the kingdom of heaven is like a landowner who went out early in the morning to hire men to work in his vineyard. He agreed to pay them a denarius for the day and sent them into his vineyard. About the third hour he went out and saw others standing in the marketplace doing nothing. He told them. 'You also go and work in my vineyard, and I will pay you whatever is right.' So they went. He went out again about the sixth hour and the ninth hour and did the same thing. About the eleventh hour he went out and found still others standing around. He asked them, 'Why have you been standing here all day long doing nothing?' 'Because no one has hired us,' they answered. He said to them, 'You also go and work in my vineyard.' When evening came, the owner of the vineyard said to his foreman, 'Call the workers and pay them their wages, beginning with the last ones hired and going on to the first.' The workers who were hired about the eleventh hour came and each received a denarius. So when those came who were hired first, they expected to receive more, but each one of them also received a denarius. When they received it, they began to grumble against the landowner. 'These men who were hired last worked only one hour,' they said, 'and you have made them equal to us who have borne the burden of the work and the heat of the day.' But he answered one of them, 'Friend, I am not being unfair to you. Didn't you agree to work for a denarius? Take your pay and go. I want to give the man who was hired last the same as I gave you. Don't I have the right to do what I want with my own money? Or are you envious because I am generous? So the last will be first, and the first will be last. Matthew 20:1-16*

*Heaven and earth have passed away and with it the measure of time they framed.*

*A new heaven and a new earth fill the void.  There is no need of sun or moon for eternity is without measure and all is lit with the glory of God and the Lamb.*

*The Holy City, the wedding chamber prepared and adorned by the Father with His glory, descends from heaven.*

*She who is undefiled, prepared and clothed in the beauty of righteousness receives her bridegroom.  The wedding contract is given to her and the blessings recited.  The bride enters the wedding chamber led by her beloved husband.  Her desire is for Him alone.*

*As they are joined as one, from the throne flows rivers of living water and the tree of life flourishes, symbols of a fruitful and prosperous union.*

# THE 8TH DAY
# MARRIAGE OF THE LAMB

At dawn of the 8th Day the final judgment is complete. With this day the prophetic Fall Feasts are concluded. It is a day considered to mark a day 'after time'. The readings from the Torah are completed. On this day the sacrifices symbolize a time of intimate communion. Jewish tradition regards this day as the time when God and His beloved people have an intimate light meal together alone. When the bride and groom retired to their earthly wedding chamber for the consummation, they broke their fast and had a small meal together. Rabbi Eleazer gives this interpretation of the 8th Day offering:

> *58. Rabbi Eleazer said: To what do the seventy bullocks [that were offered during the seven days of Sukkot] correspond? To the seventy nations [of the earth]. To what does the single bullock [offered on the Eighth Day Festival— Shemini Atzeret] correspond? To the unique nation [-Israel]. A parable of a king of flesh and blood who [for seven days] said to his servants, "Prepare a great feast for me." Then on the eighth day he said to the special friend who loved him, "Prepare a simple meal for me, that I may have the pleasure of your company."*[3]

**Before you begin, read: Revelation 21-22:5.**

> *I tell you the truth, until heaven and earth disappear, not the smallest letter, not the least stroke of a pen, will by any means disappear from the Law until everything is accomplished. Matthew 5:18*

## THE MARRIAGE

While the Son was completing His victory against the assailant, the wedding preparations were completed and the guests assembled.

### The Marriage Contract . . .

Just as a contract of marriage is presented to a Jewish bride, the Bridegroom provides a contract for His bride. For he may not live together with her until the marriage contract is written and delivered to the bride:

*He who was seated on the throne said, "I am making every-thing new!" Then he said, "Write this down, for these words are trustworthy and true." Revelation 21:5*

Her nurture and pleasure are promised:

*He will wipe every tear from their eyes. There will be no more death or mourning or crying or pain, for the old order of things has passed away. . . He said to me: "It is done. I am the Alpha and the Omega, the Beginning and the End, To him who is thirsty I will give to drink without cost from the spring of the water of life. Revelation 21:4 & 6*

The brides inheritance is described:

*He who overcomes will inherit all this, and I will be his God and he will be my son. Revelation 21:7*

And finally her protection is provided:

*But the cowardly, the unbelieving, the vile, the murderers, the sexually immoral, those who practice magic arts, the idolaters and all liars—their place will be in the fiery lake of burning sulfur. This is the second death. Revelation 21:8*

Only now may the Bridegroom come together with His bride:

*And I heard a loud voice from the throne saying, "Now the dwelling of God is with men, and he will live with them. They will be his people, and God himself will be with them and be their God. Revelation 21:3*

### The Wedding Chamber . . .

The bride and groom retire to the wedding chamber after the wedding to consummate their marriage. The earthly *chuppah* was made by the father of the bridegroom and was beautifully adorned and outfitted with every comfort.

*For he was looking forward to the city with foundations, whose architect and builder is God. . . Instead, they were longing for a better country—a heavenly one. Therefore God is not ashamed to be called their God, for he has prepared a city for them. Hebrews 11:10, 16*

*For here we do not have an enduring city, but we are looking for the city that is to come. Hebrews 13:14*

The Holy City, the New Jerusalem, is introduced by 'coming down out of heaven from God'. This city having been prepared

Lock 4-1
Book of Covenant
Page #191

Lock 5-1
Father of
Household
Page #145

*Him who overcomes I will make a pillar in the temple of my God. Never again will he leave it. I will write on him the name of my God and the name of the city of my God, the new Jerusalem, which is coming down out of heaven from my God; and I will also write on him my new name. Revelation 3:12*

Lock 5-8
Bridegroom
Page #196

Lock 5-1
Father of
Household
Page #145

by the heavenly Father is compared to the way a bride would be dressed for a wedding.

> *I saw the Holy City, the New Jerusalem coming down out of heaven from God, prepared as a bride beautifully dressed for her husband. Revelation 21:2*

Revelation 21:9-27 gives us the description of the New Jerusalem, that Holy City that represents the wedding chamber. It has high walls and shines brilliantly like a jewel. There are twelve gates made of pearls opening on four sides like the wedding canopy and the tent of Abraham. There is no Temple because God and the Lamb are the Temple. It does not need the sun or moon because God's glory gives it light and the Lamb is its lamp. Nothing impure will be allowed into it; only those who have overcome and are found written in the Lamb's Book of Life.

Lock 4-18
Wedding Chamber
Page #117

Again the city is measured, not with a rod of judgment, but with a golden rod of purity. The New Jerusalem is foursquare just like the Holy of Holies and the symbolic wedding chamber:

Lock 2-4
Holy of Holies
Page #169

> *The city was laid out like a square, as long as it was wide. He measured the city with the rod and found it to be 12,000 stadia in length, and as wide and high as it is long. Revelation 21:16*

> *You are the most excellent of men and your lips have been anointed with grace, since God has blessed you forever. Gird your sword upon your side, O mighty one; clothe yourself with splendor and majesty. In your majesty ride forth victoriously in behalf of truth, humility and righteousness; let your right hand display awesome deeds. Let your sharp arrows pierce the hearts of the king's enemies; let the nations fall beneath your feet. Your throne, O God, will last for ever and ever; a scepter of justice will be the scepter of your kingdom. You love righteousness and hate wickedness; therefore God, your God, has set you above your companions by anointing you with the oil of joy. All your robes are fragrant with myrrh and aloes and cassia; from palaces adorned with ivory and music of the strings makes you glad. Daughters of kings are among your honored women; at your right hand is the royal bride in gold of Ophir. Listen, O daughter, consider and give ear: Forget your people and your father's house. The king is enthralled by your beauty; honor him, for he is your lord. The Daughter of Tyre will*

*come with a gift, men of wealth will seek your favor. All glorious is the princess within her chamber; her gown is interwoven with gold. In embroidered garments she is led to the king; her virgin companions follow her and are brought to you. They are led in with joy and gladness; they enter the palace of the king. Your sons will take the place of your father; you will make them princes throughout the land. I will perpetuate your memory through all generations; therefore the nations will praise you for ever and ever. Psalms 45:2-17*

### The Consummation . . .

The wedding ceremony complete, those who are overcomers and written in the Lamb's Book of Life (bride) and the Bridegroom (Jesus the King) may dwell together, becoming one.

> *He who has an ear, let him hear what the Spirit says to the churches. To him who overcomes, I will give some of the hidden manna. I will also give him a white stone with a new name written on it, known only to him who receives it. Revelation 2:17*

Lock 5-6
Consummation
Page #145

Lock 4-14
Living Water
Page #98

Lock 4-20
Late to the
Banquet
Page #139

> *On that day living water will flow out from Jerusalem, half to the eastern sea and half to the western sea, in summer and in winter. Zechariah 14:8*

From the throne the water of life flows, symbolic of the new life that is created between a husband and wife. The marriage is consummated for the bride sees her husband face to face—a symbol of intimacy. She will now receive His name.

*They will see his face, and his name will be on their foreheads. Revelation 22:4*

*Now we see but a poor reflection as in a mirror; then we shall see face to face. Now I know in part; then I shall know fully, even as I am fully known. I Corinthians 13:12*

The word 'knowing', in Hebrew Yada, is sometimes used to describe sexual intimacy, i.e., in Genesis 4:1-Adam knew his wife [KJV]. The sexual encounter produces an intimate 'knowledge' of the other. This knowledge comes from the inside—the mystery of the other.

### Tree of Life . . .

The health and prosperity of the Bride and Bridegroom's union

Lock 4-19
Tree of Life
Page #143

is symbolized by the flourishing Tree of Life. That union, in turn, demonstrates a thriving kingdom.

> *He who has an ear, let him hear what the Spirit says to the churches. To him who overcomes, I will give the right to eat from the tree of life, which is in the paradise of God. Revelation 2:7*

*On each side of the river stood the tree of life, bearing twelve crops of fruit, yielding its fruit every month. And the leaves of the tree are for the heal-*

*ing of the nations. . . There will be no more night. They will not need the light of a lamp or the light of the sun, for the Lord God will give them light. And they will reign for ever and ever. Revelation 22:2b & 5*

With his victory complete and the household restored, the Son subjects himself to the Father that the Father may be all in all.

*But each in his own turn: Christ, the firstfruits; then, when he comes, those who belong to him. Then the end will come, when he hands over the kingdom to God the Father after he has destroyed all dominion, authority and power. For he must reign until he has put all his enemies under his feet. The last enemy to be destroyed is death. For he "has put everything under his feet." Now when it says that "everything" has been put under him, it is clear that this does not include God himself, who put everything under Christ. When he has done this, then the Son himself will be made subject to him who put everything under him, so that God may be all in all. I Corinthians 15:23-28*

Lock 5-1
Father of the
Household
Page #197

## THE BANQUET

According to custom, the bride and bridegroom join their wedding guests for a great feast, following their intimate communion.

Remember our promise in the introduction to answer the questions: "Why the lake of fire?" and "What's being served at the Wedding Supper of the Lamb?" The following legend is told to the Jewish children in connection with the Feast of Tabernacles. It attempts to draw a vivid picture for them of when the Messiah will arrive, the time of eternal bliss on earth. We offer it for your enjoyment. Its theme is developed out of Isaiah's account of Israel's future deliverance in:

*In that day, the Lord will punish with his sword, his fierce, great and powerful sword, Leviathan the gliding serpent, Leviathan the coiling serpent; he will slay the monster of the sea. Isaiah 27:1*

The story sets a stage of excitement as all the children look forward to the Feast:

*Their thoughts are carried still farther afield when the teacher recites, or rather sings, as he interprets Akdomus. King David descended from Ruth and Boaz, and from David's seed, it is believed, will come the Messiah.*

*They see the golden thrones, approached by seven stairs; seated on the thrones are the saints, gleaming and shining like the stars of heaven. Above them are spread canopies of light, and below ripple streams of fragrant balsam. There is no end to the joy and happiness of the saints. They dance in Paradise, arm-in-arm with God himself; He entertains them with a mammoth spectacle, arranged especially for them, the combat between the Leviathan and the Behemoth.*

Lock 4-17
Leviathan
Page #91

*So enthusiastic does the teacher become at this point that his imagination expands and grows, and he paints a picture of the two fantastic creatures that is so clear, one would think he had seen them himself. The Leviathan, he says, encircles the sea that surrounds the world. He lies coiled up, with his tail in his mouth; should he, for one moment, release his tail, then the doom of the world would come. Just as great and fearful is the Behemoth. He eats, in one day, the pasturage on a thousand hills; and when he is thirsty, all the water that flows from the Jordan into the sea makes just one gulp for him.*

> *It was you who split open the sea by your power; you broke the heads of the monster in the waters. It was you who crushed the heads of Leviathan and gave him as food to the creatures of the desert. Psalms 74:13-14*

*The teacher tells of the feast which God will prepare after the coming of the Messiah, and his imagination makes it more vivid and colorful even than its description in Akdomus. He pictures the saints seated around a table made of precious stones, eating the flesh of the Leviathan and the Behemoth. But the feasting does not interest the listening children. Their thoughts recur to the combat between the two monsters; they see the monster of the deep giving mighty blows with his powerful fins, while the Behemoth again and again gores his rival with his gigantic horns.[4]*

## IN CONCLUSION

So we've come to it—the conclusion we promised not to make, the answers we promised not to give. But we have sorted some apples and oranges for you! We hope you'll enjoy using your keys to unlock even more end times prophecies through the Feasts of the Lord.

You may have been frustrated in this final chapter that we disposed of the Beasts, the Great Tribulation and the Wrath of God in a few simple paragraphs. Certainly a library full of volumes have been written on these subjects, which we have so conveniently ignored. But while arguments about the timing and means of our rapture  and the 'true' identity of the beast have been the main focus of most studies, the glorious message of the book of Revelation has been largely ignored. Proof of this is found in the attitude of dread and confusion with which Christians approach this book.  We have endeavored to restore the glorious joy of this message and its Jewish roots.  The judgment of the Lord is tempered with patience and mercy. For it is His desire that none perish but all be brought to repentance and the joy of knowing him face to face.

> *The river of life . . . flows from birth toward death. Day follows day with wearisome monotony.  Only the holidays twine themselves together to form the circle of the year.  Only through the holidays does life experience the eternity of the river that returns to its source.  Then life becomes eternal.*
>                                             *-Franz Rosenezweig*

# APPENDIX F
# FALL FEAST DAYS COMPARISON CHART

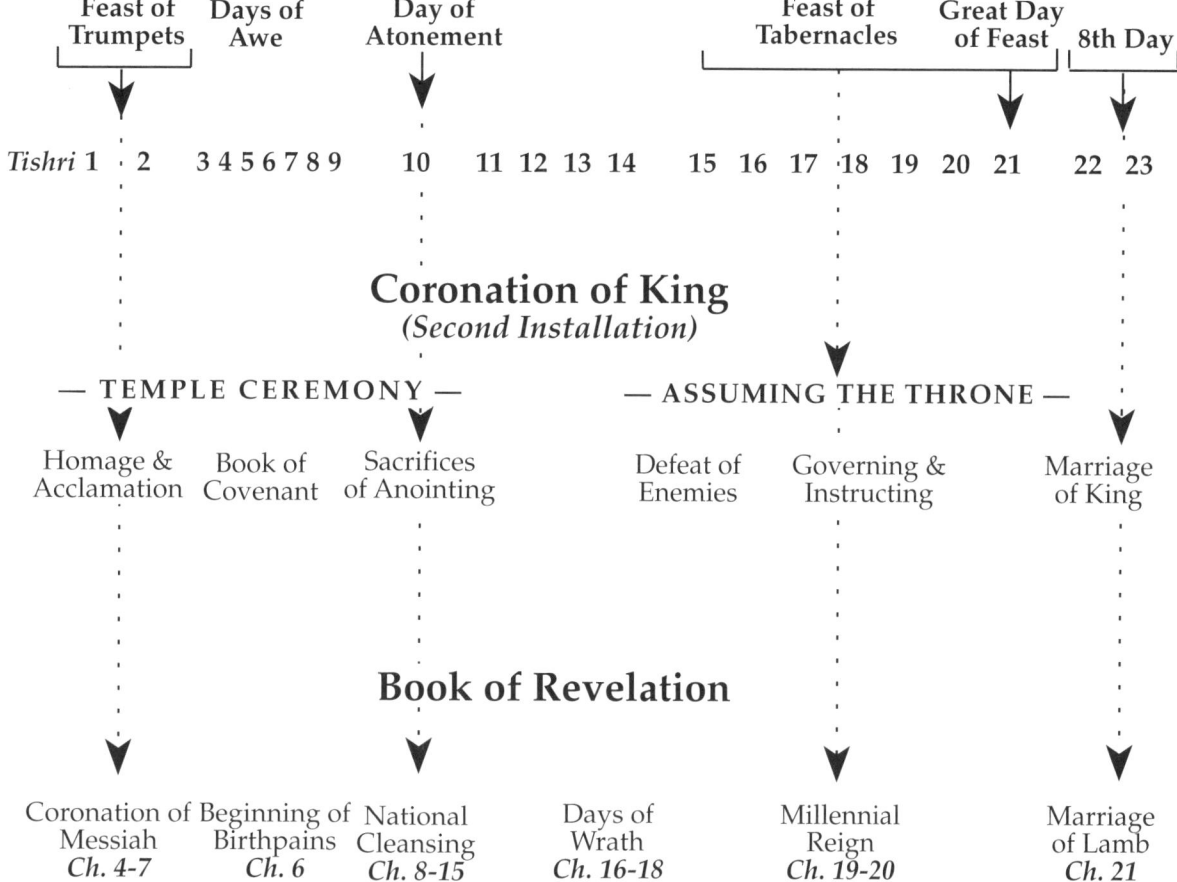

# EPILOGUE

About four years ago, I had the opportunity to share the substance of this study with my students at the New Life Bible School in Daugavpils, Latvia. During the last week of our lessons Marina Trunova, my translator, shared with me that a prominent leader of Latvia had issued, that week, an announcement asking forgiveness from Israel for the atrocities committed against the Jewish people in Latvia during the Second World War. It was quite significant to her in view of our study on national repentance.

A short time later, Marina and I had the privilege of attending a prayer conference in Budapest, Hungary attended by 27 nations. Again we observed a phenomenon significant to us; representatives of nations repenting and forgiving one another for sins committed in the present and the past.

From that momentum, individuals came before the conference confessing the sins of ancestors in the persecutions of Jews and political enemies. In response, descendants of the persecuted came forward and forgave on behalf of their nations and loved ones. Representatives of church denominations repented and forgave the persecutions of church against church and tears flowed freely. Many told of events planned in their countries that added actions to their words of repentance.

I returned to the United States and within weeks heard of a church denomination issuing a plea for forgiveness of their policies of segregation in the South. I continued to receive word from international contacts that the spirit of repentance was moving in many areas of the globe at all levels from national to personal.

As we have completed the work on this text, we have observed nations asking forgiveness for historical acts of war, churches issuing confessions of wrong doing, church leaders publicly repenting of sins, and individuals seeking reconciliation. All the while we have observed that these are not *apologies* being made, meaningless phrases of "I'm sorry", but the powerful spiritual words of "Please forgive."

These observations along with so many other significant ful-
fillments of End Times prophecies, have served to convince
us that truly the Summer Months are coming to a close and
the time for the Fall Harvest is upon us.

M. Mineer

# ENDNOTES

**INTRODUCTION**
[1]*Rosh HaShanah & The Messianic Kingdom to Come,* by Joseph Good, p. 17

**CHAPTER 1 - THE SACRED CALENDAR**
[1] *The Book of Our Heritage, Vol. 1,* by Eliyahu Kitov, p. 233-234
[2] Ibid., p. 234-235

**CHAPTER 2 - TABERNACLE OF MOSES**
[1]*The Chumash* by Rabbi Nosson Scherman, p. 475
[2]*The Temple Its Ministry and Services* by Alfred Edersheim, p. 184
[3] Ibid., p.184

**CHAPTER 3 - THE SPRING FEASTS**
[1]*The Seven Festivals of the Messiah* by Edward Chumney, p. 5
[2]*The Book of Our Heritage, Vol. 2,* by Eliyahu Kitov, pg. 209
[3]Ibid., p. 222
[4]*The Book of Our Heritage, Vol. 2,* by Eliyahu Kitov, p. 236-239
[5]Ibid., p. 173
[6]Ibid., p. 177
[7]Ibid., p. 167 & 169
[8]*The Book of Legends Sefer Ha-Aggadah,* Edited by Hayim Nahman Bialik and Yehoshua Hana
  Ravnitzky, p. 176
[9]Ibid., pg. 177-178
[10]*Days of Awe,* by S. Y. Agnon, p. 139-140

**CHAPTER 4 - THE FALL FEASTS**
[1]*The Book of Our Heritage, Vol. 1,* by Eliyahu Kitov, p. 19
[2]The Torah - A Modern Commentary, Edited by W. Gunther Plaut p. 934
[3]Ibid, p. 934
[4]*The Days of Awe,* by S. Y. Agnon, p. xvi
[5]*The Temple,* by Alfred Edersheim, p. 250
[6]Ibid, pg. 253
[7]*Mishnah, Taanith 4:8,* p. 200-201
[8] *The Book of Our Heritage, Vol. 1,* by Eliyahu Kitov, p. 159
[9]Ibid, p. 184-185
[10]*The Book of Legends Sefer Ha-Aggadah,* Edited by Hayim Nahman Bialik and Yehoshua Hana
  Ravnitzky, p. 183-184
[11]*The Jewish Festivals, History & Observance,* by Hayyim Schauss, p. 183-184
[12]*The Book of Our Heritage, Vol. 1,* by Eliyahu Kitov,  p. 204-205
[13] Ibid., p. 208
[14] *Hebrew Installation Rites,* Hebrew Union College Annual 20 (1947), Hebrew Union College:
  Cincinnati, Ohio., p. 137
[15]*The Book of Our Heritage, Vol. 1.* by Eliyahu Kitov, p. 159
[16]*The Book of Our Heritage, Vol. 1,* by Eliyahu Kitov, p. 218-219
[17] Ibid, p. 218-219
[18] Ibid, p. 220

### CHAPTER 5 - MARRIAGE & DIVORCE

[1] Tetragrammaton is the Hebrew word for God that consists of the four letters *yod, he, vav, and he*, that is transliterated consonantally usually as YHVH.

[2] *Love, Marriage, and Family in Jewish Law and Tradition* by Michael Kaufman, p. 123

[3] *Social World of Ancient Israel 1250-587 BCE,* by Victor H. Matthews & Don C. Benjamin, 1993, p. 178

[4] *Rosh HaShanah and the Messianic Kingdom to Come,* by Joseph Good, p. 149

[5] *The Mishnah*, Sotah ('The Suspected Adulteress') 2:4, by Herbert Danby, D.D., p. 295

### CHAPTER 6 KINGSHIP

[1] *Hebrew Installation Rites*, Hebrew Union College Annual 20 (1947), Hebrew Union College: Cincinnati, Ohio., p. 137

### CHAPTER 7 REVELATION

[1] *Rosh Ha Shanah and the Messianic Kingdom to Come*, by Joseph Good, p. 121

[2] Refer to Appendix A - Binding of Isaac

[3] *The Book of Legends Sefer Ha-Aggadah*, Edited by Hayim Nahman Bialik and Yehoshua Hana Ravnitzky, p. 173

[4] *The Jewish Festivals, History & Observance*, by Hayyim Schauss, p. 91-92

### APPENDIX C - THE AZAZEL GOAT

[1] *The Torah, A Modern Commentary*, Edited by W. Gunther Plaut, p. 859

# GLOSSARY

**Apocrypha**  A collection of religious writings not included in Hebrew Scriptures.

**Atzeret**  Derived from gathering or detention.  A festive gathering for the concluding day of a festive season.

**Azazel**  See Appendix C.

**Beth Ha She'Ubah**  Place or act of water drawing.

**Chametz**  Food that has been prepared with leaven; refers to all foods and utensils forbidden on Passover.  Also spelled *hametz*.

**Chuppah**  The Hebrew word for the canopy under which a pair stand at the wedding ceremony; symbolizes the home to be established and represents the wedding chamber.  Also spelled *huppah*.

**Cohen pl. Cohanim**  Hebrew word for a priest, descendant of Aaron.

**Erusin**  Hebrew word for betrothal; the formal engagement ceremony before a marriage; requires a bill of divorcement to annul.

**Etrog**  Citron fruit; part of the lulav used during Feast of Tabernacles.

**Get**  Hebrew word for a Jewish bill of divorcement.

**Haftorah (Haftarah)**  A selection read from the Prophets or chanted after the weekly Torah readings during Sabbath and holiday services.

**Hallel**  Special psalms of praise that are sung or recited during festivals.  Ps. 113-188.

**Hev Lo shel Mischeac**  Birth of Messiah into the world.

**Hev Le She Misheac**  People born into the Messiah during Day of Lord and birthpains.

**High Holy Days**  A ten day period from Feast of Trumpets to Day of Atonement.  Also known as the Days of Awe.

**Kabalah**  Mystic lore and esoteric teachings of Jewish tradition based on cosmology of divine emanations and secret names of God.  Also spelled kabbalah.

**Kedushin**  The Hebrew word for the wedding ceremony.

**Ketubah**  The written marriage contract that dealt with the duties of a wife and husband, provisions and obligations to his wife, and may contain the list of the wife's dowry.

**Kiddushin**  Means holiness in Hebrew; refers both to the wedding ceremony and to the state of matrimony.

| | |
|---|---|
| **Leviathan** | The sea monster referred to in Job, of which the righteous will eat at the resurrection. |
| **Lots** | An object used in deciding a matter by chance, a number of these being placed in a container and then drawn or cast out at random one by one. |
| **Lulav** | Palm branch, myrtle and willow branches, and etrog all attached together, used at Feast of Tabernacles. |
| **Midrash** | A Hebrew collection of works compiled between the third and twelfth centuries that seeks out underlying truths and meanings of the Bible. |
| **Mishnah** | Code of Jewish law edited by Rabbi Judah HaNazi about 200 C.E.; together with the Gemara forms the Talmud. |
| **Nissuin** | The Hebrew word for the formal wedding ceremony during ancient times. Also spelled *Nisuin*. |
| **Omer** | A sheaf or bushel of grain offered with the meal offering in the Temple. |
| **Pesach** | Hebrew word for Passover |
| **Rosh haShanah** | Hebrew word for the Jewish New Year. |
| **Sabbatical Year** | Celebrated every seven years by allowing a yearly rest for the land from cultivation and a time when debts were cancelled. Known as a Year of Sabbath and a Year of Release. |
| **Sage** | Wise, perceptive and discerning men of respect. |
| **Sanhedrin** | A High Court made up of 71 sages who served as the supreme religious, legislative and political body in Jerusalem. |
| **Shavuot** | Hebrew word for Feast of Weeks, The Day of Pentecost, beginning of the wheat harvest. |
| **Shemini Atzeret** | Hebrew word for the day following the Feast of Tabernacles and known as the Eighth Day. |
| **Shofar** | Hebrew word for the trumpet made from a ram's horn that is sounded on Rosh haShanah and Yom Kippur. |
| **Shofar HaGadol** | Hebrew word for the Shofar blown at last service of Day of Atonement at the closing of the gate. |
| **Simchat Torah** | Hebrew word that means the joy of the Torah. The day after Shemini Atzeret the annual reading of the Torah was completed and begun again. |
| **Sukkot** | Hebrew word for booths; Feast of Tabernacles celebrated in booths at the end of the Fall harvest; temporary dwelling place. Commemorates Israel's wanderings in the desert after leaving Egypt. Also spelled *Sukah*. |
| **Talmud** | A Jewish collection of legal and ethical discussions of the rabbis edited around the year 500 C.E. and is comprised of the Mishnah and Gemara. |
| **Teshuvah** | Hebrew word that means turning or returning; a Jewish term for repentance. |

| | |
|---|---|
| **Torah** | The first five books of the Bible; the Law. Also called the Pentateuch. |
| **Tsadikim** | Hebrew word that means Saints or the Righteous. |
| **Yamim Nora'im** | Hebrew word for Awesome days or The Days of Awe. |
| **Yom Kippur** | Hebrew word for The Day of Atonement. |
| **Zohar** | A central work of the kabbalistic literature, also called The Book of Splendor (Hebrew). |

# SOURCES CONSULTED

Agnon, S.Y., *Days of Awe,* Schocken Books, Inc.: New York, 1948, 1965.

Arukh, Kitzur Shulhan, *Code of Jewish Law*, Hebrew Publishing Company: New York, 1993.

Bloch, Abraham P., *The Biblical and Historical Background of Jewish Customs and Ceremonies*, KTAV Publishing House Inc.: New York, 1980.

*The Book of Jubilees or The Little Genesis*, Translated from The Editor's Ethiopic Text and Edited, with Introduction, Notes, and Indices by R. H. Charles, D. D., Adam and Charles Black: London, 1902.

*The Book of Legends, Sefer Ha-Aggadah, Legends from the Talmud and Midrash*, Edited by Hayim Nahman Bialik and Yehoshua Ana Ravnitzky, Schocken Books, Inc.: New York, 1992.

Cardozo, Arlene Rossen, *Jewish Family Celebrations, The Sabbath, Festivals, and Ceremonies*, St. Martins Press: New York, NY, 1982.

Chumney, Edward, *The Seven Festivals of the Messiah*, Treasure House: Shippensburg, PA, 1994.

Conners, Kevin J., *The Feasts of Israel*, Bible Temple-Conner Publications: Portland, Oregon, 1980.

Cornwall, Judson, *Let Us Draw Near,* Logos International, 1977.

Danby, Herbert, D.D., *The Mishnah*, Oxford University Press: Oxford, New York, 1989.

Edersheim, Alfred, *Sketches of Jewish Social Life,* Photolithoprinted by Eerdmans Printing Co.: Grand Rapids, Michigan, 1976.

Edersheim, Alfred, *The Temple, Its Ministry and Services,* Henderickson Publishers, Inc.: Peabody, Massachusetts, 1994.

Epstein, Louis M., *The Jewish Marriage Contract, A Study in the Status of the Woman in Jewish Law,* Arno Press, New York, 1973.

Feldheim, Philipp, *Elitahu Kitov, The Book of Our Heritage, Volumes 1, 2, & 3,* Feldheim Publishers, Ltd. : Jerusalem, Israel-New York, 1978.

Fishbane, Michael, *Biblical Interpretation in Ancient Israel,* Oxford Univeristy Press: Oxford, New York, 1985.

*Fragments of a Zadokite Work,* Translated from the Cambridge Hebrew Text and Edited with Introduction, Notes and Indexes by R. H. Charles, D.Litt., D. D., Oxford at the Clarendon Press, London, New York, 1912

Good, Joseph, *The High Holy Days,* Port Arthur, Texas: Hatikva Ministries.

Good, Joseph, *Rosh HaShanah and the Messianic Kingdom to Come,* Port Arthur, Texas: Hatikva Ministries.

*Hebrew Union College Annual #12-13 (1937-38) "Amos Studies",* by Julian Morgenstern, pp 1-34.

*Hebrew Union College Annual #14 (1939), "The Mythological Background of Psalm 82",* by Julian Morgenstern.

Hoehner, Harold W., *Chronological Aspects of the Life of Christ,* Grand Rapids: Zondervan Publishing House, c1977.

Hooke, Samuel H., *The Labyrinth,* Society for Promoting Christian Knowledge, London, New York, The Macmillan Company, 1935.

Hooke, Samuel H., *Myth & Ritual,* 1933 London, Oxford University Press, H. Milford, 1933.

Hooke, Samuel H., *The Origins of Early Semitic Ritual,* 1938 London Pub. for the British Academy by H. Milford, Oxford University Press, 1938.

Irstam, Tor, *The King of Ganda: "Studies in the Institutions of Sacral Kingship of Africa",* 1944 Lund, H. Ohlssons boktr. 1944.

*Jews and Divorce,* Edited by Jacob Freid, Commission on Synagogue Relations of the Federation of Jewish Philanthropies of New York, KTAV Publishing House, Inc., New York, 1968.

Karp, Abraham J., *The Jewish Way of Life,* Prentice-Hall, Inc.: Englewood Cliffs, N.J.,1962.

Kaufman, Michael, *Love, Marriage, and Family in Jewish Law and Tradition,* Jason Aronson, Inc, Northvale, New Jersey, London, 1996.

Kitov, Eliyahu, *The Book of Our Heritage, Vol. 1-4,* Feldheim Publishers: Jerusalem-New York, 1978.

Klein, Isaac, *A Guide to Jewish Religious Practice*, 1979 New York: Jewish Theological Seminary of America; distributed by KTAV Publishing House, c1979.

*The Life and Works of Flavius Josephus*, translated by William Whiston, A.M., The John C. Winston Company, Philadelphia.

*Maimonides' Mishneh Torah (Yad Hazakah),* Edited from Rare Manuscripts and Early Texts, Vocalized, Annotated and Provided with Introductions by Philip Birnbaum, Hebrew Publishing Company, Brooklyn, New York, 1989.

*Marriage*, Edited by Hayyim Schneid, JPS Popular Judaica Library, Jewish Publication Society of America, Philadelphia, PA.,1973.

Matthews, Victor H. and Don C. Benjamin, *Social World of Ancient Israel 1250-587 BCE,* Hendrickson Publishers, Inc., Peabody, Massachusetts, 1993.

Morgenstern, Julian, *American Journal of Semitic Languages & Literature 55 (1938), "A Chapter in the History of the High Priesthood".*

Patai, Raphael, *On Jewish Folklore,* 1983 Detroit: Wayne State University Press.

Pesikta Rabbati (Midrash for festivals and outstanding Sabbaths). Ed. Meir Friedmann, Vienna 1880.

Price, Walter K, *Next Year in Jerusalem,* 1975 Chicago: Moody Press, 1975.

Rosenau, William, Ph.D., L.H.D., *Jewish Ceremonial Institutions and Customs*, Singing Tree Press: Detroit, 1971.

Rosenthal, Marvin, *The Pre-Wrath Rapture of the Church*, Thomas Nelson Publishers, Nashville, 1990.

Routtenberg, Lilly S. and Ruth R. Seldin, *The Jewish Wedding Book*, Third and Revised Edition, Harper & Row, Publishers, New York, Evanston, and London.

Rowley, H. H., *Worship in Ancient Israel, Its Forms and Meaning*, Edward Cadbury Lectures delivered in the University of Birmingham, American Edition: Fortress Press, Philadelphia, 1967.

Schauss, Hayyim, *The Jewish Fesivals, History and Observance,* Union of American Hebrew Congregations, Schocken Books Inc.: New York, 1938.

Scherman, Rabbi Nosson, *The Chumash*, Mesorah Publications, Ltd., New York, 1993.

Slemming, C.W., *Temple, Made According to Pattern*, Christian Literature Crusade, Fort Washington, Pennsylvania, 1971

*Strong's Exhaustive Concordance*, by James Strong, Dugan Publishers, Inc., Gordonsville, TN.

*The Talmud of the Land of Israel, A Preliminary Translation and Explanation, Volume 16 Rosh Hashanah*, Translated by Edward A. Goldman, The Univeristy of Chicago Press, 1988.

*The Talmud of the Land of Israel, A Preliminary Translation and Explanation, Volume 17 Sukkah,* Translated by Jacob Neusner, The Univeristy of Chicago Press, 1988.

*The Torah, A Modern Commentary,* Edited by W. Gunther Plaut, Union of American Hebrew Congregations: New York, 1981.

Unger, Merrill F., *Unger's Bible Dictionary,* The Moody Bible Institute of Chicago: Chicago, Illinois, 1982.

*The World of Ancient Israel, Sociological, Anthropological and Political Perspectives,* Edited by R. E. Clements, Cambridge University Press: Dambridge, New York, 1989.

*Young's Analytical Concordance to the Bible*, Robert Young, LL.D., Wm. B. Eerdmans Publishing Company, Grand Rapids, Michigan,1977.

*Zondervan Pictorial Encyclopedia of the Bible.* Merrill C. Tenny, General Editor, Zondervan Publishing House, Grand Rapids, Michigan, 1976, 1976.

# KEYS & LOCKS INDEX

# ORDER FORM

# UNLOCKING THE MYSTERIES OF REVELATION

### USING THE KEYS OF THE FEASTS OF THE LORD

Name: _____

Address: _____

_____

City, State, Zip: _____

Phone Number: _____

E-Mail: _____

(If you provide your e-mail address we will confirm receipt of your order.)

_____ Number of Copies @ $24.95    $ _____

Postage/Handling @ $3.00 per book    $ _____

Arizona Residents Only
Sales Tax @ 8.3%    $ _____

TOTAL    $ _____

Please enclose check or money order payable to Marilyn Mineer and mail order form to:

Carlton/Mineer Publishing
Marilyn Mineer
P. O. Box 7026
Page, AZ 86040
1-435-675-3908

*Thank you for your order!*